Customer Service for Hospitality and Tourism

Simon Hudson

Louise Hudson

Goodfellow Publishers Ltd

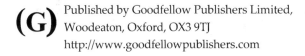 Published by Goodfellow Publishers Limited,
Woodeaton, Oxford, OX3 9TJ
http://www.goodfellowpublishers.com

British Library Cataloguing in Publication Data: a catalogue record for this title is available from the British Library.

Library of Congress Catalog Card Number: on file.

ISBN: 978-1-908999-33-7

 Design and typesetting by P.K. McBride, www.macbride.org.uk

Printed by Baker & Taylor, www.baker-taylor.com

Cover design by Cylinder, www.cylindermedia.com

Cover photo courtesy of Seabourn

Contents

Preface

We've all sat in restaurants waiting interminably for a drink, fruitlessly hailing oblivious blinkered servers while patrons who arrived later are unaccountably served first. Finally, we are perfunctorily attended by a harried waitress who then tries to deliver everything at once to make up for the wait and get us out of the door in record time, muddling orders, delivering courses all at once and forgetting any particular requests in the process. Underwhelming service has become so common in restaurants, hotels, airports and other tourism and hospitality settings that when the service is actually smooth, friendly and accommodating, we are surprised and gratified. But in a competitive global retail market, it should not be like this. What happened to 'service with a smile' and 'the customer is always right'? How come, after all those customer service training manuals and courses and all the high tech gadgets which facilitate transactions, the computer still says no?

Providing high quality customer service should be at the top of every CEO's agenda. In the last few decades, businesses have changed dramatically as the economy has shifted from a dependence on manufacturing to a focus on providing timely, quality service. The service economy has been in full swing for some time now, driven by increased technology, globalization, de-regulation and changing consumer behavior, among other factors. Customer service is therefore more important than ever before, especially during difficult economic times when customers are looking to increase value for money and are less forgiving of mediocre service.

But despite its importance, quality customer service is the exception rather than the norm in many parts of the world. There are a number of reasons for this fall in standards. When economic conditions become more demanding, many organizations focus on cost cutting and acquiring new customers which invariably puts the relationships with their existing customers at risk. Quite often training budgets are the first to get cut. Also, many companies wrongly believe they are providing service excellence. A study by the Bain Company, reported in the *Harvard Management Update*, revealed that 80% of 362 companies surveyed believed they delivered superior service to their customers. When the customers of those same firms were surveyed, only 8% agreed. Nine out of ten companies who confidently assert the high level of their customers' satisfaction are completely misinformed. In addition, many organizations simply don't understand the significance of customer service, despite the exhaustive literature that has made the connection between service excellence, satisfaction and loyalty – and therefore profits. Customer service training is often viewed as a cost rather than an investment. Finally, even if companies recognize the importance of customer service, they don't know how to deliver consistent, high quality customer service on an on-going basis.

Given the critical importance of customer service for the tourism and hospitality sector, it is remarkable that (until now) there is no comprehensive text that deals with this important topic. There are a number of service marketing textbooks that are strong theoretically, but they only pay lip-service to the actual delivery of customer service. There are also many customer service handbooks with worksheets for practitioners to use, but they lack the theory behind the practice. So this book is useful for both students and practitioners as it explains not only the theory behind the importance of customer service but also acts as a guidebook for those wishing to put this theory into practice. In essence it is the 'whys' and 'hows' of customer service. By focusing on tourism and hospitality businesses, this text makes a unique contribution to the literature – no other book of this kind exists. In addition to making a theoretical contribution, the text will also be of great value to those planning to join – or already working in – the service industry, since customer service is critical to most businesses in this sector.

The book is easy to read, very current, and full of references to the latest research from both academic and practitioner literature. Chapters cover important topics such as the financial and behavioral consequences of customer service, consumer trends influencing service, developing and maintaining a service culture, managing service encounters, the importance of market research, building and maintaining customer relationships, providing customer service through the servicescape, the impact of technology on customer service, the importance of service recovery, and promoting customer service internally and externally.

An 'At Your Service' spotlight at the beginning of each chapter focuses on the achievements of successful individuals related to the art of customer service. In the middle of each chapter there is a 'Service Snapshot' – short, real-life cases to illustrate a particular concept or theoretical principle presented in the chapter. At the end of every chapter there is an up-to-date, relevant and detailed 'Case study', and as a collection, these case studies will cover a variety of sectors, organizations and regions. Designed to foster critical thinking, the cases illustrate actual business scenarios that stress several concepts found in the chapter. All cases have been developed following a personal visit or in-depth interviews conducted by the authors, and there is an international flavor throughout the book. Cases analyse customer service in the USA, South America, South Africa, Europe, Russia, Australia, China, Canada, Korea and Dubai.

The last chapter of the book is a handbook that practitioners can use to implement a generic customer service program. The handbook has a number of structured activities and each exercise is accompanied by a facilitator's guide that a trainer can follow (with an explanation of their purpose and learning outcomes).

About the authors

Dr Simon Hudson is an Endowed Chair in Tourism at the University of South Carolina. He has held previous academic positions at universities in Canada and England, and has worked as a visiting professor in Austria, Switzerland, Spain, Fiji, New Zealand, the United States, and Australia. Prior to working in academia, Dr Hudson spent several years in the tourism industry in Europe, and he now consults for the industry in North America. Dr Hudson has written five books. His first, *Snow Business*, written in 2000, was the first book to be written about the international ski industry, followed by *Sports and Adventure Tourism*, published by Haworth in 2003. His third book, *Marketing for Tourism and Hospitality: A Canadian Perspective*, has sold over 8000 copies, and is in its second edition. *Tourism and Hospitality Marketing: A Global Perspective* was published by Sage in 2008, and his most recent book, *Golf Tourism* was published by Goodfellow in 2010. He has written a number of journal articles and case studies on customer service. He is frequently invited to international tourism conferences as a keynote speaker and one of his specialist subjects is customer service.

Louise Hudson is a freelance journalist living in South Carolina (www.tourismgurus.com). She has collaborated with Dr Hudson on many of his books and research projects and co-wrote *Tourism and Hospitality Marketing: A Global Perspective* and *Golf Tourism* with him. Originally trained in journalism in England, she now writes for many publications including *USA Today, LA Times, Dallas Morning News*, Canada's *Globe and Mail* and *Dreamscapes Magazine, Calgary Sun, Calgary Herald* and canada.com network, *Edmonton Sun, Ottawa Citizen*, Canada's *MORE magazine, Sheen Magazine, Wink Magazine, Alberta Parent, Calgary's Child, Travel Alberta, Fresh Tracks, Alberta Hospitality* and *BC Inn Focus* magazine among others. With a side-line in the fashion industry, Louise has also collaborated with Dr Hudson in writing and presenting retail workshops and handbooks to help small businesses in marketing and advertising. She also runs fashion workshops at the University of South Carolina – www.hrsm.sc.edu/fashioncamp.

1 Introduction to Customer Service

A Disney employee invites children to dance during the parade at Hongkong Disneyland Park.

Photo courtesy of Allison Zhang

What is Disney's edge? It stems in part from Walt Disney's precept that money is not the most important factor in business. Instead he focused on identifying the customers' needs and giving them what they wanted. His business philosophy stemmed from his strong family values, morals, religious beliefs, creative goals and innate psychographic awareness. As he said back in the 1960s: 'Disneyland is a work of love. We didn't go into Disneyland just with the idea of making money'.

During an NBC interview in 1966 Walt stressed that excellence of products and service are more crucial than profits at his theme parks: '... my young group of executives are convinced that Walt is right, that quality will win out, and so I think they will stay with this policy because it's proven it's a good business policy. Give the public everything you can give them, keep the place as clean as you can keep it, keep it friendly – I think they're convinced and I think they'll hang on after – as you say, "after Disney"'.

He laid the framework for the future with his focus on animated films and the invention and development of the quintessential theme park. Today's Walt Disney Company has diversified further to incorporate cruise lines, TV channels and film studios, and an international professional business training institute. So, how has the company managed to maintain high standards since the pioneering founder's demise?

Although he died back in 1966, the company still holds true to his basic beliefs. One of Walt's well-known maxims was that nothing is ever finished, there is always room to grow and improve: 'Just do your best work — then try to trump it.' This is borne out in Disney's quest to expand, renovate and diversify as well as surprising customers by both meeting and then exceeding their expectations in regard to product and service.

Having invented the modern day concept of the theme park back in 1955, the company does not rest on its laurels; it is always going a step further. Disney doesn't just cater for kids, but also considers adults, bundling (and unbundling) services and attractions to enable customized packages to suit all age groups both during the day and evening at its parks and cruises. Films are made with an overt attraction for kids and an underlying message to adults.

At its theme parks, attractions are not designed with purely the bottom line in mind. Disney designers look at the audience, evaluating the time needed for a full experience, including the ride, interaction with other customers, and immersion in the imaginary environment. It is this painstaking focus on customer satisfaction that Disney execs have dubbed 'imagineering' – a concept fully explored in *The Imagineering Workout*. In this book there are tips for travel agents, for example, to stimulate their imaginations in attracting more customers. These include sharing personal experiences with prospective clients and using 'what ifs' to paint pictures - and as a positive alternative to saying 'no' - to even seemingly impossible requests. Imagineering also counsels research to enhance credibility and confidence and breaking routines to stimulate creative thinking.

Customer service naturally depends partly on staff/customer interaction. Walt Disney introduced a novel way of training his employees by providing a new internal language based on Hollywood terminology. Staff are cast members, customers are guests, shifts are performances, a job description is a script, the HR department is casting, and being on duty is being on stage. This analogy with show business helps immerse both staff and guests in the imaginary world of Disney, putting everyone in the spotlight.

1

Disney also believed that the front-line is the bottom-line, with a company judged by its face-to-face staff. Staff trainers (presumably 'directors') encourage the cast to discover the guests' 'wow' moments and share the knowledge and celebrate it with other cast members. One question which has often caused inappropriate responses is 'What time is the three o'clock parade?' Despite the occasion for mirth or sarcasm, Disney trains staff to answer with a confirmation of the time, place and other information about nearby facilities. Disney is also meticulous in sustaining the mystique by keeping backstage activities out of sight – for example, Snow White cannot be seen smoking in the park's public areas!

Disney has even turned a 'no' into a 'yes' to some extent without compromising its strict safety rules. Many of its rides have a height minimum but whenever a child is turned away from a ride for not being tall enough, he is given a priority pass for him and his family to return when he is tall enough.

Disney's commitment to its customers is defined by their term 'guestology'. Like 'imagineering', it focuses on the guest experience rather than traditional business efficiencies. The customer point of view – both child and adult – is considered critical, resulting in such innovations as child-height peepholes in hotel room doors as well as the usual adult ones and bins located at 27-foot intervals – designated after calculating the average time people will go before dropping litter.

Disney's meticulous customer service training attracted other executives from a wide variety of businesses around the world, resulting in the development in 1986 of the Disney Institute, a Florida-based corporate customer training unit of the Walt Disney Co. Trainers – with around ten years' Disney service – teach principles created and tested by decades of research, data collection and visitor surveys. Attention to details, removing barriers and keeping customers informed were just some of the principles which attracted Miami International Airport to the Institute. Simple ideas such as clothing staff in bright colors and providing easy-to-read name tags were adopted by the airport which had previously had very low ranking for its service culture. Miami Airport - which handles over 30 million travelers each year - paid around $28,000 per day for a series of full-day training sessions which then empowered company leaders to train those who worked under them in the polished precepts. Ideas such as 'it's not my fault, but it is my problem' are general enough to be easily incorporated into any business.

Over a million professionals have come through the institute earning their Mickey Mouse ears along with new standards for effective leadership, people management, customer service and creative business practices. One of the most recent advocates of 'Disneyfication' is the Federated Hospitality Association of South Africa (FEDHASA) which was responsible for customer service improvements for the 2010 FIFA World Cup. The Disney Institute trained 15,000 South African front-line workers over nine provinces in a 34-day program.

Sources:

Dickson et al. (2005); Anon (2002); Anon (2006); Solnet et al. (2010); Anon (2008); Associated Press (2011); http://afterthemouse.com/node/2223;

www.disneyinstitute.com; http://disneyinstitute.com/topics/quality_service.aspx; www.disneydreamer.com

Customer service defined

The opening case study is an excellent example of how a strong customer service philosophy is often driven by one person (in this case Walt Disney) and how that philosophy can lead to an enduring service culture that can differentiate an organization from competitors. In fact, this chapter puts a spotlight on three individuals who have made customer service a priority and succeeded in becoming market leaders – Walt Disney, Cliff Roberts of the Augusta Masters, and Eustasio Lopez of the Lopesan Group in the Spanish Canary Islands. Unfortunately, these individuals are exceptions rather than the rule, and this chapter will allude to falling customer satisfaction levels and the reasons for poor customer service in today's environment. The chapter will also discuss some of the services marketing models that illuminate the importance of customer service, providing a platform for the remainder of the book.

Many attempts have been made to define customer service. Zethalm et al. (2007) simply define it as 'the service provided in support of a company's core product' (pp. 5). Fisk, Grove and John (2000) agree although they extend the definition to include the importance of customer relationships. They say customer service is 'all customer-provider interactions, other than proactive selling and the core product delivery that facilitate the organization's relationship with its customers' (pp. 177). Lovelock and Wright (1999) have a similar view suggesting that the concept is 'the provision of supplementary service elements by employees who are not specifically engaged in selling activities' (pp.252). The Institute of Customer Service (2011) prefer to stress the importance of customer expectations and satisfaction in their definition calling customer service 'the sum total of what an organization does to meet customer expectations and produce customer satisfaction'.

Perhaps the most comprehensive definition comes from Lucas (2009) who defines customer service as 'the ability of knowledgeable, capable, and enthusiastic employees to deliver products and services to their internal and external customers in a manner that satisfies identified and unidentified needs and ultimately results in positive word-of-mouth publicity and return business' (pp. 6). What this definition does not consider is that customer service may not always be satisfactory and can also lead to bad word-of-mouth and a loss of business. In addition, customer service is more than the interaction between employees and internal or external customers. It also relates to the physical infrastructure in a retail space or hospitality servicescape. Disney for example, a truly customer-focused organization (see *Spotlight*), has two peepholes in its hotel room doors – one at the usual height, and another at a child's level. The definition of customer service used in this book therefore builds on that of Lucas and is as follows:

> *Customer service is the practice of delivering products and services to both internal and external customers via the efforts of employees or through the provision of an appropriate servicescape.*

A history of customer service

The modern concept of customer service has its roots in the craftsman economy of the 1800s, when individuals and small groups of manufacturers competed to produce arts and crafts to meet public demand (Free Books Online, 2011). Customized orders were taken for each customer, and the customer care was highly individualized. During that era, customer service differed from what it is today by the fact that the owners of businesses were also motivated frontline employees working face-to-face with their customers and they had a vested interest in providing good service and in succeeding (Lucas, 2009).

As the era of mass production eased in early in the 20th century, it became more and more difficult to cater to the needs of individual customers. The explosion in the demand for goods after the Second World War further reduced the importance of customer service, as the power of suppliers surpassed that of the consumer. This balance shifted in the 1970s as the dominance of Western manufacturers was challenged by Asia and the increased competition caused producers to improve the quality of their products and services. The economic boom of the 1990s again increased the power of the suppliers, who, while not completely reverting to lower standards of service, were able to be more selective in which customers to serve, and of what levels of service to provide.

Today, businesses have changed dramatically as the economy has shifted from a dependence on manufacturing to a focus on providing timely, quality service (Lucas, 2009). The service economy has been in full swing for some time now, driven by increased technology, globalization, deregulation and changing consumer behavior amongst other factors. Customer service is therefore more important than ever before, especially during difficult economic times, when customers are looking to increase value for money and are less forgiving of mediocre service (Miller, 2011). A 2011 study found that seven in ten Americans are willing to spend an average of 13% more with companies they believe provide excellent customer service. Three in five would try a new brand or company for a better service experience (AMEX, 2011).

But despite its importance, quality customer service is the exception rather than the norm in many parts of the world (Bigger and Bigger, 2010). In the same American Express study referred to above, 60% of Americans believe businesses had not improved their customer service – up from 55% in 2010. Worse, 21% felt that companies took their business for granted. A number of reasons have been proposed for this fall in standards. When economic conditions become more demanding, many organizations focus on cost cutting and acquiring new customers which invariably puts the relationships with their existing customers at risk (Miller, 2011). Quite often training budgets are the first to get cut. In the UK, where the country came a disappointing 14th in the 2010 international customer service rankings from the Nation Brand Index, one excuse given is that the issue of service is a class problem, with service viewed as subservient and a second-class occupation by many (Waites, 2011). Others say that the slip in customer service dates back to the booming economy of the late 1990s, when the unemployment rate slipped so low, that many countries in the west were at full employment. Businesses were forced to hire workers who were often less committed to their jobs, and many of those workers knew that treating customers poorly rarely resulted in being fired(Brokamp, 2007).

The authors of this book believe there may be three further reasons for the fall in standards of customer service. First, many companies wrongly believe they are providing service excellence. A study by the Bain Company, reported in the Harvard Management Update, revealed that 80% of 362 companies surveyed believed they delivered superior service to their customers (see Figure 1.1). When the customers of those same firms were surveyed, only 8% agreed (Allen et al., 2005). Nine of 10 companies who confidently assert the high level of their customers' satisfaction are completely misinformed. According to the Bain Study, many companies get wrong-headed about their customer's satisfaction because they rely on indirect metrics to measure service, rather than designing the right offers and experiences for the right customers.

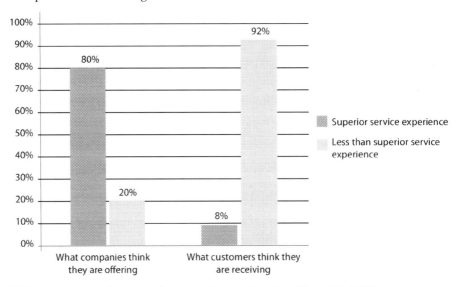

Figure 1.1. The customer service perception gap . (Source: Based on Allen et al., 2005)

1

Second, organizations simply don't understand the significance of customer service, despite the exhaustive literature that has made the connection between service excellence, satisfaction and loyalty – and therefore profits. Customer service training is often viewed as a cost rather than an investment. Finally, even if companies recognize the importance of customer service, they don't know how to deliver consistent, high quality customer service on an on-going basis. Companies need to commit research funds to understand employees, their needs and wants, how to motivate them, how to offer them good incentives, how to encourage them, how to train them and how to help them deliver the kind of experiences that are promised in external communications to customers (Schultz, 2002).

The role of customer service

In response to the tremendous growth and economic contributions of the service sector, several models and frameworks have been developed to assist in making services marketing and management decisions at both the strategic and implementation levels. Some of these frameworks will now be discussed, and the role and significance of customer service for businesses can be seen in all of these frameworks.

■ Unique characteristics of services

Service products are commonly distinguished from goods products by four unique characteristics; intangibility, inseparability, heterogeneity, and perishability. These are described in Table 1.1. Services tend to be more intangible than manufactured products, and often cannot be seen, felt, tasted or touched in the same manner that one can sense tangible goods. This intangibility presents several marketing challenges. Services cannot be inventoried, and therefore fluctuations in demand are difficult to manage, particularly in the accommodation and airline sectors. Services cannot be easily patented, so can be easily copied by competitors. The inseparability of services means that the quality of service and customer satisfaction will be highly dependent on the interactions between employees and customers, although the real time nature of services provides opportunities to customize offerings for individual customers. The heterogeneity of services means that service delivery quality depends on who provides the services, so ensuring consistent quality is challenging. Finally, the perishability of services means that for the tourism sector, empty airline seats, hotel rooms, daily ski passes, restaurant covers, etc. cannot be sold the next day. Demand forecasting and creative planning for capacity utilization are therefore very important. The fact that services cannot typically be returned or resold also suggests a need to have a service recovery strategy in place should things go wrong.

Table 1.1: The four unique characteristics of services

Characteristic	Description
1) Intangibility	Service products cannot be tasted, felt, seen, heard, or smelled. Prior to boarding a plane, airline passengers have nothing but an airline ticket and a promise of safe delivery to their destination. To reduce uncertainty caused by service intangibility, buyers look for tangible evidence that will provide information and confidence about the service.
2) Inseparability	For many services, the product cannot be created or delivered without the customer's presence. The food in a restaurant may be outstanding, but if the server has a poor attitude or provides inattentive service, customers will not enjoy the overall restaurant experience. In the same way, other customers can affect the experience in service settings.
3) Heterogeneity	Service delivery quality depends on who provides the services. The same person can deliver differing levels of service, displaying a marked difference in tolerance and friendliness as the day wears on. Lack of consistency is a major factor in customer dissatisfaction.
4) Perishability	Services cannot be stored. Empty airline seats, hotel rooms, daily ski passes, restaurant covers—all these services cannot be sold the next day. If services are to maximize revenue, they must manage capacity and demand since they cannot carry forward unsold inventory.

■ The services marketing triangle

The services marketing triangle is another framework that address the challenges inherent in services, and can be used to assess and guide strategies, as well as provide a roadmap for implementation planning. The triangle in Figure 1.2 shows the three interlinked groups that work together to develop, promote, and deliver services. These key players—the company, the customers, and the providers—are labeled on the points of the triangle. Between these three points there are three types of marketing that must be successfully carried out for a service to succeed: external, interactive, and internal marketing. For all services, especially for tourism and hospitality services, all three types of marketing activities are essential for building and maintaining relationships.

Through its *external* marketing efforts, a company makes promises to its customers regarding what they can expect and how it can be delivered. Traditional marketing activities facilitate this, but for services, other factors such as the servicescape and the process itself help to establish customer expectations.

Keeping promises, or *interactive* marketing, is the second kind of marketing activity captured by the triangle. Interactive marketing occurs in the 'moment of truth' when the customer interacts with the organization and the service is produced and consumed. From the customer's point of view, the most vivid impression of service occurs in the service encounter or the moment of truth. It is in these encounters that customers receive a snapshot of the organization's service quality, and each encounter contributes to the customer's overall satisfaction and willingness to do business with the organization again.

Figure 1.2: The services marketing triangle. *Source:* Based on Zeithaml and Bitner (2000).

Finally, internal marketing takes place through the enabling of promises. Promises are easy to make, but unless providers are recruited, trained, provided with tools and appropriate internal systems, and rewarded for good service, the promises may not be kept. Internal marketing was first proposed in the 1970s (Berry et al, 1976) as a way to deliver consistently high service quality, but despite the rapidly growing literature on internal marketing, very few organizations actually apply the concept in practice. One of the main problems is that a single unified concept of what is meant by internal marketing does not exist. Lack of investment in internal marketing may also be the result of corporate distraction. Companies that are busy trying to boost revenues and cut costs may not see why they should spend money on employees, thus missing the point that these are the very people who ultimately deliver the brand promises the company makes.

However, there is growing awareness that an effective internal marketing program will have a positive effect on service quality, customer satisfaction and loyalty, and eventually profits. The main objective of internal marketing is to enable employees to deliver satisfying products to guests. This takes place through a four-step process: the establishment of a service culture, the development of a marketing approach to human resource management, the dissemination of marketing information to employees, and the implementation of a reward and recognition system. This internal marketing process will be discussed in more detail in Chapter 4.

Snapshot: Customer service at the Augusta Masters

Cliff Roberts

The Masters in Augusta, Georgia, is a golf tournament conceived, nurtured and run for nearly forty years by a man called Cliff Roberts. More than three decades after his death, the Masters still operates as if he were at the controls. Customer service excellence was the guiding principal behind Robert's perfectionism and his conception of almost every aspect of the club and the tournament. His practice of calling spectators 'patrons' was a reflection of his belief that the purpose of the club during Masters week was to serve the people whose support had made the tournament possible in the first place. He had a similarly solicitous attitude towards the players who competed in the tournament and the media who covered it. Asked what they are playing for, the competitors still name an article of clothing (the 'Green Jacket') and not a sum of money.

The Masters is still viewed almost universally as the best-run golf tournament in the world, if not the best-run sporting event, and it has maintained its standing without acquiring the modern trappings of success. Spectators can still buy lunch for half the price of any other tournament, because Roberts believed that anyone who had to travel two hundred miles to watch a game of golf ought to be able to buy a decent meal at a decent price. Teams of uniformed workers constantly clean up after spectators because Roberts felt that litter detracted from the beauty of the course and the dignity of the event. In fact, the cups and sandwich bags are green, making them nearly invisible to television cameras – a major issue with Roberts. Members still wear their green coats all week, as they have done since 1937, because Roberts felt that knowledgeable sources of information ought to be easily identifiable to spectators in need of assistance.

Many key features of professional golf tournaments were introduced in Augusta. Early tour events were not professionally run, whereas at Augusta, the needs of spectators

1

were anticipated and satisfied from the moment they arrived. There were a number of refreshment stands, excellent picnicking grounds, and plenty of lavatories. It was the first tournament that spared spectators from having to carry a bulky program around all day; instead daily pairing sheets with a diagram of the course on the reverse side were provided for free. The Masters was the first seventy-two-hole tournament to be played over four days. It was the first played on terrain that was routinely reshaped to provide better sight lines for spectators. It was the first to use bleachers or observation stands. It was the first to systematically rope galleries and to allow only players, caddies, and officials inside the ropes. It was the first tournament to be covered live on nationwide radio, and the first to develop an on-course scoreboard network, in which scores were gathered over dedicated telephone lines as they occurred.

After several early years of financial difficulties, Roberts later said that the hospitality for which the Masters is legendary had been the produce of necessity. To sell enough tickets to cover costs, the club had to pamper spectators. The prices had to be low, the food good, the views unobstructed, the course perfect and the bathrooms clean. Focusing on the needs of his customers was a priority for Roberts. In his quest for improvement, Roberts accepted suggestions from every quarter, and many of the tournaments amenities were ideas from outsiders. All recommendations from patrons or others were taken seriously. In 1961, an executive of a fire hydrant company in Alabama, suggested that the television broadcast of the tournament be shown on closed-circuit TV sets situated on the course itself, to make it easier for spectators to follow the action of the more popular players – an idea that Roberts liked and implemented.

The Masters is still the competition by which other competitions are judged, and the credit belongs largely to Roberts. Mark Lockridge, Clubhouse Manager says: 'We use our history to drive our culture and we use our culture to drive service excellence.' Principles for providing service excellence that were created by Roberts are still used as the guiding philosophy. These include keeping it simple, making it measurable, providing training and coaching, soliciting feedback and ideas from the team, and recognizing and rewarding performance. Approximately 3,500 staff are employed at the Masters every year, and they are all trained to understand the critical importance of service. Don Pritchard, Head of Concession Planning and Operations, says the purpose of training is to get everyone moving in the same direction. 'Genuine hospitality is not teachable', he says, 'so we look for a special type of person to work here.' All staff are trained to offer a sincere greeting to spectators, make eye contact, offer assistance with a 'My Pleasure' response, thank patrons for their business, and offer customers a sincere farewell with wishes for a great day. 'In the race for excellence, there is no finishing line' says Lockridge.

Sources: Owen, D. (1999). *The Making of the Masters*. New York: Simon and Schuster; Presentations by Mark Lockridge and Don Pritchard, 14 February 2012; personal visit to the Masters, 8 April 2012.

The marketing mix for services

Another framework that highlights the importance of customer service is the expanded marketing mix for services. The marketing mix may be defined as 'the mixture of controllable marketing variables that the firm uses to pursue the sought level of sales in the target market' (McCarthy, 1981). The original four Ps of the marketing mix, introduced in 1961, (AMA, 1985) are product, place, promotion, and price. Because services are usually produced and consumed simultaneously, customers are often part of the service production process. Also, because services are intangible, customers will often be looking for any tangible cue to help them understand the nature of the service experience. These facts have led service marketers to conclude that they can use additional variables to communicate with and satisfy their customers. Acknowledgement of the importance of these additional variables has led service marketers to adopt the concept of an expanded marketing mix for services, shown in Table 1.2. In addition to the traditional four Ps, the services marketing mix includes people, physical evidence, and process.

Table 1.2: Expanded marketing mix for services. Source: Booms and Bitner (1981)

Traditional 4 'P's of Marketing

Product	Place	Promotion	Price
1) Physical good features	1) Channel type	1) Promotion blend	1) Flexibility
2) Quality level	2) Exposure	2) Salespeople	2) Price level
3) Accessories	3) Intermediaries	- *Number*	3) Terms
4) Packaging	4) Outlet locations	- *Selection*	4) Differentiation
5) Warranties	5) Transportation	- *Training*	5) Discounts
6) Product lines	6) Storage	- *Incentives*	6) Allowances
7) Branding	7) Managing channels	3) Advertising	
		- *Targets*	
		- *Media types*	
		- *Types of ads*	
		- *Copy thrust*	
		4) Sales promotion	
		- *Publicity*	

Additional 3 'P's of Services Marketing

People	Physical evidence	Process
1) Employees	1) Facility design	1) Flow of activities
- *Recruiting*	2) Equipment	- *Standardized*
- *Training*	3) Signage	- *Customized*
- *Motivation*	4) Employee dress	2) Number of steps
- *Rewards*	5) Other tangibles	- *Simple*
- *Teamwork*	6) Reports	- *Complex*
2) Customers	7) Business cards	3) Customer involvement
- *Education*	8) Statements	
- *Training*	9) Guarantees	

The people element includes all human actors who play a part in service delivery and thus influence the buyer's perceptions—namely the firm's personnel, the customer, and other customers in the service environment. The physical evidence is the environment in which the service is delivered and where the firm and customer interact, and any tangible components that facilitate performance or communication of the service. Table 1.2 gives some examples of tangible evidence or cues used by service organizations. Finally, the process is the actual procedures, mechanisms, and flow of activities by which the service is delivered. The three new marketing mix elements are included in the marketing mix as separate elements because they are within the control of the firm and any or all of them may influence the customer's initial decision to purchase a service and the customer's level of satisfaction and repurchase decisions. The traditional elements as well as the new marketing mix elements are explored in depth in later chapters.

Customer service in the tourism and hospitality sector

Tourism is a powerful economic force providing employment, foreign exchange, income, and tax revenue. The United Nations World Tourism Organization (UNWTO) defines tourism as comprising the activities of persons travelling to and staying in places outside their usual environment for not more than one consecutive year for leisure, business and other purposes not related to the exercise of an activity remunerated from within the place visited. The tourism market reflects the demands of consumers for a very wide range of travel and hospitality products, and it is widely claimed that this total market is now being serviced by the world's largest industry. The number of international arrivals has risen from just 50 million in 1950 to 983 million in 2011 (UNWTO, 2011). While this represents an annual growth rate of 6.5% over more than half a century, the receipts generated by these tourists have increased nearly twice as fast – global tourism receipts for 2009 amounted to $851 billion. This growth rate for tourism far outstrips the world economy as a whole, and tourism now represents a quarter of all exports of services. In 2010 employment in the travel and tourism economy comprised over 200 million jobs or 8.2% of total employment. The UNWTO Tourism 2020 Vision forecasts that international arrivals will reach over 1.56 billion by the year 2020. Of these 1.18 billion will be intra-regional and 377 million will be long-haul travelers. The top three receiving regions are expected to be Europe, East Asia and the Pacific, and the Americas, followed by Africa, the Middle East and South Asia.

Although tourism continues to grow in certain parts of the world, in western countries the industry could be considered mature. In this sector, in a mature industry, characterized by severe competition, low product differentiation, and limited promotional costs, standing out from competitors is not an easy task. In the case of branded hotels and airlines for example, the product offering of rivals is nearly identical (Gagnon and Roh, 2008). Customer service is therefore increasingly becoming a differentiator in this sector. Some organizations do excel in the art of customer service. Solnet et al. (2010) recently analyzed hospitality firms that were frequent subjects of positive customer storytelling, and they identified seven exemplar firms (see Table 1.3 below). These firms were The Ritz-Carlton, Harrah's Entertainment, The Walt Disney Company, Four Seasons, Club Med, Southwest Airlines, and Singapore Airlines. A single theme – related to customer and employee obsession – was determined to be the common thread. Effective leadership and direction from a single founder or entrepreneur was also evident in all the organizations, an attribute that is similarly obvious from the three case studies in this opening chapter.

Table 1.3: Customer service superstars. *Source:* from Solnet et al, 2010, pp. 895

Name of firm	Short description
1) The Ritz-Carlton Hotels and Resorts	Luxury hotel; renowned for its personalized service and famous (and generous) employee empowerment policy; has its own Leadership Centre, often used by other companies for development and training; motto, 'We are ladies and gentlemen serving ladies and gentlemen' has impact internally and externally.
2) Harrah's Entertainment	Gaming/entertainment; CEO is co-author of the service profit chain; uses leading edge database system to do 'surgical marketing'; belief that business should be grown by investing heavily to focus the firm on the customer rather than investing on the tangible assets of the firm only.
3) The Walt Disney Company	Entertainment; in addition to its reputation as the provider of family entertainment and fun, Disney is known for many customer-focused approaches such as 'guestology' and the 'imagineers.'
4) Four Seasons	Luxury hotel; embodies a true 'home away from home' experience with exceptional personal service; ranked number two in recent *Business Week* survey of best customer service.
5) Club Med	Resorts; the carefree, all-inclusive holiday package company, in search of the 'alchemy of happiness,' has been able to make necessary adjustments along with demographics of customer base.
4) Southwest Airlines	Airline; innovation of the 'low cost' carrier—has continually run contrary to most of the airline industry through its customer-service culture; considers itself a 'customer service business which just happens to provide transportation.'
4) Singapore Airlines	Airline; at the premium end of the market, has consistently outperformed its competitors throughout its three-and-a-half decade long history; have sustained their competitive advantage by effectively implementing a dual strategy: differentiation through service excellence and innovation, together with simultaneous cost leadership.

However, as consumers have come to expect more and more, satisfaction rates for some tourism and hospitality players are lagging behind other sectors. In the US, satisfaction ratings for airlines are below those of other industries, while hotels and restaurants are comparable to other sectors. Customers seem to be more satisfied with the quality provided by full-service restaurants than they are with hotels or airlines. In fact, as Figure 1.3 shows, airlines perform quite poorly according to the American Customer Satisfaction Index (ACSI, 2012). The ACSI is a national economic indicator of customer evaluations of the quality of products and services available to household consumers in the US. Data from interviews with approximately 70,000 customers annually are used as inputs into an econometric model to measure satisfaction with more than 225 companies in 47 industries and 10 economic sectors, as well as with more than 130 federal government departments, agencies, and websites. Results are released on a monthly basis with all measures reported using a 0-100 scale. For 2012, airlines received a score of 67 out of 100, while hotels (77) and full-service restaurants (80) performed much better.

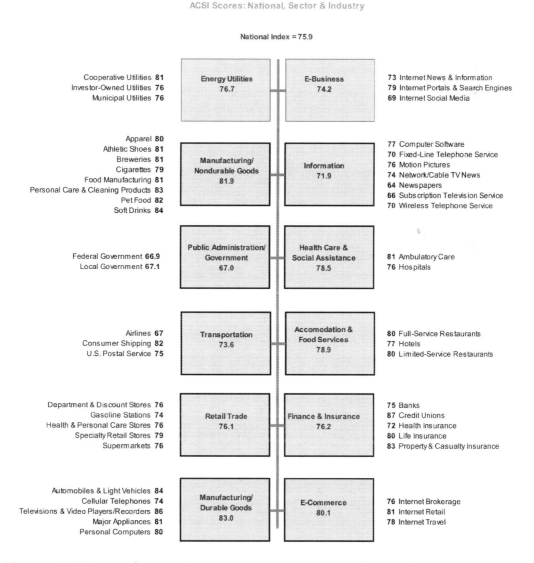

Figure 1.3: ACSI scores for 2012. *Source:* American Customer Satisfaction Index, 2012.

Table 1.4: Bloomberg Business Week's customer service elite, 2010. *Source:* Business Week, 2010.

Rank	Brand	Industry	Quality of Staff	Efficiency of Service	Total Score	Change in Score from 2009 (%)	Definitely Recommend Brand (%)	Definitely Repurchase Brand (%)
1	L.L. Bean	Online/Catalog Retail	A+	A+	1055.95	10.71	58	59
2	USAA	Insurance	A+	A+	1042.76	1.48	78	84
3	Apple	Computers & Electronics	A+	A+	1016.55	9.92	66	58
4	Four Seasons Hotels &Resorts	Hotel	A+	A+	1000.9	3.65	55	41
5	Publix Super Market	Supermarket	A+	A+	992.02	2.64	72	66
6	Nordstrom	Department Store Retail	A	A	974.71	7.26	60	53
7	Lexus	Automotive	A+	A+	966.44	-5.52	58	38
8	The Ritz-Carlton	Hotel	A+	A+	950.74	2.73	54	39
9	Barnes & Noble	Big Box Retail	B+	A-	944.32	NA	51	50
10	Ace Hardware	Home Improvement Retail	A	A	939.69	-0.05	37	29
11	Amazon.com	Online/Catalog Retail	A+	A+	933.55	-5.67	61	57
12	Wegmans Food Markets	Supermarket	A	A+	923.85	NA	78	62
13	Starbucks	Restaurant	A-	A-	923.77	2.24	40	41
14	Amica Mutual Insurance	Insurance	A+	A+	920.8	1.01	61	67
15	Charles Schwab	Brokerage	A-	B+	918.68	-1.69	47	NA
16	Jaguar	Automotive	A+	A+	916.34	-6.07	48	27
17	WestJet	Airline	B+	B+	909.6	NA	56	47
18	American Express	Credit Card	B+	B-	900.46	-0.69	44	NA
19	Enterprise Rent-A-Car	Rental Car	B	B	900.02	-0.83	36	34
20	Branch Banking & Trust	Banking	B+	B-	895.91	2.97	40	37
21	Panera Bread	Restaurant	B+	B+	892.45	NA	45	40
22	True Value	Home Improvement Retail	A-	A	879.02	0.41	26	22
23	Dell	Computers & Electronics	B+	A-	872.64	5.74	44	47
24	Southwest Airlines	Airline	B	B+	871.84	1.52	50	40
25	Fairmont Hotels & Resorts	Hotel	A+	A+	871.65	1.16	51	32

Bloomberg BusinessWeek produces an annual Customer Service Elite ranking with its research partner, J.D. Power & Associates (see Table 1.4). Based on consumer surveys about customer satisfaction, Bloomberg rates what customers perceived about the friendliness and competency of a company's workers, and what customers think of its processes, such as return policies or reservation procedures. Eight of the top 25 companies in the list are in the tourism and hospitality sector, including Four Seasons, The Ritz-Carlton, and WestJet, all profiled in this book.

In the UK, according to the Institute of Customer Service (2011) customer satisfaction levels rank higher for the tourism industry than many other industry sectors including finance, public services, telecommunications, transport and utilities. Virgin Atlantic, Marriott and Virgin Holidays appear in the list of ten highest scoring names organizations. However, as mentioned earlier, the country came a disappointing 14th in the 2010 international customer service rankings from the Nation Brand Index, in terms of its 'welcome' by visitors.

Customer service levels may be inconsistent in the West, but in Asia the tourism and hospitality sector is often commended for its high levels of service. In a recent customer satisfaction study in Singapore, the tourism sector performed particularly well, with The Ritz-Carlton, Singapore Airlines, Swissotel The Stamford, Shangri-La and Grand Hyatt, taking the top five spots across all sectors. The Ritz-Carlton's director of sales and marketing, Mr. Andres Kohn said: 'Knowing our guests and their preferences helps us to understand their needs, and in turn, we are able to anticipate their requests before they even ask for assistance' (Xuanwei and Chan, 2011). The satisfaction index, implemented by Singapore Management University, measures customer satisfaction across eight economic sectors and 102 organizations.

Case study: The Lopesan Group, Gran Canaria, Spain

Everything is topnotch at Lopesan's Meloneras resort in Gran Canaria, a Spanish island off the northwest coast of Africa. Owner, Eustasio Lopez had a vision to create an upmarket enclave in the sandy south of the island, incorporating five-star hotels, beach, restaurants, shopping malls, golf course, conference center and entertainment facilities. Since 2000 he has built several huge, high-class hotels in the resort and also taken over existing properties to revamp and reinvent.

It is a huge undertaking but Lopez is unfazed by scale. His signature hotel, the four-star Costa Meloneras comprises 1250 rooms amidst opulent décor and lavish landscaping featured prominently by Condé Nast magazine. It is the company's cash cow, with high occupancy almost year round. Gran Canaria hoteliers benefit from the mild winter weather - which attracts millions of European visitors every year - as well as a dependable summer season. The five-star, 570-room Villa del Condé is modeled after his home town of Aguimes and includes all the buildings that a typical Canary village would incorporate as well as a gigantic, central cathedral which is actually the hotel reception. Many of the visitors to Gran Canaria are quintessential sun, sea and sand seekers and so Lopez has brought the culture of the island to the guests rather than have them go out and find it.

The African-themed Baobab Hotel in Gran Canaria

His latest hotel, the African-themed Baobab cost 110,000,000 Euros to build, and exudes Africa with jungle foliage, rivers, bridges, thatched roofs, bamboo furniture, animal pelts and wood-posted balconies, emulating the architecture in rotunda-style villages. Lopez doesn't stop at architecture and interior design – he wants to appeal to every sense and fills his hotels with smells and sounds appropriate to the ambiance. At the Baobab, guests are surrounded by jungle calls as they enter the reception area over a draw bridge. All the hotels have exotic scents pumped out via the air conditioning. One concrete way of providing better customer service is in the amenities of a hotel. As patrons enter any of the Lopesan resorts, they are immediately aware of the spaciousness. There has been much attention directed towards keeping a reasonable ratio of guests to available square footage both in the rooms and in the public areas. By the pools, there are far more sunbeds available than guests. With multiple interests to cater to – from families, to honeymooners, to golfers, to seniors – there are many different areas and pools in each resort. Each pool area is protected – and effectively soundproofed - from the next by dense foliage and interestingly shaped landscaping.

Naturally customer service is high on Lopez's list of priorities and the first inkling of this is when waiters deliver cooled cocktails to anyone waiting to check in at reception. According to Lopesan's quality control manager, Pablo Lorenzo, Lopez holds to the Spanish saying 'there's no second chance for a first impression'. His aim is to make guests feel as if they have stepped into a different planet. 'The president wanted to promote a different conception of Canary Island tourism in this area,' says Lorenzo. 'I think his vision is a bit like Vegas, not for the casinos, but he would like a very big resort with thematic variety, hence the African and colonial themes.'

The Lopesan mandate is to give more value for money and attract a high-class segment of tourism to Gran Canaria, a destinations which has habitually promoted cheap package deals since the 1960s. Exceptional service doesn't stop at reception though. Once in their rooms, Lopesan guests find televisions already tuned into the correct language channel for them. Later, if they order a particular drink on their room key card, the next day the waiters will already know their favorite tipple. 'This makes a customer feel special,' explains Lorenzo, who says that innovative ideas come from both customer and staff feedback. If guests return more than three times, they are considered 'repeaters' and will be greeted in their rooms with complementary drinks and fruit.

But how does he ensure consistently high standards of customer service with 3500 employees and 12,000 beds in his Canary Island properties? Lorenzo says the group invests a lot of money and time on training the staff, 50 % of whom are on fixed contracts and the remainder on seasonal, six month contracts. 'It is very important to keep high standards in training to keep a consistent top level of service across the whole hotel chain,' he says. They also offer higher wages than other competitors in order to attract the best employees. Staff is incentivized by career opportunities within the huge company which owns hotels in the Canary Islands, Germany and Punta Cana. 'We have a large human resources department with a section each for every department within each hotel. Each hotel is audited regularly and there are financial bonuses for managers and second-tier managers,' says Lorenzo. He compares his job to that of 'fireman', putting out fires in all the departments. He also has special personnel responsible for service recovery when problems arise, trained to calm customers and negotiate compensation within already decreed limits.

So where does Lopesan get its high standards for service? Firstly the business is family-run, employing both of Lopez's sons as well as his wife, who were all brought up on Gran Canaria. Also, son Francisco - manager for golf, conferences, marketing and communications - studied in the US, bringing back many ideas and influences from his years in Florida. With 40 % of the customers designated 'repeaters', he is very aware of the need to keep thinking of new things with which to wow guests. Son Roberto is operational manager, also responsible for supervising HR. The family keeps a tight rein on the architecture, interior design, culture and ambiance of the hotels, retaining as much Canary Island heritage as possible. Lopez and his wife still live nearby in the south of Gran Canaria.

Lopez hasn't finished building his dream resort yet. Right next to the Baobab Hotel there is a huge acreage of land – thoughtfully shielded from view by a dense thicket of banana trees – where there are forward plans to build another shopping center, utilizing an underground area, with extravagant flowers and trees above. All around Meloneras, visitors see the Lopesan logo, a dynamic dolphin leaping out of the water – it is Lopez's symbol for leaping up a notch and it will be very interesting to see what he puts his progressive logo on next.

Sources

Interview with Pablo Lorenzo, 2011; Personal visit, 2011; www.lopesan.com

References

Allen, J., Reichheld, F.F. and Hamilton, B. (2005)'Tuning in to the voice of your customer', *Harvard Management Update*, Harvard Business School Publishing, Article Reprint No. U0510C.

American Customer Satisfaction Index (2012)*ACSI Scores: National Sector and Industry*. Accessed 10/14/2011 from http://http://www.theacsi.org/acsi-results/acsi-sectors-and-industries

AMA (1985) 'AMA board approves new marketing definition', *Marketing News*, 1 March, p.1.

AMEX (2011) 'AMEX Global Service Barometer 2011 Press Release', accessed 09/01/2011 from http://www.thetrainingbank.com

Anon (2008) 'Disney helps agents 'imagine' more bookings', *Destination Florida.*

Anon (2009) 'Eight Disney Customer Service Rules'. Accessed 09/06/2011 from http://afterthemouse.com/node/2223_

Associated Press (2011) 'What time is the 3 o'clock parade?' Accessed 09/06/2011 from http://www.msnbc.msn.com/id/20941885/ns/business-us_business/t/what-time-oclock-parade/

Berry, L. L., Hensel, J. S. and Burke, M.C. (1976) 'Improving retailer capability for effective consumerism response', *Journal of Retailing,* **52**(3), 3–14.

Bigger, A.S. and Bigger, L.B. (2010) 'Customer service: Serve today as our jobs may depend on it tomorrow', *Executive Housekeeping Today*, August.

Booms, B. H. and Bitner, M. J. (1981)'Marketing strategies and organizational structures for service firms,' In J. H. Donnelly and W. R. George (Eds.), *Marketing Services*. Chicago: American Marketing Association.

Brokamp, E. (2007) 'Right customer service wrongs', *The Motley Fool*, 24 March. Accessed 09/02/2011 from http://www.fool.com/personal-finance/shopping/2007/03/24/right-customer-service-wrongs.aspx

BusinessWeek (2010)'Customer service champs 2010', accessed 09/04/2011 from http://images.businessweek.com/ss/10/02/0218_customer_service_champs/index.htm

Dickson, D., Ford, R., and Laval, B. (2005) 'Managing Real and Virtual Waits in Hospitality and Service Organizations', *Cornell Hotel and Restaurant Administration Quarterly*, **46**(1), 52-68.

1

Fisk, R.P., Grove, S.J. and John, J. (2000) *Interactive Services Marketing*, Boston: Houghton Mifflin Company.

Free Books Online (2011b)'History of Customer Service', accessed 09/01/2011, http://free-books-online.org/marketing/customer-relationship-management-marketing/history-of-customer-service/

Gagnon, G.B. and Roh, Y.S. (2008)'The impact of customization and reliability on customer satisfaction in the US lodging industry', *Journal of Quality Assurance in Hospitality & Tourism*, **8**(3), 60-78.

Institute of Customer Service (2011)'Public services satisfying customers in tough times', July, accessed 09/02/2011 from http://www.instituteofcustomerservice.com/files/UKCSI_July_2011_summary.pdf

Jackson, D. (2005) 'The importance of being earnest', *The Global Future Forum*. Accessed 09/02/2011 from http://feedback.precise.com/documents/the_future_of_service.pdf

Lucas, R.W. (2009) *Customer Service. Skills for Success*, Boston: McGraw Hill.

McCarthy, E. J. (1981) *Basic Marketing, a Managerial Approach* (7th ed.). Georgetown, ON: Irwin.

Miller, R. (2011)'Customer focus in a slow economy', *Customer Service Excellence*, October, 16-17.

Owen, D. (1999). *The Making of the Masters*, New York: Simon and Schuster.

Schultz, D.E. (2002)'Study internal marketing for better impact', *Marketing News*, **14** October, 8-9.

Solnet, D., Kandampully, J. and Kralj, A. (2010) 'Legends of service excellence: The habits of seven highly effective hospitality companies', *Journal of Hospitality Marketing & Management*, **19**, 889-908.

UNWTO (2012) *UNWTO Tourism Highlights, 2012 edition*.

Waites, R. (2011) 'Why is service still so bad in the UK?', *BBC News Magazine* 12 January, accessed 09/01/2011 from http://www.bbc.co.uk/news/magazine-121234

Xuanwei, T. and Chan, W. (2011) 'Tourism sector gets top marks', *Today*, 10 February, p. 6.

Zeithaml, V. A., Bitner, M. J., Gremler, D., Mahaffey, T. and Hiltz, B. (2007) *Services Marketing: Integrating Customer Focus across the Firm*, Canadian Edition. New York: McGraw-Hill.

Zeithaml, V. A. and Bitner, M. J. (2000). *Services Marketing: Integrating Customer Focus across the Firm*. New York: McGraw-Hill, p. 16.

Scan here to get the hyperlinks in this chapter

2 The Financial and Behavioral Impacts of Customer Service

Photo Courtesy of Scott Dunn Travel

A British luxury travel company has spent over 25 years wowing its customers. From its first ski season when the owner personally drove to France with huge supplies of bacon to perfect its English breakfasts, Scott Dunn has gone the extra mile for service and for quality. 'From day one we wanted to be the best,' says founder Andrew Dunn. The company was established in 1986 initially as a ski chalet business, operating out of two chalets in Verbier, Switzerland. Despite first year losses, 22-year-old Dunn ploughed on, opening up chalets in neighboring resorts and differentiating on comforts such as down duvets and morning tea in bed. Launching his London office in 1988, he provided his own staff and British nannies for his Swiss and French properties, establishing a benchmark for Alpine chalet holidays with his emphasis on opulence and personal service. Up until then, most competitors had provided quaint but adequate accommodation, basic catering, and very low-budget wines.

When Giles Tonner joined the Scott Dunn team in the 1990s, worldwide tailor-made adventure holidays were added to the mix – this was soft adventure without compromising comfort. Seeing a bigger profit margin in high-end travel, Dunn also added long-haul luxury and Mediterranean villas with private chefs, hosts, nannies and exclusive children's clubs. He was following the advice of his grandmother who told him when he started his business: 'Andrew, you never want to be selling the cheapest – people will always pay for the best'.

A graduate in Psychology and Biology from Oxford Brookes University, Dunn has always been astute in consumer behavior. 'I was acutely aware that a guest is not just a single purchase; they are a multiple purchase and there's potentially a lifetime journey with them'. He looks to woo each customer early on and retain them through the different phases of their lives: marriage, parenthood and beyond. 'It's a massive responsibility because if you screw up it's not just that booking you are going to lose; you've probably lost another six bookings over the next couple of years,' he says. His education helped out with recruitment and training, too. 'I've always had a knack for finding the right people to work for me. It's a question of whether I like an individual and a lot about chemistry. I need to know "do they care" and "do they want to give the guests the best experience possible" or do they just want to travel the globe,' says Dunn. Unlike many travel companies, he retains a strong base of year-round staff in order to ensure consistency and high standards with a permanent management team in the UK and seasonal workers in resort – around a third of whom return year round.

Dunn also employs consultants to scope out destinations in Africa, Asia-Pacific, Europe, India, Arabia, Latin America, the Caribbean and South Pacific. They then write Travelogs for the company website about their experiences and also work as advisors to potential customers. 'What makes us different is that nothing is too much trouble,' explains Dunn. 'That mantra is just as important today as it was 25 years ago. If you worry and you care and you want your guests to have a good time, then they will.' The Scott Dunn website promises to craft something special for each customer. This type of one-on-one service has led to more than 70% repeat business through loyalty and referral. The Scott Dunn service philosophy includes unexpected acts of kindness (U.A.K.s) – a term Dunn coined – for guests, and there's a behind-scenes budget for this. The price tag of such extras is never questioned. 'We obviously try to mitigate costs as much as we can but nothing that would affect a guest. If you're part of the DNA of the company, you understand the importance of the guest,' Dunn asserts.

It has not been easy weathering two economic slumps during Scott Dunn's years in business. But, quick to react to external pressures, Dunn circumvented disaster early in his career when the 1992 recession compromised his company. He reached out to a dozen new investors by offering both a 1% share in the company as well as free holidays. Profits grew 20% year-on-year between 1992 and 2008 and potential dangers from the 2008 recession were averted by cutting back on quantity rather than quality, reducing the amount of accommodation offered and securing more performance-linked contracts. By 2011 profits had soared again with sales of $40 million, zero debt and seven-figure profits from the 10,000 yearly holidaymakers who average more than $19,000 per booking.

One thing in his favor, particularly during economic downturns, is that the high-spending clientele is relatively recession-proof: 'When we're negotiating our rates (with chalets, hotel rooms), we explain to the resorts that they will want our guests rather than someone booking on Expedia, for example, as they are going to spend more and be more value. They're buying a caliber of guest who is not afraid to spend.' When asked how Scott Dunn has outlived many competitors over the past quarter century, Dunn explains: 'We've been consistent; we've always undersold and over-delivered and provided you do that, you manage people's expectations and they wax lyrical as you exceed their expectations. It's then all about having the right people working with you.' He also thinks too many travel companies focus on the bottom line rather than on keeping customers: 'they are too busy counting beans.'

While still the controlling shareholder, Dunn expanded his senior management in 2010 by recruiting a chairman, Clive Beharrell, and a managing director, Simon Russell, who brought a wealth of experience from working for Thomas Cook and British Airways Holidays. Dunn remains the ideas person, also in charge of guest loyalty and brand enhancement. In 2011 Scott Dunn was voted Favorite Specialist Tour Operator in Condé Nast Traveller Readers' Travel Awards. Scores were particularly high in relation to reliability, staff and service. 'We call it guest service rather than customer service,' insists Dunn. He thinks his style of exemplary service is why Scott Dunn has survived while other 'young pretenders' have failed. Dunn says the award will give the company 'collateral for the next 12 months or so' for marketing, advertising and online clout. But he also rates highly the value of good press. 'PR is very important for us, more so than advertising,' he says. A recent coup was a three page feature story in *The Sunday Times* Saturday Travel section. 'It helps us create that warm, fuzzy feeling,' explains Dunn.

How to sustain the personal touch and strong service culture during future growth is obviously something that concerns Dunn: 'Of course if I didn't worry about this, there would be something wrong. We're growing around 20% a year but I think we can still maintain this culture.' He advocates a family-orientation throughout all levels of personnel and encourages open lines of communication. 'I had two staff members come to see me earlier on this morning. We have regular open communication to reinforce why we're the company we are, why we are different. So I asked them what do you think is the most important thing in dealing with guests and they said "nothing is too much trouble.'"

Sources

Personal interview with Andrew Dunn, 1 October 2011; O'Connell (2011); http://www.scottdunn.com

http://www.thesundaytimes.co.uk/sto/public/roadtorecovery/article661649.ece

The relative importance of the service economy

As world economies shift from a dependence on manufacturing to a focus on providing timely, quality service, customer service becomes more and more critical to business success – particularly in the service sector. The opening spotlight featuring Scott Dunn Travel is a good example. The tourism industry is just one part of the growing service sector, and there is an increasing dominance of services in economies worldwide. The services sector employs around 45% of the world's total labor force, and in many western countries, the service sector is responsible for over three-quarters of the Gross Domestic Product. In North America today over 75% of people employed work in the service sector and only 10% are employed in manufacturing. The service sector accounts for nearly 80% of GDP. This is the same in many European economies (United Kingdom, Netherlands, Luxembourg, Sweden, France, Denmark and Belgium) and, outside Europe, other manufacturing countries have moved to services as well. For example, in Korea service activities represented 53.8% of total employment in 1995 and ten years later they reached 65% (Rubalcaba, 2007).

The growth in the service sector has exceeded overall economic performance for decades, which has resulted in the share of services in total economic activity increasing over time. The rising trend can be expected to continue, or even accelerate, in light of the increasing prominence of knowledge-based, service-oriented activities. The growing role reflects higher consumer and business demand, outsourcing of service-related activities from manufacturing firms and the major role played by information technology. With swifter communication and data gathering available, companies can no longer afford to neglect more personal customer interaction and service.

Services also play an important intermediary role that is not easily reflected in statistics. Well-established financial, transportation and distribution systems, for example, are critical for the smooth functioning of all businesses and, for that matter, governments. In the field of international trade, although services themselves are not as widely traded as manufactured goods, they are associated with, and support, every export and import transaction. In the absence of such services, international trade would grind to a halt (OECD, 2000).

Stahel (1994) has argued that as a company moves from maximizing sales of material products to the delivery of customer satisfaction, its long-term source of competitive advantage will become the ability to provide the needed service, and that economic value will be based in utilization (customer satisfaction in the service gained). With seven out of ten people employed within the global service industries, many service providers are increasingly under pressure to provide value for money and meet service consumer expectations. Service consumers expect consistent standards in all service encounters (McManus, 2009). As Isadore Sharp, founder of the Four Seasons (see *Spotlight* in Chapter 4) says: "Quality is far and away the chief factor in competitiveness" (Sharp, 2009: 91).

Impact of service quality on market share growth, prices and profits

Service quality has been increasingly identified as a key factor in differentiating service products and building a competitive advantage in tourism. The spotlight on Andrew Dunn at the beginning of this chapter clearly demonstrated such differentiation. The process by which customers evaluate a purchase, thereby determining satisfaction and likelihood of repurchase, is important to all marketers, but especially to services marketers because, unlike their manufacturing counterparts, they have fewer objective measures of quality by which to judge their production. Service quality can be defined as customers' perceptions of the service component of a product, and these perceptions are said to be based on five dimensions: reliability, assurance, empathy, responsiveness, and tangibles (Parasuraman et a., 1988).

Many researchers believe that an outgrowth of service quality is customer satisfaction, measured as the difference between the service that a customer expects and the perceived quality of what is actually delivered (Reichheld and Sasser, 1990). Satisfying customers has always been a key component of the tourism industry, but never before has it been so critical. In these uncertain times, and with increased competition, knowing how to win and keep customers is the single-most important business skill that anyone can learn. Customer satisfaction and loyalty are the keys to long-term profitability, and keeping the customer happy is everybody's business. Becoming customer-centered and exceeding customer expectations are requirements for business success.

Well-publicized research shows that companies can increase profits from 25% to 85% by retaining just 5% more of their customers (Reichheld and Sasser, 1990), but the newest research indicates that merely 'satisfying' customers is no longer enough to ensure loyalty (Heskett et al, 1997). There is little or no correlation between satisfied (versus highly satisfied) customers and customer retention (see Figure 2.1). This means that it is not enough just to please customers. Each customer should become so delighted with all elements of their association with an organization that buying from someone else is unthinkable.

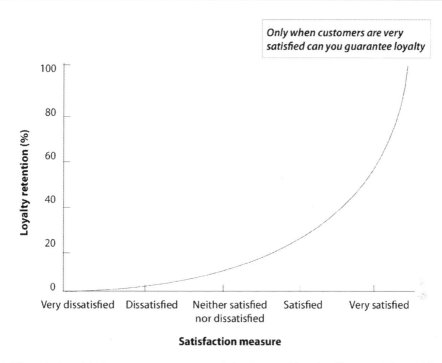

Figure 2.1: The relationship between customer satisfaction and loyalty (Source: Adapted from Heskett et al, 1997)

Today the issue of highest priority related to service quality involves understanding the impact of service quality on profit and other financial outcomes of the organization. Executives of many companies in the 1980s were willing to trust their intuitive sense that better service would lead to improved financial success. They therefore committed resources to improving service prior to having documentation of the financial payoff. Some of these companies, such as Four Seasons (see Chapter 4) and Loews Hotels & Resorts (see *Snapshot* in this chapter) have been richly rewarded for their efforts. But executives in other companies have been reluctant to invest in service improvements without solid evidence of their financial soundness. As Andrew Dunn commented in the opening spotlight, too many companies focus on the bottom line rather than on keeping customers – 'they are too busy counting beans,' he says.

However, research on the relationship between service quality and profits has begun to accumulate. Findings from these studies show that companies offering superior service achieve higher than normal market share growth (Buzzell and Gale, 1987); that the mechanisms by which service quality influences profits include increased market share and premium prices (Phillips et al, 1983); and that businesses in the top quintile of relative service quality realize on average an 8% higher price than their competitors (Gale, 1992).

The American Customer Satisfaction Index data referred to in Chapter 1 have proven to be strongly related to a number of essential indicators of micro and macroeconomic performance (ACSI, 2011). For example, firms with higher levels of customer satisfaction tend to have higher earnings and stock returns relative to competitors. Stock portfolios based on companies that show strong performance in ACSI deliver excess returns in up-markets as well as down-markets. And, at the macro level, customer satisfaction has been shown to be predictive of both consumer spending and gross domestic product growth, as exemplified by the upcoming snapshot on Loews Hotels and Resorts..

Consumers worldwide are willing to spend more on service excellence. It was mentioned in Chapter 1 that seven in ten Americans are willing to spend an average of 13% more with companies they believe provide excellent customer service (AMEX, 2011). The same study found a similar willingness in other countries (Australia and Canada, 12%; Mexico, 11%; UK, 10%; France, 9%; Italy, 9%; Germany, 8%; and Netherlands, 7%). In India, consumers would spend 22% more for excellent customer service. One recent study found that the value of great customer service in the US economy is a staggering $267.8 billion per year (STELLAService, 2010). This figure was calculated based on the average spend per person per year with each type of company. Value is the extra percentage that people are willing to spend if they know they will receive great service. If the consumers surveyed received great customer service, 70% would use the same company again, and 50% would make recommendations to family and friends (see Figure 2.2). In the hotel sector, the study found that consumers are willing to spend 11% more for great service, higher than most other sectors.

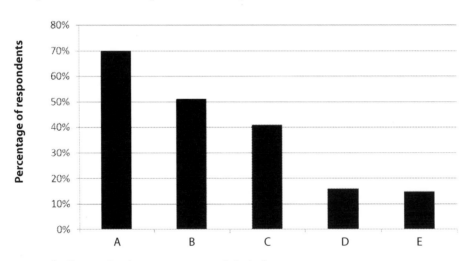

A   Plan on using the same company again in the future
B   Recommend company to friends or family
C   Bought a second product or service form the company, following the great customer experience
D   Added more products or services at the time of purchase
E   None

Figure 2.2: The value of great customer service (Source: STELLA Service, 2010, p.7)

Jonathan M. Tisch is a master multi-tasker. He is co-Chairman of the Board and a member of the Office of the President of Loews Corporation, one of the largest diversified financial holding companies in the US, as well as the Chairman of its subsidiary, Loews Hotels & Resorts. He also manages to be a successful author, television host, public speaker, holds various national leadership roles in the travel and tourism industry in addition to his work with the arts and his role as a co-owner and a member of the Board of Directors of the New York Giants and the team's Treasurer.

Jonathan Tisch, Loews Hotels & Resorts

After graduating from Tufts University, Tisch worked as a cinematographer and producer for WBZ-TV in Boston where he was nominated twice for local Emmy Awards, gaining useful media experience which he later brought to Loews Hotels. Tisch has used his production expertise and public relations acumen to elevate the recognition of the Loews Hotels brand.

Loews Corporation, founded by Tisch's father, Preston Robert "Bob" Tisch, and uncle, Larry Tisch, is a financial holding company with interests in oil, natural gas, insurance and hotels. Its subsidiary, Loews Hotels, founded in 1946, owns and/or operates 18 hotels and resorts throughout the US and Canada. For more than two decades, Tisch's role has been to expand Loews Hotels, developing the four-diamond brand with an innovative corporate culture which focuses on partnerships.

Tisch has been at the forefront of Loews Hotels' renewed growth plan. In 2012, with the goal of doubling the size of the company within the next five years, Tisch appointed renowned hospitality executive, Paul Whetsell, to the position of President and CEO. Their task is to continue to operate the unique properties in the Loews Hotels portfolio, while also looking for additions to the brand through acquisition, development and management. Loews' long tradition of owning and operating high quality hotels and delivering great guest experiences continues with the objectives of further developing and growing the brand while delivering superior financial operating results.

Tisch's strategy is that profitability will be improved by establishing partnerships that empower employees, satisfy customers and contribute to communities. The crux of his message is that he could never have achieved his career success alone. He has spent his working life building relationships with colleagues, customers, communities and even competitors. He advocates reaching the customer beyond the usual advertising campaigns by engendering 'buzz' in order to create ever-increasing ripples of word-of-mouth marketing. He does this by creating experiences for customers rather than relying on just products or services.

In the aftermath of the 9/11 terrorist attacks, Tisch was Chairman of New York Rising, a task force created to rebuild the city by revitalizing tourism. In recognition of his work he was named one of Crain's New York Business 'Top Ten Most Influential Business Leaders' and the 2006 'CEO of the Year' by the Executive Council of New York.

Another prong of Tisch's approach is linking business with the communities where Loews Hotels operates, particularly through volunteerism, speaking engagements, activities and social media networking. At the forefront of corporate responsibility, he initiated the Loews Hotels Good Neighbor Policy over 20 years ago. The Good Neighbor Policy was the hospitality industry's first comprehensive outreach program to address social responsibility in our communities and is a recipient of the US President's Service Award from the Points of Light Foundation.

Having applied his relationship and partnership philosophy to business, Tisch is not reticent in sharing his success with competitors and potential customers, worldwide. Thanks to his three published books and his TV shows, the secrets to Loews' success are internationally famous. His first book, *The Power of We: Succeeding Through Partnerships*, explains his partnership philosophy. In his second book, *Chocolates on the Pillow Aren't Enough: Reinventing the Customer Experience*, he explores customer service and product enhancement to meet customers' changing needs. And his third book, *Citizen You: Doing Your Part to Change the World*, emphasizes corporate responsibility and community volunteerism.

Drawing on his television expertise, Tisch participated in The Learning Channel's role reversal reality show, *Now Who's Boss?* where he demonstrated his understanding of his employees' roles within the company by doing all of their different jobs over one week at the Loews Miami Beach Hotel. From cook to bellhop, housekeeper to working at check-in, Tisch did each job to get a better understanding of his co-workers' various challenges. With his Emmy-nominated and Gracie Award-winning program, *Beyond the Boardroom with Jonathan Tisch*, he speaks with some of America's preeminent CEOs and business luminaries in one-on-one interviews. Viewers discover that business is about more than just numbers, rather, it's the successful combination of people, hard work, guts, and imagination. He further spreads the word through speaking engagements and social media, and with his Huffington Post blogs. These address diverse issues such as active citizenship, volunteerism, unemployment, infrastructure, promoting New York and also America in general, the arts, parenthood and the lost art of customer service.

Sources: Personal communication with Jonathan Tisch, Loews Hotel & Resorts, and Jennifer Farley, Walnut Hill Media, August 2012

The behavioral consequences of customer service

Another fruitful area of research is that which examines the relationship between service quality and behavioral intentions. Zeithaml et al (1996) have developed a conceptual model that depicts the behavioral consequences of service quality as intervening variables between service quality and the financial gains or losses from retention or defection (see Figure 2.3). The top half of the model is at the level of the individual customer and proposes that service quality and behavioral intentions are related and, therefore, that service quality is a determinant of whether a customer ultimately remains with or defects from a company.

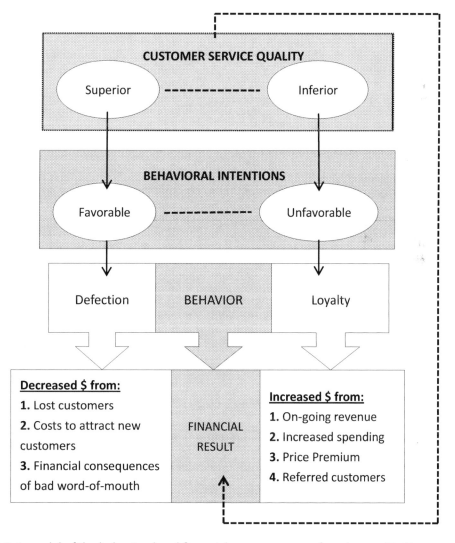

Figure 2.3: A model of the behavioral and financial consequences of service quality (Source: Adapted from Zeithaml and Parasuraman, 1996)

By integrating research findings and anecdotal evidence, a list of specific indicators of customers' favorable behavioral intentions can be compiled. These include saying positive things about the company to others, recommending the company or service to others, paying a price premium to the company, and remaining loyal to the company. Loyalty may be manifested in a variety of ways – for example, by expressing a preference for a company over others, by continuing to purchase from it, or by increasing business with it in the future. Customers perceiving service performance to be inferior are likely to exhibit behaviors signaling that they are poised to leave the company or spend less money with the company. These behaviors include complaining, which is viewed by many researchers as a variety of negative responses that stem from dissatisfaction and predict or accompany defection.

After testing this model, the authors found strong empirical support for the intuitive notion that improving service quality can increase favorable behavioral intentions and decrease unfavorable intentions. The findings demonstrate the importance of strategies that can steer behavioral intentions in the right directions, including (1) striving to meet customers' 'desired-service' levels (rather than merely performing at their 'adequate-service' levels), (2) emphasizing the prevention of service problems, and (3) effectively resolving problems that do occur. However, multiple findings suggest that companies wanting to improve service, especially beyond the desired-service level, should do so in a cost-effective manner.

One popular model that interprets the behavioral consequences of service is the Apostle Model, developed at Harvard Business School (Jones and Sasser, 1995). Based on satisfaction and loyalty, this approach segments customers into four quadrants: Loyalists, Hostages, Mercenaries, and Defectors. The Apostle Model has been adopted and refined by Market Metrix into a practical tool for grouping hospitality industry segments, brands and individual customers (Barsky and Nash, 2007). Based on results from the 2006 Market Metrix Hospitality Index (140,000 customer surveys completed during the year), hotel brand scores for customer satisfaction (horizontal axis) and loyalty (vertical axis) were plotted on a chart (see Figure 2.4).

Loyalists are customers who have high satisfaction and high loyalty. Sub-segments are Apostles, who have the highest satisfaction and loyalty scores, and Near Apostles, who give high ratings for both, but at a slightly lower level. Some 80% of Starbucks' revenues come from Apostles who visit their stores an average of 18 times a month. Hotel brands create Apostles when they deliver not only superior products and services, but also create an emotional connection derived from the total experience. These customers are loyal because they love a business. The Ritz-Carlton and Four Seasons have created apostles who are so satisfied that they want to convert others to share their experience. Defectors are those who have low satisfaction and low loyalty. A sub-segment comprises the Terrorists, with the lowest satisfaction and loyalty scores. In addition with the costs associated with losing them, these customers are so unhappy that they speak out against a brand at every opportunity. Hotel brands found in the Defector quadrant include a number of chains whose products and services have not evolved as quickly as customer expectations have changed.

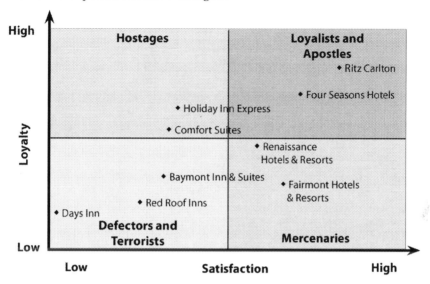

Figure 2.4: The Apostle Model applied to the hospitality industry (Source: Adapted from Barsky and Nash, 2007)

Hostages are customers who have low satisfaction, but still report high loyalty. This typically is due to lack of competition or high switching costs. Customers in this category feel 'trapped.' Hotel brands in this category often win business simply due to their location (when no suitable alternatives are nearby) or, because of the strength of their loyalty club. However, these customers exhibit 'false loyalty' – acting loyal even when they are just waiting for a chance to jump ship. Mercenaries are those who have high satisfaction, but low loyalty. These customers are often price-sensitive and will switch easily when they have the opportunity. Companies in this category may provide superior products and services but do not stand out from the competition. They may be seen as interchangeable with other similar level hotels because they have not created a passion for their brand (like the Loyalists have).

The service profit chain

The snapshot on Loews Hotels & Resorts illustrated the financial rewards of delivering superior guest experiences. Chairman Jonathan Tisch's strategy is that profitability will be improved by establishing partnerships that empower employees, satisfy customers and contribute to communities. The logic connecting employee satisfaction and loyalty to customer satisfaction and loyalty – and ultimately profits – is illustrated by the service profit chain (Heskett et al, 1997). The chain suggests there are critical linkages among internal service quality; employee satisfaction/ productivity; the value of services provided to the customer; and ultimately customer satisfaction, retention, and profits. The model implies that companies that exhibit high levels of success on the elements of the model will be more successful and profitable than those that do not.

In Figure 2.5, the profit chain is applied to the Lopesan hotels featured in Chapter 1. The chain begins with internal service quality where human labor is of critical importance to the hotel industry. Efforts need to be made internally to enhance the professional skills of employees and motivate them to satisfy the specific needs and wants of guests. This was evident in the Lopesan case in Chapter 1 where the group spent considerable resources training its 3500 staff. The theory is that employee satisfaction will lead to increased productivity and higher retention levels, which will in turn increase the value of hotel services for customers, resulting in satisfaction and loyalty. Staff retention at Lopesan is higher than average, with 50% of staff on fixed contracts. They are also paid higher wages than other competitors and are incentivized by career opportunities and financial bonuses. The resulting external value for customers comes in the form of exceptional service. From the minute customers arrive at the hotel they are treated like valued guests; waiters deliver cooled cocktails to anyone waiting to check in at reception, and once in their rooms, Lopesan guests find televisions already tuned into the correct language channel for them. Later, if they order a particular drink on their room key card, the next day the waiters will already know their favorite tipple. Satisfied guests tend to make repeat visits and share their positive experiences with other potential guests, leading to greater profits and the growth of hotel enterprises. At the Lopesan hotels, a 40% loyalty rate contributes to higher than average occupancy, and a healthy balance sheet, completing the profit chain for the Canary Island's hotel group.

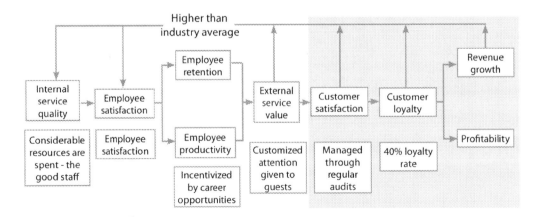

Figure 2.5: The service profit chain at work in the Lopesan hotels (Source: Based on Heskett et al, 1997).

To understand the financial value of building long-term relationships with customers, companies sometimes calculate lifetime values. The lifetime value of a customer is a calculation that considers customers from the point of view of their potential lifetime revenue and profitability contributions to a company. This value is influenced by the length of an average lifetime, the average revenues generated in that time period, sales of additional products and services over time, and referrals generated by the customer. For example, Snowsports Industries America has estimated that each skier beginning at the age of ten, has a life time value to the industry of $52,024. In Disney's case, a typical household of 3.6 people has a lifetime value of more than $50,000 to the company (Schlaifer, 2006). But is not just the lifetime value of consumers that is important to tourism providers. In the Bahamas, where diving is a multimillion dollar industry, and sharks are an ever increasing draw, experts have calculated that a single shark in a healthy habitat is worth as much as $200,000 in tourism revenue over its lifetime (Holland, 2007).

Offensive and defensive marketing effects of service

Companies can use marketing as an offensive or defensive tool to grow their businesses (see Figure 2.6). Offensive marketing refers to the practice of attracting more and better customers to the business, and quality service can play an important role here by improving market share, reputation and price premiums. When service is above average, a company gains a positive reputation and through that reputation a higher market share and the ability to charge more than its competitors. This is certainly the case for Canadian Mountain Holidays (CMH) profiled at the end of this chapter. They have the largest market share in the business and never have to discount.

When it comes to keeping existing customers, the approach is called defensive marketing (Fornell and Wernerfelt, 1987). The CMH case shows how when service is good, a company can gain a positive reputation and through that reputation a higher market share and the ability to charge more than its competitors for services – ultimately resulting in higher profits. CMH also makes a concerted effort to retain customers. Research has shown that the longer a customer remains with a company, the more profitable the relationship is for the organization.

The money a company makes from this retention comes from four sources – lower costs, volume of purchases, price premium and word of mouth communication. Attracting a new customer can be five times more costly than retaining an existing one (Zeithaml et al, 2007), and as mentioned earlier, companies can increase profits from 25% to 85% by retaining just 5% more of their customers. Customers who are satisfied with a company's services are likely to increase the amount of money they spend with that company or the types of services offered (Reichheld and Sasser, 1990). Regular skiers at CMH lodges will spend more on vertical feet skied, and more on clothing and equipment in the lodges. Research has also shown that customers who value services provided will pay a premium for those services, and that is certainly the case for CMH's guests, who spend well over $1000 a day for the privilege to heli-ski. Finally, satisfied customers will advocate the services provided to them, and for CMH, 'encouraged word of mouth' plays a significant role in the company's success.

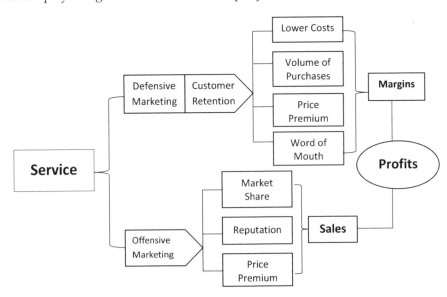

Figure 2.6: The offensive and defensive marketing effects of service on profits (Source: Adapted from Zeithaml et al, 2007).

The financial implications of poor customer service

Negative service takes its toll. According to an American Express study, 81% of Americans will never do business with a company again because of poor customer service (AMEX, 2011). Half of those surveyed say it takes two poor service experiences before they stop doing business with a company. But consumers are far more forgiving if a company has earned their trust over time. Almost nine out of ten consumers say they are willing to give a company a second chance after a bad experience if they have experienced great customer service with that company in the past. Companies that do get it wrong should realize there is a cost: 52% expect something in return after a poor customer experience, even if the problem has been resolved; 70% want an apology or reimbursement. It has been estimated that reducing customer defections by as little as 5% can double an organization's profits (Reichheld, 1996).

According to research by IBM, dissatisfaction has a clear impact on shareholder value (IBM, 2002). Consumer spending trends correspond closely with customer satisfaction. When customers are not happy, they spend less, and corporate profitability suffers. Those frustrated customers may share their unfavorable opinions, driving away potential new customers. The impact doesn't stop with lost revenue; costs go up too. Businesses are forced to spend more on customer acquisition, trying to replace losses in their customer base. Companies also have to absorb costs associated with resolving customer complaints.

A study of business-to-business (B-to-B) customer service in 2009 found that 30% of companies switched vendors due to poor customer service costing the companies they ditched, on average, $15 million each in lost business (Sprague, 2009). A superior experience with a provider encouraged loyalty for two thirds of recipients. Two important factors created such a superior and differentiated customer service experience: the quality/competence of service personnel and the ability to address the problem on the first call or email. Another B-to-B study in Europe looked at the impact of poor customer service on businesses' likelihood of getting paid. Apparently poor customer service impacts Europe's top 1000 businesses' profits by over $11 billion a year and creates a cash flow gap of about $220 billion (Bielenberg, 2006). The more unhappy customers are, the more unlikely they are to delay or withhold payment. This in turn inflates write-offs and bad debt, and impacts cash flow and working capital – ultimately destroying profits and shareholder value.

As was mentioned previously, some customers that defect after poor service can turn into what are called 'terrorists,' who are desperate to tell others about their unhappy experiences. The Starbucks 'coffee terrorist' is a good example (Zeithaml et al, 2007). In 1995, a Starbucks customer purchased a defective cappuccino maker and demanded the company replace it with its top-of-the-line machine, worth approximately $2000 more than the one he had purchased. He threatened to take out a full-page ad in the *Wall Street Journal* if Starbucks did not comply. The company refused his demands so he went ahead and published the ad – and of course received national media attention. The ad read as follows: 'Had any problems at Starbucks Coffee? You're not alone. Interested? Let's talk. (800) 510-3483.' Nearly 3000 unhappy customers of Starbucks responded with their tales of ill-treatment by Starbucks.

Of course, with the advent of social media, customer service terrorists can vent their anger in less expensive ways, and still reach a very wide audience. Berger and Milkman (2010) took a psychological approach to understanding the diffusion of online content. They found that anxiety- and anger-inducing Internet content is highly shared. In fact, the most powerful predictor of email 'virality' in their study was how much anger an article evokes. A good example of such virality was the complaint letter from a Virgin passenger in 2008 that was circulated around the world and has been almost universally praised for its directness and humor. In fact, Oliver Beale's letter to Virgin Atlantic chairman Richard Branson is generally acknowledged as the best customer service complaint letter (Daily Telegraph, 2009).

The complainant contacted Branson after a flight from Mumbai to Heathrow, to convey his disappointment with the food served on board the airline. In his 2008 missive, Beale, an ad agency employee, deconstructs a flight from London to Mumbai. His tirade mocks the food ('a crime against bloody cooking'), the in-flight movie ('Is that Ray Liotta?'), and pokes fun at Branson ('I can't imagine what dinner round your house is like, it must be like something out of a nature documentary') – all in 1070 hugely entertaining words. The letter also included five photographs of the 'offending' dishes. The London-based passenger afterwards received a call from Sir Richard inviting him to come to the airline's catering house next month, to help select the food on future Virgin flights. 'While we investigated his complaint seriously, and following Richard Branson's phone call we've invited him to our catering house to select the next range of meals and wines we serve on board,' said a spokesman for Virgin Atlantic. 'Then we can ensure his personal taste is well and truly catered for' (Daily Telegraph, 2009). At the time of writing, the YouTube version of the complaint letter had been viewed by over 17,000 people.

Case Study: Profiting from fun in the Canadian Rockies

Photo Courtesy of CMH

Canadian Mountain Holidays (CMH), a helicopter tourism pioneer, was founded in 1965 and operates in 12 mountain areas of southeastern British Columbia. The Banff-based business claims a market share of around 52% in the global heli-skiing domain and boasts a 65% repeat-booking figure in the winter. CMH has the leasehold rights from the BC government to 15,765 km^2 of remote territory in the Purcell, Cariboo, Selkirk, and Monashee mountain ranges. It operates 21 helicopters over 11 ski areas including eight remote lodges – many accessible in winter only by helicopter. Lodges have been designed specifically to meet the needs of heli-tourists. Each lodge has a dining room and a fully stocked lounge and is equipped with a sauna and a jacuzzi. There are even resident qualified massage practitioners who can rejuvenate skiers' tired muscles. The company divides its business into three strands: heli-skiing, heli-hiking, and mountaineering.

According to Chief Marketing Officer, Marty von Neudegg 'CMH is just a bunch of mountain guides taking people into the mountains to have fun, and the company philosophy reflects this attitude.' But is having fun a good enough foundation for a successful business model? Back in 1965, the late Hans Gmoser – the founder of CMH – took a few friends up in a helicopter to go skiing in untracked powder while working as a mountain guide. It didn't take long to catch on. 'Demand literally exploded. Suddenly there were no four-five hour walks and areas became so accessible. I was driven because I had such a good time myself, but it was infectious, and it rubbed off on the guests,' Gmoser explained in a 2008 interview.

About 50% of CMH customers nowadays are from Europe and 45% from the USA. A seven-day package cost between $6,600 and $11,820 for the 2012 season and included 100,000 vertical feet of skiing, and accommodation and food for seven nights. CMH invented heli-hiking (an abbreviation for helicopter-assisted hiking) in 1978, and from June to September it runs high altitude hiking excursions that depart from five mountain lodges. All-inclusive packages range from family adventures and photography workshops to alpine ecology. Stays can be at one or a combination of five lodges, and three-night heli-hiking packages cost approximately $2000. Helicopters transport guests to remote wilderness areas around BC, where participants can decide from day to day whether they want to be mountaineers scaling steep ridges or hikers, strolling leisurely along the glaciers and flower-filled meadows.

Marketing at CMH is very unique. The company's greatest marketing vehicle is 'encouraged word of mouth' and CMH does very little advertising. Marty von Neudegg says that there are three marketing areas for the company: sales, advertising, and service. However, 90% of the marketing budget is spent on service, in order to encourage customer loyalty. It must be working as repeaters account for over 65% of business. CMH produces colorful brochures for each of its three activity strands (winter brochures being produced in six languages), expensive videos are made for all three products, and a website exists for each activity.

Another critical ingredient of CMH's marketing strategy is search engine optimization and social media, according to Media Manager, Sarah Pearson. 'This is an increasingly integral and important factor in our marketing strategy. The more we can drive traffic to our website and convert those viewers into active leads, the more successful our marketing strategy is. Engaging both our potential and existing guests through social media is a very powerful tool for increasing referrals, retaining guest connections, and spreading the culture of CMH.' CMH also hosts marketing events called 'An Evening with CMH' through-out North America, Europe, Japan, and Australia. These are invitation-only evenings at which CMH staff and guides entertain and provide information to past guests and their friends. These events are very successful, generating high conversion rates. Pearson feels these events are well worth the investment: 'It's hard to track the conversion rate to book-ings right away as that really spans a two year period. But we feel it is very worth doing as it builds customer loyalty in the markets we're going into and we see an immediate pick up on bookings from those regions. Over time, where we put a lot of energy into events, they continue to grow and we get more names in the system and more people in the marketing funnel.'

When CMH began marketing in Europe during the late 1960s and early 1970s, Europe-ans had no knowledge of Canadian heli-skiing opportunities. Rather than following the normal route of mass-media advertising, CMH chose to place no advertisements at all. Instead, the company found one person in each nation to be the CMH agent, and this person had to know the product and its market intimately. These agents sold heli-skiing to one person at a time, in a very personal interaction. This took place many years before the term 'one-to-one' marketing had been coined. Although the distribution system has become more sophisticated over the years, these 16 agents still work in Europe and bring in 55% of the business. For the US and Canadian markets CMH employs its own travel agency, based in Banff.

CMH is also part of the 'Adventure Collection,' a group of nine adventure companies that have joined together to form an alliance based on the principle that each company is deeply committed to the environment and culture through which it takes its guests. The alliance prints a collective brochure that is sent to guests of all nine companies, and the companies jointly promote each other's trips. They also combine itineraries to create new trips in order to give travellers more choices.

Although the company may not have changed much in culture over the years, the ownership structure has. Gmoser himself found the only way he could detach himself emotionally from the company was to sell it to Alpine Helicopters in 1995. Two years later, Intrawest Corp. of Vancouver purchased a 45% stake in Alpine, and in November 2005 bought the remaining 55%. Involved in 15 mountain resorts in North America and Europe, Intrawest invests heavily in real estate developments and tourism infrastructure, adding retail, lodging and restaurants to attract people to its resorts and keep them there. So far, Intrawest has left the CMH culture intact.

Sources: Personal interviews with Marty Von Neudegg, Hans Gmoser, CMH Media Manager, Sarah Pearson.

References

AMEX (2011) 'AMEX Global Service Barometer 2011 Press Release', accessed 09/01/2011 from http://www.thetrainingbank.com

Barsky, J. and Nash, L. (2007) 'What percent of your customers are loyalists?', *Market Metrix*, 15 May, accessed 09/01/ 2011 from http://www.marketmetrix.com/en/default.aspx?s=research&p=whatpctloyal

Berger, J. and Milkman, K. (2009) 'Social transmission emotion, and the virality of online content', accessed 06/10/ 2011from SSRN: http://ssrn.com/abstract=1528077

Bielenberg, D. (2006) *The Financial Impact of Bad Customer Service*, The Customer Value Group, May, accessed 09/01/ 2011 from http://www.customervaluegroup.com

Buzzell, D. and Gale B. T. (1987) *The PIMS Principles*, New York: Free Press.

Daily Telegraph (2009) 'Virgin: the world's best passenger complaint letter?', Travel section, 26 January, accessed 09/11/2011 from http://www.telegraph.co.uk/travel/travelnews/4344890/Virgin-the-worlds-best-passenger-complaint-letter.html

Fornell, C. and Wernerfelt, B. (1987) 'Defensive marketing strategy by customer complaint management: A theoretical analysis', *Journal of Marketing Research*, **24** (November), 337-346.

Gale, B. (1992) 'Monitoring customer satisfaction and market-perceived quality', *American Marketing Association Worth Repeating Series*, Number 922CSO I. Chicago: American Marketing Association.

Heskett, J. L., Sasser, W. E., Jr. and Schlesinger, L. A. (1997) *The Service Profit Chain: How Leading Companies Link Profit and Growth to Loyalty, Satisfaction, and Value*, New York: Free Press, 83.

Holland, J.S. (2007) 'An eden for sharks', *National Geographic*, **211**(3), 116-137.

IBM (2002) *Customer Satisfaction: Do You Know the Score*, Report for the IBM Institute for Business Value prepared by Melody Badgett, Whitney Connor and Jennifer McKinley.

Jones, T.O. and Sasser, W.E. (1995) 'Why satisfied customers defect', *Harvard Business Review*, **73** (November-December), 88-99.

McManus, J. (2009)'The service economy', *Management Services*, Summer, 16-20.

OECD (2000) *The Service Economy*, Organization for Economic Co-operation and Development, accessed 09/05/ 2011 from http://www.oecd.org/dataoecd/10/33/2090561.pdf

O'Connell, D. (2011) 'Long-haul holidays keep their place in the sun', *The Sunday Times*, accessed 10/10/ 2011 from http://www.thesundaytimes.co.uk/sto/public/roadtorecovery/article661649.ece

Parasuraman, A., Zeithaml, V. A. and Berry, L. L. (1988) 'SERVQUAL: A multiple item scale for measuring consumer perceptions of service quality', *Journal of Retailing*, **64**, 12–20.

Phillips, L. D., Chang, D. R. and Buzzell, R. (1983) 'Product quality, cost position and business performance: A test of some key hypotheses', *Journal of Marketing*, **47**(Spring), 26–43.

Reichheld, F. F. and T. Teal (1996), *The Loyalty Effect the Hidden Force Behind Growth, Profits, and Lasting Value*. Boston, Mass: Harvard Business School .

Reichheld, F. F. and Sasser, W. S., Jr. (1990) 'Zero defections: Quality comes to services', *Harvard Business Review*, **68**, 105–111.

Rubalcaba, L. (2007) *The New Services Economy: Challenges and Policy Implications for Europe*, Cheltenham, UK: Edward Elgar Publishing.

Schlaifer, A.N. (2006) 'Build customer and employee loyalty you can be proud of', *The Resort Trades*, July, accessed 09/15/ 2011 from http://www.resorttrades.com/articles. php?showMag=Resort&act=view&id=190

Sharp, I. (2009) *Four Seasons. The Story of a Business Philosophy*, New York: The Penguin Group.

Sprague, B. (2009) 'Customer service is crucial in a downturn', *Bloomberg Businessweek*, 15 May, accessed 11/29/ 2011 from http://www.businessweek.com
Stahel, W. (1994) 'The utilization-focused service economy: Resource efficiency and product-life extension,' In Allenby and Richards, *Greening of Industrial Ecosystems*, National Academy of Engineering, Washington DC. Available through the National Academy Press Office (202-334-3313)

STELLA Service (2010) *The Value of Great Customer Service: The Economic Impact for Online Retail and Other Consumer Categories*, accessed 09/07/ 2011 from http://media. stellaservice.com/public/pdf/Value_of_Great_Customer_Service.pdf

Zeithaml, V. A., Berry, L. L. and Parasuraman, A. (1996) 'The behavioral consequences of service quality', *Journal of Marketing*, **60**, 31–46.

Zeithaml, V. A., Bitner, M. J., Gremler, D., Mahaffey, T. and Hiltz, B. (2007) *Services Marketing: Integrating Customer Focus Across the Firm*, Canadian Edition, New York: McGraw-Hill.

Scan here to get the hyperlinks in this chapter

3 Understanding the Consumer

'At Your Service' Spotlight: Joe Nevin – understanding the needs of the traveling baby boomer

Photo Courtesy of Bumps for Boomers®

When Joe Nevin set up Bumps for Boomers® in Aspen, Colorado in 2003, he had already carefully chosen his market segment: baby boomers (those born between 1946 and 1964) who he felt were keen to carry on skiing into their old age. These are often dubbed Zoomers – boomers with zip – and have no intention of slowing down in passive retirement and are looking for more active travel pursuits in which health and fitness play prominent roles. With life expectancy over 80, there will be 115 million people 50 or older in the US by 2020, 50% more than now.

Having investigated all the latest research into boomer skiers, Nevin produced the tagline Ski For Life™. 'Boomers are slowing down and concerned about injury. They are also worried about skiing on overcrowded runs where they could get knocked down. But they want to go on skiing as long as possible,' says Nevin. His program instructs on moguls and powder, expanding the terrain that boomers can enjoy and spreading their skiing away from the crowded groomed runs where most collisions occur.

He devised a program specifically to satisfy boomers' needs as well as a delivery that would have them raving about their experiences to all their friends. His focus is on longevity and safety, coupled with fun. Choosing Aspen was also a key: it is one of the most luxurious ski resorts in the world. Outside the B4B offices, the sidewalk has underground heating, so no-one has to negotiate icy patches in their slippery ski boots. There is a ski valet just up the stairs by the lift station and a kiosk dispensing free coffee nearby. On the slopes there are ski-in, free cider and water bars. And the on-mountain lodges feature in-house masseurs along with all the typical cold-weather comfort food.

Choosing boomers was already a smart move. The senior travel market is both lucrative and unique because it is less tied to seasonal travel, involves longer trips, and is not wedded to midweek or weekend travel, so it can boost occupancy rates for business and leisure travel opportunities. But this group has 'been there, seen it, done it all' in their decades of travel. So, what does Nevin do to make his boomers feel pampered and at home in Aspen?

The service starts before they even arrive with personal phone contact and booking. 'We do not use an automated booking system because we want to talk to prospects and make sure that we have fully answered any and all questions and safety/physical concerns about taking a mogul program,' explains Nevin. Next follows free mogul and powder skiing tips by email to give them a head start on the learning process. Prospective clients are also directed to the Mogul Techniques Learning Center on the website for additional information and are encouraged to take advantage of two free ski fitness video training programs to help them get into optimum shape for their holiday. The site also features encouraging testimonials from other boomers who have taken the program.

Nevin's coaching team consists of boomer-age instructors with whom his clients can readily identify. Nevin recognizes the comfort and camaraderie of being in a peer group: 'You can't take a 30-year-old instructor and expect them to know what it's like to be 50, 60, 70 or even 80,' he says. His motto is 'Designed by Boomers, Taught by Boomers, For Boomers' and he helps out with coaching himself.

Skiers are carefully grouped by pace so that no-one either holds a group up or races ahead. Short skiboards are used to reduce terrain anxiety and minimize speed with their shorter turn radius. 'This in turn accelerates learning due to less concern regarding injury,'

3

says Nevin. 'We introduce mogul techniques on groomed runs so people can easily learn new techniques without worrying about terrain anxiety, emphasizing good balance and speed control rather than fast skiing.' Not only do his concepts increase skiing efficiency, they also counteract fatigue and reduce knee and back strain.

Nevin has also noted subtle differences between the way men and women learn and makes an effort to cater for this in the program. 'I have taken a number of women's fear clients run by the PSIA (Professional Ski Instructors of America). Over at Snowmass there's a clinic called "The Women's Edge" – a female-specific program. They get a kick out of it when I'm there because I am the only guy at the training session,' says Nevin. He maintains that both genders get more fearful of injury as they age and equally appreciate his emphasis on finesse and control. One of his mantras is 'you are the CEO of your own skiing' which reassures all students that pace, direction and style is an individual choice and there is no need to try to keep up with younger, macho mogul-munchers.

Nevin has spent considerable time in analyzing the best ways to teach his demographic. He realized that the first day is always the most overwhelming in any kind of instruction program. Although skiing is essentially a practical sport, Nevin developed several pages of 'homework' reading for his students, setting out all his theories on paper with diagrams to help the message sink in. This is given to each student at the end of day one and is very rare with ski teaching which traditionally uses the basic 'follow me' method.

He adds the personal touch by going round to each group of students during the day, troubleshooting specific issues and adding extra reinforcement for the B4B philosophy. He also waits for the perfect weather and takes group photographs for all the clients with their coaches which he provides for free. Nevin's five-star service continues after the holiday with a survey for all participants designed to encourage feedback which will be integrated into teaching improvements. Results of the surveys are provided on the website. Due to demand Nevin has also introduced a follow-up course, Master of Bumps Academy program for graduates of the regular B4B course.

Sources: Personal interview with Joe Nevin on 20 October 2011; Hudson, S. (2010); http://www.bumpsforboomers.com/

Customer expectations

In a highly competitive environment, customers increasingly expect service providers to anticipate their needs and deliver on them. It is therefore important that customer expectations are understood by those delivering customer service, and the opening spotlight provided an excellent example of a service provider – Joe Nevin in Aspen – totally in tune with customer expectations. Customers evaluate service quality by comparing what they expected with what they perceive they received from a particular service provider. If their expectations are met or exceeded then customers will usually believe that they have received high quality service and they are more likely to remain loyal to that supplier. Customer expectations are likely to vary, even within the same sector. Travelers may expect a low level of service on an EasyJet short-haul flight across Europe, whereas they would expect much higher levels of service on a Singapore Airlines long-haul flight from Europe to the Far East. Expectations will also change over time; airline passengers have much lower expectations in terms of customer service than they did twenty years ago as flying has moved from being a luxury experience to more of a commodity.

Expectations embrace several elements, and Zeithaml, Berry and Parasuraman (1993) suggest that customers have three levels of expected service; desired, adequate and predicted. A zone of tolerance falls between the desired and adequate service levels. All these service elements are depicted in the model shown in Figure 3.1. The desired service is a 'wished for' level of service, and is influenced by personal needs, explicit and implicit promises from the service provider, word-of-mouth comments, and the customer's previous experiences. Adequate service is the minimum level of a service that a customer will accept without being dissatisfied, and is influenced by perceived service alternatives, the self-perceived service role, and situational factors. The level of service that customers actually anticipate receiving is known as the predicted service, which directly affects how they define adequate service.

As mentioned in Chapter 1, one of the unique characteristics of service is heterogeneity which means that ensuring continuity and consistency with service quality is challenging. The extent to which customers recognize and are willing to accept a variation in customer service is called the zone of tolerance. When service is outside this range, customers will react, either positively or negatively. If service falls below adequate levels then customers will become frustrated and are likely to complain. If service performs higher than desired service then customers are likely to be highly satisfied and remain loyal to the service provider. As an example, one can consider the zone of tolerance for waiting at an airport security check-point. After 9/11, screening procedures greatly increased the amount of time Americans had to spend waiting in security lines at airports. At the time, passengers' zone of tolerance for waiting in lines at airports was wide as they recognized the need for extra security measures; passengers expected at least 30 minute wait lines. However, as memories faded, people became less tolerant of security waiting lines. Five years later, a 2006 study found that airports had only 15 minutes before passenger satisfaction levels dropped below the 'adequate' level (Boehmer, 2006). Today, as the zone of tolerance continues to shrink, airport officials are constantly looking at ways to shorten waiting lines. For example, Copenhagen Airport is experimenting with a new program that tracks travelers' movements based on the Wi-Fi-emitting devices they carry (Negroni, 2011). Airport officials can get a real-time picture of where travelers go and what they do, and can use this information to improve the design of the airport, direct the flow of passengers or shift employees to improve the efficiency of security check-points. Meanwhile, travelers can download the associated iPhone application to receive location-specific information on their devices so that they can find the shortest security line.

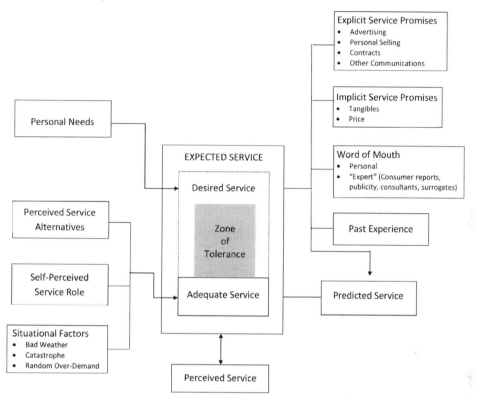

Figure 3.1: Factors influencing customer expectations of service (Source: Adapted from Zeithaml, Berry and Parasuraman, 1993, p.5).

There has been some debate over the merits of constantly exceeding the 'desired' level of expectations, providing customer delight. Delight is a positive form of affect resulting from a combination of pleasure, elation, and unexpected levels of surprise, and has been proposed as an important determinant of loyalty. Delight arises where service performance positively exceeds customers' expectations to a surprising degree resulting in highly positive disconfirmation[1] and loyalty (Oliver, Rust and Varki, 1997). However Bowden and Dagger (2011) have found that in a luxury restaurant setting, customer delight did not necessarily lead to loyalty. Satisfaction was the key driver of customers' intentions to repurchase and to recommend the restaurant. The authors concluded that while moving beyond satisfying customers to delighting them may add value to the customer experience, it may not translate into the development of enduring loyalty bonds

---

1 Disconfirmation means that the results of a service experience are inferior (or superior) to what was expected by the consumer when he/she made a decision to purchase.

for new or repeat purchase customers.

Surprising customers has however been shown to be an effective strategy to connect emotionally with them and build loyalty. Hyatt Hotels and Resorts, for example, have found that rewarding customers with random acts of kindness can have a strong impact on loyalty. In fact, through consumer research, they found that customers who had benefited from such acts, whether it be a free breakfast or drink at the hotel bar, remained loyal because they felt guilty staying with a competitor. Months of consumer research preceded their 'random acts of kindness' campaign, the idea being that the unexpected nature of the gifts will leave the customer not just pleased but also grateful. Gratitude is a powerful, and potentially quite profitable, emotion to inspire (Palmatier et al, 2009).

The customer experience

Much has been written recently about customer experiences and their important role in influencing consumer behaviour (Zeithaml et al, 2007), and companies in the tourism and hospitality sector are being admonished to create memorable experiences for their customers. Research has shown that consumer experiences are derived through a unique combination of responses to physical environment dimensions and human interaction dimensions. A conceptual model for the structure of the consumer experience in a luxury hotel context is presented in Figure 3.2 (Walls et al, 2011). The physical environment has an important influence on experience of consumers in many service settings, and the 'servicescape' will be explored in more detail in Chapter 8. Walls et al found that in the hotel setting, the ambience, the multisensory impact of the hotel, the space and function, and the signs and symbols were four themes that emerged from their research as key constructs of the physical environment.

Human interaction dimensions, both with employees and fellow guests, are another key influence on the consumer experience. Studies by Lin et al (2008) and Wang (2009) referred to later in this chapter reinforce the impact that employees' roles have on customers' experience in a service setting. As service consumption often takes place in the presence of other customers, customer-to-customer interactions can have a substantial impact on consumption experiences. Positive interactions among consumers, in a variety of service settings, have been shown to be important to both consumers and companies, and research shows that managerially facilitated positive customer-to-customer interactions enhance consumer satisfaction and enjoyment (Levy, Hudson and Getz, 2011).

The consumer experience is also significantly impacted by personal characteristics, and the last section of this chapter shows how cultural differences can affect the experience of customers. Americans, for example, in a hospitality setting, are more likely to tell a friend, return to the same place, and be motivated to increase the amount of the tip, in comparison to Asians (Manzur and Jogaratnam, 2006).

Finally, the consumer experience is impacted by trip-related factors. Andersson and Mossberg (2004), for example, in studying the customer experience in a restaurant, found that customers expect evening restaurants to satisfy social and intellectual needs whereas lunch restaurants mainly cater for physiological needs.

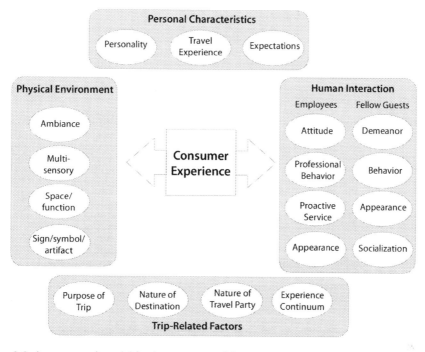

Figure 3.2: A conceptual model for the structure of the consumer experience in a hotel context (Source: Walls et al, 2011, pp. 177).

Delivering a consistent and distinctive customer experience has always been a central concern of brand management. In the early 1900s, retail pioneers like Gordon Selfridge were similarly clear about delivering such experiences. The man who first coined the phrase 'the customer is always right' described his original vision for his new department store, Selfridges, as 'delighting them with an unrivalled shopping experience' (which included such innovations as in-store coffee shops) and training his staff in the 'Selfridges Way' to ensure a distinctively consistent level of customer service (Mosley, 2007).

Because customer service is an experience, service blueprinting or mapping can be a particularly useful tool for outlining the customer experience. A blueprint will describe the critical service steps objectively and depict them so that employees, customers and managers alike know what the service is, can see their role in its delivery, and understand all the steps and flows involved in the service process. Figure 3.3 shows a blueprint for an overnight hotel stay, and depicts a guest first checking in, then going to a hotel room where a variety of steps take place, and then finally checking out. The blueprint makes clear which employees with whom the guest interacts as well as the variety of employees involved over

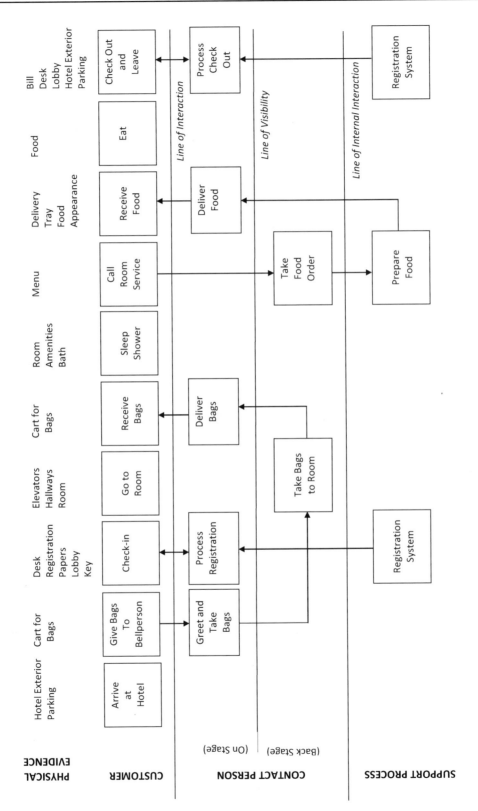

Figure 3.3: A blueprint for an overnight hotel stay (Source: Adapted from Zeithaml et al, 2007, pp. 232).

several interactions. All these points of contact are service encounters, and can be further explored using critical incident techniques (see Chapter 6). Each step of the blueprint is also associated with various forms of physical evidence, from the hotel parking area to the lobby, the room and the food.

Outstanding tourism and hospitality organizations will use blueprints to plan the service experience and ensure that every detail of the entire service experience is understood, tested and measured (Ford and Heaton, 2010). Careful analysis of each contact point in the blueprint will reveal where problems might occur so they can be anticipated and avoided. Moments of truth at which service failure is most likely to happen can be identified on the blueprint and early-warning mechanisms included.

3

Snapshot: Welcoming the world at the London Olympics

Volunteers at the London 2012 Olympics. Photo courtesy of John Grady

With the Olympics and Paralympic Games in 2012, the Ryder Cup and Commonwealth Games in 2014 and the Rugby World Cup in 2015, the UK faced a customer service challenge potentially worth billions of dollars to the economy. But there were fears that front-line staff and volunteers would not be able to deliver the kind of service that international visitors would expect.

The People 1st Training Company was given the mandate to bring UK service standards up to scratch. With the British reputation for sloppy, rude and slow service in a country where complaining is 'not the done thing', they had their job cut out for them. Research from YouGov in 2010 showed that 73% of the general public in Britain agreed that the country needed to improve customer service ahead of the Olympics, especially with around half a million daily spectators expected from 205 countries. The UK also had to overcome bad publicity generated by the 2011 riots, security worries, and years of economic depression and high costs which had undermined its perceived value for money in the eyes of tourists. Traditionally service in Britain was considered a second-class occupation, a stop gap or student job and not a career move. This had led to a weak service training culture with reluctant body language, poor eye contact and grudging service delivery proliferating throughout tourism, hospitality and retail.

Planning for the 2012 Summer Olympic Games in London had two main thrusts: 1) infrastructure and 2) people power. Once the redevelopment of venues in various areas of London was set in motion, it was the issue of peopling the Games that was paramount for planners. LOCOG – the London Organizing Committee of the Olympic Games and Paralympic Games – was set up to organize the 17-day event which, if leveraged correctly, could boost England's ailing tourism industry and prompt positive economic impacts for years to come. The initiatives set up in advance of the Games included Blue Badge tourist guides, responsible for spreading the word about the Olympics during daily public walking tours around the 2012 site. In 2010 they guided 220 school and college trips and over 1000 new visitors and tourists per day during the summer. As well as transportation improvements to trains and underground systems, a public waterbus was also planned for the area for 2011 and a flagship bike-hire scheme inaugurated with thousands of bikes available. But the main mandate was to infuse the frontline service providers with a new, topnotch customer service culture.

To train the 70,000-strong cohort of volunteers (dubbed Games Makers by LOCOG), People 1st looked to a Canadian company for help. With customer service training programs honed during the Vancouver Games, British Columbia's WorldHost™ provided an ideal toolkit for the UK. People 1st adapted the program for the UK market, supported by leading employers such as McDonalds in sponsorship collaboration. The customized program included modules on serving customers with disabilities, service across cultures and an ambassador workshop for volunteers assisting overseas visitors.

Through the five-year, renewable license with WorldHost™, People 1st also intended the training program to be a lasting legacy of the Games, with 2000 people living in the vicinity of the main Olympic park gaining hospitality skills transferable to future careers. In a press release, Brian Wisdom, chief executive of People 1st, said: 'We are also campaigning to train 200,000 front-line staff ahead of the Olympics throughout the wider visitor economy, so that we can effect a cultural change in the perception of the warmth of the UK welcome, which currently lags far behind other countries. It's essential we improve on this if we are to reap the long-term benefits of a successful Games.' Almost a million people worldwide have been trained using WorldHost™ - including 40,000 volunteers and tourism staff who helped make the Vancouver Winter Olympics in 2010 such a success.

The WorldHost™ UK website paints the Games as a chance for the British to impress: 'This presents a unique opportunity for hospitality, tourism, leisure and retail businesses to showcase the best of Britain and increase their sales by providing a warm welcome and impeccable service to visitors to the UK'. WorldHost™ Manager, Yahvel Velazquez says that their training workshops encourage frontline professionals to go beyond service with a smile: 'It's not just about being nice and friendly….some situations require more tact and very strong listening and communication skills and those are the skills taught and developed by our service professionals.' Intrinsic to WorldHost™'s program is the message that service providers are a key part in the overall visitor experience. 'They are part of a long chain of interaction that visitors will experience during their stay and if we can collectively deliver good service, individuals will go away with a positive experience.' Velazquez ascribes the effectiveness of the workshops to the holistic manner in which customer service is viewed: 'We encourage people to believe themselves to be part of a greater mandate, to believe it is something not to be undervalued or underestimated.' This motivation, he says, helps them overcome the often draining and exhausting nature of their daily workload.

A sturdy customer service culture can seriously impact a country's brand strength, affecting goodwill towards the country and boosting its tourism, business and immigration. There are various factors which help create a strong country brand, ranging from tourism, heritage and culture, business, quality of life and value systems. Having a successful Olympics – which is in effect a showcase to the world – can alter or reinforce elements about a nation that people continue to associate it with for years after the event. Positive attributes for the UK's street cred already included music, nightlife, sport, fashion, film, literature, celebrity culture, heritage and, of course, the Royal family. Recognizing this, VisitBritain came up with an etiquette guide for interactions with visiting foreigners. Called 'Delivering a First Class Welcome', it was based on input from those nationalities featured. It included all the cultural no-no's from mistaking Canadians for Americans to pouring wine incorrectly for Argentinians.

Boris Johnson, London's charismatic Mayor, also took on the job of improving London's customer service standards. In the July 2011 issue of *Traveller*, he stressed the importance of a 'warm welcome' for all visitors. He announced the recruitment of 8000 London Ambassadors from diverse cultural backgrounds, to help out at airports, stations and other key visitor spots. The Queen's Diamond Jubilee in June 2012 was planned as a precursor to the Games, stressing Britain's biggest brand differential – Royal pageantry.

Sources

Personal interview with Yavhel Velazquez, Nov 4 2011; Edwards, S. (2010); King, M. (2010); Phillips, L. (2008); Phillips, L. (2008); Woods, D. (2011); Anon. (2010); Anon. (2011); Wilkes, D. (2010); Johnson, B. (2011); Wardrop, M. (2010); Waites, R. (2011); 2010 Country Brand Index (2010).

http://www.instituteofcustomerservice.com/1746/National-Customer-Service-Week.html;

http://www.instituteofcustomerservice.com/5976-7188/Will-London-2012-provide-a-great-customer-experience.html

The importance of emotions in the service experience

With the trend today toward commoditization and increasing price and quality parity, engaging with customers emotionally – through the brand experience – often provides the best opportunity for differentiation. A number of studies have shown that consumption emotions have an impact on behavioral intentions, including word of mouth communications and loyalty (Crosby and Johnson, 2007). Ladhari (2007), for example, found that pleasure and arousal have significant effects on word of mouth. Palmatier et al (2009) found that gratitude, the emotional appreciation for benefits received, accompanied by a desire to reciprocate, is an important construct for understanding relationship marketing effectiveness.

Emotions are a person's positive (i.e. pleased or relaxed) and negative (i.e. nervous or annoyed) feelings (Lee, Back and Kim, 2009). Although emotions are ubiquitous throughout marketing, we are only beginning to understand the role they play in modern communications (Bagozzi, Gopinath and Nyer, 1999). Consumers are often highly emotional and intuitive in their behavior, operating through the emotional centers of the brain, dictated by their 'heart' or 'gut feel' and often independent of conscious control (Pawle and Cooper, 2006).

A considerable number of studies in psychology and marketing have proposed measures of consumer emotions, and some researchers have studied emotions in the tourism and hospitality setting. Han et al (2010) have developed their own consumption emotion scale specifically for a restaurant setting. This scale involved 32 refined items, and four dimensions – excitement, comfort, annoyance and romance. Their findings indicate the significant relationship between these emotional factors and customer loyalty, with comfort being the most significant determinant of loyalty. They suggest that recognizing the importance of customers' emotional experiences, managers and operators should carefully observe the characteristics of the service encounter and ensure that their customers are pleased and expectations are met. These efforts may generate favorable emotional experiences, thereby increasing customer loyalty.

Namking and Jang (2010) also looked at emotions in a restaurant setting, analyzing the effects of perceived service fairness on emotions and behavioral intentions in restaurants. They grouped customers' emotional responses into six categories: joy (happy pleased, welcomed, warm-hearted); peacefulness (comfortable, relaxed, at rest); refreshment (refreshed, cool); anger (angry, furious, and outraged); distress (frustrated, disappointed, upset, downheartedness); and disgust (disgusted, displeased, bad). What they found was that setting reasonable prices and providing efficient services in a timely manner was the key to negate negative emotion. At the same time, the findings suggest that providing high-quality tangible outcomes and intangible service were critical to evoke positive emotions and eventually to generate future favorable behaviors.

A study by Lin et al (2008) reinforced the impact that employees' roles have on customers' emotions in a service setting. They found that service personnel's appearances, attitudes, and behaviors relate positively to customers' emotions, which affect customers' satisfaction. Moreover, customers' emotions mediate the influence of service personnel's emotional expressiveness on customer satisfaction. Because emotion represents part of a service transaction, when customers feel positive emotions during a service encounter, they also feel satisfied and likely will repurchase in the future. If, however, they experience negative emotions, their unsatisfied feelings may hinder their repurchase intentions.

Wang (2009) also examined the relationships between emotions displayed by service personnel and consumer patronage intentions. His study results showed that positive displays of emotions by employees are a strong predictor of positive consumer emotions and consumer satisfaction with contact personnel. He suggests, therefore, that marketers should invest time and effort in selecting (and rewarding) employees who individually possess positive characteristics, performance abilities (such as the ability to listen to others and empathize with their emotions, and the ability to express emotions), and a willingness to express positive emotions expected by their organizations.

Bigne et al (2005) tested two competing models of emotions in order to analyze how visitor emotions in a theme park influence satisfaction and behavioral intentions. The first model was derived from environmental psychology research where the visitor's arousal generates pleasure, and, in turn, approach/avoidance behavior. The second model was based on the cognitive theory of emotions, whereby emotions are elicited by visitors' disconfirmation of the theme park. Disconfirmation means that the results of a service experience are inferior (or superior) to what was expected by the consumer when he/she made a decision to purchase. Using confirmatory factor analysis, the researchers found that the cognitive theory of emotions better explains the effect of pleasure on satisfaction and loyalty. Disconfirmations evoke arousal which, in turn, influences feelings of pleasure.

Crosby and Johnson (2007) have developed a brand-infused causal model of customer loyalty (see Figure 3.4). Moving from left to right, the model hypothesizes that customer experiences at each touch point shape a brand essence: the salient images, personality, and feelings that customers associate with the brand. Those brand associations in turn, activate both rational and emotional motivation, and these two combine to influence customer loyalty. Rational motivation encompasses the calculative reasons for being attached to the brand, such as price. Emotional motivation in contrast has more to do with the personal and symbolic reasons for being loyal to the brand, such as social acceptance, brand identification and internalization and feelings activation.

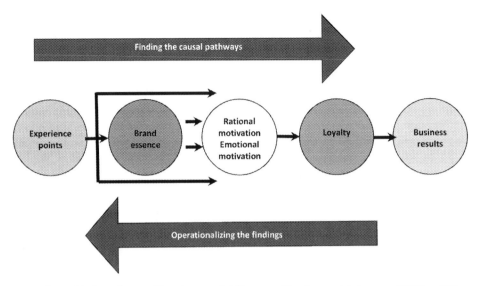

Figure 3.4: Brand-infused causal loyalty model (Source: Crosby and Johnson, 2007, p. 22).

The authors conducted a meta-analysis (a study of studies) of loyalty models, and looked at the relative impact of rational motivations versus emotional motivations on loyalty across 16 industries and 123 country segments. Using sophisticated causal modeling they found that across the almost 120 cases in the meta-analysis, the impact of emotional motivation on loyalty outweighed rational motivation by a ratio of about 5 to 3. Emotional motivation also had a very strong influence on loyalty in B2B markets (see Figures 3.5 and 3.6).

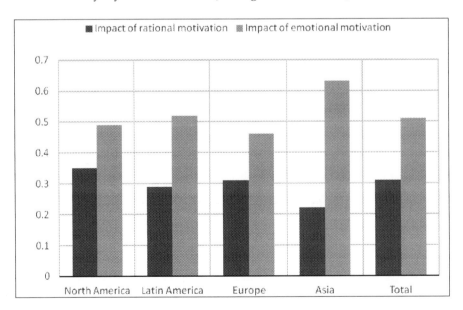

Figure 3.5: Impact of rational and emotional motivation on loyalty across regions (Source: Crosby and Johnson, 2007, p. 24).

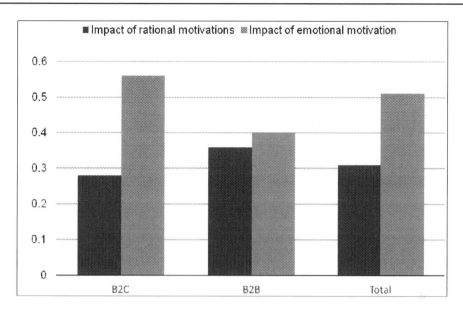

Figure 3.6: Impact of rational and emotional motivation on loyalty in business-to-consumer (B2C) and business-to-business (B2B) markets (Source: Crosby and Johnson, 2007, p. 24).

These findings suggest that organizations should quickly get the basics right (e.g. price, product durability, service reliability, etc.) and then move on to building emotional bonds with customers through some of their social and personal motivation needs. Many global brands (like Nike) develop these higher-level bonds and build loyalty by creating customer experiences that connect to self-esteem and self-actualization needs. These brands meet the customer's rational and functional needs, but then offer something additional, such as a learning opportunity or a chance to help others. Tourism and hospitality brands featured in this book such as Starbucks, WestJet, Canadian Mountain Holidays and Virgin, have demonstrated how to build brands with very little mass media advertising. Each offers a unique value proposition and focuses on the customer experience (Crosby and Johnson, 2007).

Roberts (2004) has suggested that in order to connect emotionally with consumers, brands need to evolve into 'Lovemarks'. Lovemarks as defined by Roberts are 'super-evolved brands' which maximize their connection with consumers by creating strong emotional bonds. A strong emotional bond reinvigorates loyalty and creates advocacy. The core model developed by Roberts is the Lovemark grid (see Figure 3.7).

To create a Lovemark marketers need to build not just respect but to overlay onto that a loving and close relationship. Lovemark high love is infused with three intangible, yet very real, ingredients: mystery, sensuality, and intimacy. The mystery component of a Lovemark keeps someone guessing, intrigued and coming back for more. Sensual elements of design, sound, scent, texture and flavor – things that appeal directly to the senses – influence responses over and above the more rational product arguments. And for a brand to evolve into a Lovemark, it must touch directly on the personal aspirations and inspirations of consumers: commitment, empathy and passion.

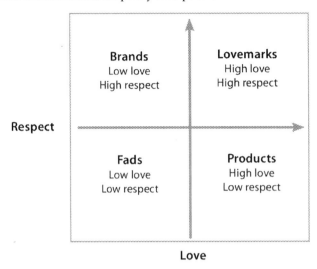

Figure 3.7: The Lovemark grid (Source: Roberts, 2004, p.77).

Understanding cross-cultural differences

The snapshot on welcoming the world at the London Olympics, discussed how volunteers were trained in delivering customer service across cultures and in assisting overseas visitors. The last few decades have witnessed an increased interest in cross-cultural studies, driven by forces such as the globalization of the market and an increase in cross-cultural encounters in daily life (Marsella, 1998). Culture is now widely recognized as an important, if not crucial, variable to be integrated in theory and research on all aspects of human behaviour. Although there is no accepted definition of culture in anthropology, sociology, or psychology today, human culture is generally defined as a meaning and information system shared by a group and transmitted across generations.

To understand the source of cross-cultural differences, psychologists have identified meaningful dimensions of cultural variability that can describe the subjective elements of culture. Hofstede (1980), for example, developed a well-known set of four dimensions: Individualism versus Collectivism, Power Distance, Uncertainty Avoidance, and Masculinity. More recently Hofstede (2001) incorporated a fifth dimension called Long- versus Short-Term Orientation. Of Hofstede's five dimensions, individualism-collectivism has become the most widely studied and has been conceptually linked to many psychological differences across cultures. Triandis (1994, 1995, 2001) in particular has championed this dimension and used it to explain many cross-cultural similarities and differences in relationships.

Another landmark study by Markus and Kitayama (1991) linked individualism-collectivism on the cultural level with the concept of self on the individual level. They posited that individualistic cultures foster the development of independent self-construals, which in turn have consequences for mental processes and behaviors. Likewise, they suggested that collectivistic cultures foster the development of interdependent self-construals, which have different consequences.

According to Markus and Kitayama, while people in North America and Western Europe are more likely to have independent self-construals (and, therefore, value being unique, asserting oneself, expressing one's inner attributes, and promoting one's own goals), people in or from Asia, Africa, and Southern Europe are more likely to have interdependent self-construals (and, therefore, value belonging, fitting in, maintaining harmony, restraining oneself, and promoting others' goals). Triandis (1995) concurs, although he contends that a second aspect of self-construal also exists; that is, equality (i.e., being 'horizontal') and hierarchy (i.e., being 'vertical'). Thus, in Triandis' conceptualization, there are four types of self-construal: horizontal individualism, vertical individualism, horizontal collectivism, and vertical collectivism.

In the last few decades, players in the tourism and hospitality industry have witnessed a form of cultural globalization as Western consumption and lifestyle patterns have spread throughout the world, a process facilitated by the flow of travelers from the West to the Third World. However, it is still critical for tourism and hospitality providers to have an understanding of different cultures in markets in which they operate. For example, Koreans are one of the most homogenous people in the world with few cultural or racial variations and virtually no ethnic minorities among them. In Myanmar, on the other hand, there are an estimated 135 ethnic minority groups with over 100 languages and dialects spoken in the country.

Other aspects of culture that are appropriate to customer service include languages, societal practices, institutions, and subcultures. The transmission of culture is primarily through the spoken and written word, but also through symbolic gestures, including the ways in which people are expected to be greeted by others. Cultural practices include how we divide the day and our attitudes toward opening hours for shops or restaurants. Institutions, such as the church, the media, and educational systems, will affect cultural patterns. The church, for example, seeks to retain a special day for worship and hence is reluctant to sanction secularization of this day, often in opposition to the promoters of tourism. Finally, most societies comprise a number of subcultures that exhibit variations of behavior as a result of ethnicity or regional differentiation.

Despite the cultural homogenization mentioned above, there are still important differences across cultures that impact customer service. Figure 3.5, for example, showed how emotional motivations are higher for Asian consumers than they are for Westerners. Asians also differ from North Americans and Europeans in their attitudes towards service in the airline industry. A recent survey found that premium-class passengers from different parts of the globe have different priorities in choosing an airline (Jones, 2011). Europeans tend to want new planes. Asian travelers are more interested in the quality of an airline's food and technology, such as in-flight access to the Internet. American passengers, on the other hand, covet the ability to access first-class and other premium-class seats. In the US, upgrading with frequent flyer miles is more prevalent than anywhere else in the world. For all cultures, an airline's safety record and reputation matter most when deciding which carrier to fly: 84% of premium-class flyers agreed on this, and 67% say it is important that the carrier offers seats that fully recline.

A study by Manzur and Jogaratnam (2006) looked at cross-cultural differences in customer perceptions of employee behavior, intentions to return, and tipping between Americans and Asians living in the US. They found, in general, American respondents were more satisfied than Asian respondents with ingratiation and exemplification techniques used by employees. Employees may use ingratiation techniques to get others to like, reward and view them favourably, whereas exemplification involves managing the impressions of integrity, self-sacrifice and moral worthiness. When employees demonstrated behaviors that were associated with good customer service, American respondents agreed that they would be more likely to tell a friend, return to the same place, and be motivated to increase the amount of the tip, in comparison to Asian respondents.

Smith (2006) examined cross-cultural differences in emotional responses to negative service encounters and the consequent impact on behavioural intentions. Focusing on West African and UK consumers, she found that while both cultural groups described the basic emotion 'anger' as a response to frustrated goals, African participants in particular projected feelings of 'sadness'. While UK respondents blamed service employees for failing to provide the required customer response after a service failure, Africans emphasized the need to conform to rules, suggested that staff were as helpful as they could be, and attributed the problem, or blame to the consumer. Africans were therefore less likely to complain or switch services.

A study of business-to-business (B2B) customer service in 2009 found that North Americans are the most loyal customers when they receive good service and Asians are the least loyal (Sprague, 2009). The Chinese have the highest switching rate (55%) due to poor customer service, and Argentineans have the lowest (7%). According to the study, France is a particularly tough place to provide and receive good customer service, and the Japanese are the toughest self-critics of the quality of their customer service. Finally, the study found that Indians have highly inflated evaluations of the quality of customer service compared with how well their customers evaluate them.

Global trends in consumer behaviour

Despite cultural differences, there are some key trends affecting the tourism industry worldwide. Below are six key trends or demands in consumer behavior that are influencing customer service in the tourism and hospitality sector today.

■ Experiences

According to Pine and Gilmore (1998), a service experience occurs when a company intentionally uses services as the stage, and goods as props, to engage individual customers in a way that creates a memorable event. More and more travel organizations are responding by explicitly designing and promoting such events. As services, like goods before them, increasingly become commodified, experiences have emerged as the next step in the progression of economic value. From now on, according to Pine and Gilmore, leading-edge companies – whether they sell to consumers or businesses – will find that the next competitive battle-ground lies in staging experiences. Experiences have always been at the heart of the entertainment business – a fact that Walt Disney and the company he founded have creatively exploited (see Chapter 1). But today the concept of selling an entertainment experience is taking root in businesses far removed from theatres and amusement parks. At theme restaurants such as the Hard Rock Cafe, Planet Hollywood, and the House of Blues, the food is just a prop for what's known as 'eatertainment.' And stores such as Niketown, Cabela's, and Recreational Equipment Incorporated draw consumers in by offering fun activities, fascinating displays, and promotional events (sometimes labeled 'shoppertainment' or 'entertailing'). But experiences are not exclusively about entertainment; companies stage an experience whenever they engage customers in a personal, memorable way. For example, WestJet and Southwest airlines go beyond the function of transporting people from point A to point B, and compete on the basis of providing an experience. The companies use the base service (the travel itself) as the stage for a distinctive en route experience—one that attempts to transform air travel into a respite from the traveler's normally frenetic life (see the WestJet case in Chapter 4).

■ Ethical products

In the last few decades, responsible tourism has emerged as a significant trend in the western world, as wider consumer market trends towards lifestyle marketing and ethical consumption have spread to tourism. Tourism organizations are beginning to realize that promoting their ethical stance can be good business as it potentially enhances a company's profits, management effectiveness, public image and employee relations. International leisure travelers are increasingly motivated to select a destination for the quality of its environmental health and the diversity and integrity of its natural and cultural resources. Studies of German and US travel markets indicate that environmental considerations are now a significant aspect of travelers' destination-choosing process, down to – in the case of the Germans – the environmental programs operated by individual hotels. Certainly in the United States, the growth in special-interest, nature-oriented travel reflects an increasing concern for the environment.

■ Health-consciousness

A more health-conscious society is often attributed to the influence of the baby boomer. Boomers are generally healthier, financially better off, better educated, and more interested in novelty, escape, and authentic experiences than were previous cohorts of older people. Many baby boomers and senior adult groups are consequently opting for more physically challenging and 'adrenalin-driven' activities as exemplified in the spotlight earlier in the chapter on Bumps for Boomers. The demographics of the baby-boom bulge are also having an impact on the health and wellness industry. Health and wellness centers are springing up in many tourism destinations, and tourists are also looking to eat healthier foods on vacation. Hotel chains are responding to this demand for healthier options. Hyatt Hotels and Resorts, for example, made significant changes to its menus in the US and Canada in 2011, including the use of cage-free eggs in all restaurant and room service menu items, as well as sourcing beef from Meyer Farm, which is known for raising its cattle humanely and naturally. Hyatt's commitment to health and wellness is part of Hyatt's global corporate responsibility program, Hyatt Thrive, which is creating programs that enhance the health and wellness of associates, neighbors and guests. These efforts range from promoting active lifestyles in the hotels to supporting programs that empower the people in Hyatt's communities to live more healthy lives. Through Hyatt Thrive, the company's operating philosophy focuses on delivering more healthful food and beverage choices, using fresh ingredients, and serving authentic dishes that are reflective of the local community and culinary heritage surrounding each hotel.

■ Customization

Requests for customized and personalized vacations are also rising sharply, and both agents and traditional tour operators are changing their businesses to meet that demand – as seen in the spotlight on G Adventures at the end of the chapter. In addition to booking air and hotel reservations, agents and outfitters today are arranging customized wine tastings, visits to artisan workshops, and private after-hour tours of the British crown jewels and the Vatican. Even at companies like Butterfield and Robinson and Abercrombie and Kent – both of which have been primarily associated with pre-arranged tours – requests for customized trips are increasing. The spotlight on Scott Dunn Travel in Chapter 2 showed how the company promises to craft something special for each customer – despite serving 10,000 holidaymakers every year. This type of one-on-one service has led to more than 70% repeat business for the luxury travel company through loyalty and referral.

■ Convenience and speed

The increasing desire for convenience and speed is having a great impact on various sectors of the tourism industry. In the restaurant sector, drive-through sales are on the rise; in transportation, self-check-in terminals are increasingly popular; and in accommodation, business travelers are seeking convenient rooms for shorter stays. Theme parks are also responding to the desire for convenience and speed. At both Universal's Orlando theme parks (Islands of Adventure and Universal Studios) visitors can get priority access to all rides and attractions at no extra cost. In front of each attraction is a Universal Express Kiosk with a computer touch screen. Guests insert their park ticket or pass and chose from a selection of times to return later in the day. The distribution center prints out a Universal Express Pass with the attraction name and return time, and guests can use this later to proceed directly inside, by-passing the regular line-ups. The Universal Express Plus program as it is called allows customers to create their own schedule and maximize their Universal Orlando experience with shorter wait times at the attractions.

■ Service quality

Service quality has been increasingly identified as a key factor in differentiating service products and building a competitive advantage in tourism. The process by which customers evaluate a purchase, thereby determining satisfaction and likelihood of repurchase, is important to all marketers, but especially to services marketers because, unlike their manufacturing counterparts, they have fewer objective measures of quality by which to judge their production. Many researchers believe that an outgrowth of service quality is customer satisfaction. Satisfying customers has always been a key component of the tourism industry, but never before has it been so critical. With increased competition, and with more discerning, experienced consumers, knowing how to win and keep customers is the single-most important business skill that anyone can learn. Customer satisfaction and loyalty are the keys to long-term profitability, and keeping the customer happy is everybody's business. Becoming customer-centered and exceeding customer expectations are requirements for business success. This book gives numerous examples of individuals or companies that have succeeded in the tourism industry by being customer focused. The following case study is no exception.

Case Study: Bruce Poon Tip, G Adventures – understanding today's traveller

Bruce Poon Tip discovered a gap in the tourism industry back in 1990 at the age of 21 when staying with hill tribes in Thailand. Since then he has cornered the adventure tourism market with G Adventures, capitalizing upon a trend towards sustainable long-haul travel with adventurous overtones.

'It wasn't my first visit, but it was my most genuine,' says Poon Tip, who has since consulted on the TV show, *Survivor*. 'That was when I knew others would want authentic travel experiences'.

Just as baby boomers were maturing and realizing the detrimental effects of their hedonistic youth,

Bruce Poon Tip, G Adventures®

Poon Tip positioned his Toronto-based company as a vehicle to do some good while traveling via environmentally-friendly, experience- and adventure-oriented tourism. Today, G Adventures is one of the largest adventure companies in the world, employing around 1350 staff worldwide and transporting over 100,000 travellers in small group excursions to hundreds of destinations on every continent.

Understanding the consumer has certainly been Poon Tip's speciality: 'In 1990, I launched G Adventures with the belief that other travelers would share my desire to experience authentic adventures in a responsible and sustainable manner'. He was reacting savvily to the consumer trend towards more authenticity in holidays, more experiential travel and green tourism. Both the baby boomer age group and younger generations wanted to return from vacations with stories to tell from sustainable tourism and voluntourism opportunities. Poon Tip realized, too, that many of these adventurous travelers also wanted to get their kicks within a safe and comfortable package.

In a world where people are living longer and staying fit and healthier later in life, the company has always targeted those who are 'young at heart'. For 'adventure with a bit of comfort' G Adventures offers small group excursions throughout South and Central America, Africa, Asia, North America and Europe, plus expeditions to the Antarctic, the

Arctic and the Panama Canal onboard the ship *M/S Explorer*. With a slant towards wildlife, culture, history and the environment, these expeditions are putting leisure and entertainment in an educational package rather than the traditional, mindless over-indulgence of typical cruise holidays. G Adventures uses small-scale lodging and local transportation. The company supports locally-owned businesses and incorporates community-based ecotourism projects into the majority of tours.

Recognizing the spirit of adventure among *all* ages and demographics of travellers, Poon Tip has gone on to develop four different levels of service to accommodate their needs. 'Some trips are like a stroll on the beach; while others have you trekking alpine passes,' he explains on his website, asking his potential customers if they prefer camping, lodges, camel rides or private vans with AC. The 'Basic' level utilizes public transport or vans for small group travel at a competitive price with lots of authentic, local colour. The next level, 'Standard', features tourist class hotels and guesthouses in keeping with a destination's character and a combo of public and private transportation. The third level, 'Comfort' trips, includes upgraded transportation as well as accommodations which Poon Tip says is 'Ideal for travellers looking for great value and a softer landing'. The 'Superior' level combines topnotch travel by planes, train, private bus or touring vehicle with upscale accommodation and dining.

In 2010 Poon Tip went a step further to segment his customers by launching YOLO – You Only Live Once. His tours have always been designed to appeal to different age groups but in the past the demographics haven't necessarily followed his plan. 'We thought people would choose different trips based on demographics,' he says. 'It just didn't happen on every trip. On basic trips we would have 60-year-olds and on every comfort class trip we would have 25-year-olds because the market has changed that much. We wanted to start differentiating a younger kind of traveler that wants more remote, more rustic and is willing to be a bit more rough and ready with their travel experience.' The YOLO program is organized backpacking for the 18-30 age group.

With a commitment to offer 'the best customer service on the planet', Poon Tip provides incentivized online surveys. 'We get a huge feedback because we offer 5% off the next trip,' he says. Having started this 15 years ago – when it was extremely innovative to offer incentives – he has accrued vast quantities of data. G Adventures racks up 95% satisfaction figures in an industry where figures in the 60s are more usual. Highest satisfaction is called the 'raver' number, which runs at around 78% of clientele. 'These are the people who come back as raving fans who can't stop talking about their trip on blogs and social media,' says Poon Tip. This figure has leapt from 66% to 78% since 2008.

One of Poon Tip's most innovative customer service inventions has been life-time deposits for which he won a Global Vision Award. The travel industry has traditionally made money out of unused holiday deposits. 'We innovated in that space. If you leave a deposit with us, it is good for life,' says Poon Tip. It can alternatively be re-gifted or donated to charity. Another differential is his 'Bear-an-Tee' for his polar bear sighting trips in the Arctic. 'We had a record with our ship which is very small and specialized,' he explains. 'We have a kind of expedition experience and we always see polar bears.' The guarantee was emphasized on the front cover of the 2011 brochure with a big paw print.

Despite the growth of G Adventures, it still remains true to its founding values. 'What hasn't changed is our passion for making sure you get behind the scenes to experience the real world in an authentic and sustainable manner. G Adventures are the Great Adventure People. We are a team of energetic explorers seeking to experience the real world with a grassroots approach to travel. We create amazing adventures that are meaningful and memorable,' says Poon Tip. The company's enthusiasm for its own product is instrumental, too, in creating customer and staff loyalty. Poon Tip explains: 'We are a company of travellers and our employees share a true passion for the industry. We are a work hard/ play hard company that is dedicated to our entrepreneurial spirit'.

Sources

Interview with Bruce Poon Tip, 18 November 2011; Interview with Bruce Poon Tip, 15 December 2006; Baginski, M. (2002); Anon (2005); Anon (2010);

http://www.gadventures.com/trips/service-levels/;

http://www.greatplacetowork.net/index.php?option=com_content&view=category&layout=blog&id=62&Itemid=213

References

Andersson, T. D. and Mossberg, L. (2004) 'The dining experience: Do restaurants satisfy customer needs', *Food Service Technology*, **4**, 171-177.

Anon. (2005). 'Travel for the Fifty Plus', *Travelweek magazine*, 26 May 2005, 16.

Anon. (2010). 'New explorations', *Spotlight*, Vol. 501. Accessed 11/07/2011 from http://www.grouptour.com/spotlight/detail.php?recid=477&issue=501

Anon. (2010). 'Thousands to be trained as 2012 Olympic volunteers', *BBC News London*, 7 September 2010.

Anon. (2011). 'Customer Journey Mapping for London 2012', *Customer Champions*. Accessed 17 October 2011 from http://www.customerchampions.co.uk/customer/olympic-customer-journey.php

Baginski, M. (2002). 'GC acquisition fills large G.A.P.' Accessed 10/10/2002 from http://www.canadatourism.com/en/ctc/ctx/ctxnews/search/newsbydateform.cfm

Bagozzi, R., Gopinath, M. and Nyer, P. (1999) 'The role of emotions in marketing', *Journal of the Academy of Marketing Science'*, **27**, 184-206.

Bigne, J. E., Andreu, L. and Gnoth, J. (2005) 'The theme park experience: an analysis of pleasure, arousal and satisfaction', *Tourism Management*, **26**, 833-844.

Birkner, C. (2011) 'Sharing the LOVE', *Marketing News*, **45**(3), 20-21.

Boehmer, J. (2006) 'Las Vegas' McCarran, New York's LaGuardia top J.D. Power's airport customer satisfaction survey', *Business Travel News*, July 17.

Bowden, J.L.H. and Dagger, T.S. (2011) 'To delight or not to delight. An investigation of loyalty in the restaurant industry', *Journal of Hospitality Marketing & Management*, 20(5), 501-524.

Country Brand Index 2012, Futurebrand in partnership with BBC World News, 2010.

Crosby, L. and Johnson, S. (2007) 'Experience REQUIRED', *Marketing Management*, **16**(4), 20-28.

Edwards, S. (2010). 'Why customer service is the most important competition at the 2012 Olympics', *MyCustomer.com*. Accessed 10/17/2011 from http://www.mycustomer.com/topic/customer-experience/2012-olympics-world-class-service-fit-champions-and-visitors/115062

Ford, R.C. and Heaton, C.P. (2001) 'Lessons from hospitality that can serve anyone', *Organizational Dynamics*, **30**(1), 30-47.

Han, H., Black, K-J. and Barrett, B. (2010) 'A consumption emotion measurement development: A full-service restaurant setting', *Service Industries Journal*, **30**(2), 299-320.

Hofstede, G.H. (1980) *Culture's Consequences: International Differences in Work-Related Values*, Beverly Hills, CA: Sage Publications.

Hofstede, G.H. (2001) *Culture's Consequences: International Differences in Work-Related Values* (2nd ed.), Beverly Hills, CA: Sage Publications.

Hudson, S. (2010). 'Wooing zoomers: Marketing tourism to the mature traveler', *Marketing Intelligence & Planning*, **28**(4), 444 – 461.

Jones, C. (2011) '1st-class fliers: safety first but next up is lie-flat seat', *USA Today*, 23 August, 6B.

Johnson, B. (2011). 'It's time for London to shine', *Traveller*, July 2011, 69-72,

King, M. (2010). 'Public services will fall short at 2012 Olympics', *The Guardian*. Accessed 09/28/2010 from http://www.guardian.co.uk/uk/2010/sep/28/public-services-london-2012-olympics

Lee, Y., Back, K. and Kim, J. (2009) 'Family restaurant brand personality and its impact on customer's emotion, satisfaction, and brand loyalty', *Journal of Hospitality & Tourism Research*, **33**(3), 305-328.

Lin, M-Q, Huang, L-S. and Chiang, Y-F. (2008) 'The moderating effects of gender roles on service emotional contagion', *The Services Industries Journal*, **28**(6), 755-767.

Levy, S., Hudson, S. and Getz, D. (2011) 'A field experimental investigation of managerially facilitated consumer-to-consumer interaction, *Journal of Travel & Tourism Marketing*, **28**(6), 656-674.

3

Manzur, L. and Jogaratnam, G. (2006) 'Impression management and the hospitality service encounter: Cross-cultural differences', *Journal of Travel & Tourism Marketing*, **20**(3/4), 21-31.

Markus, M. and Kitayama, S. (1991) 'Culture and the self: Implications for cognition, emotion, and motivation', *Psychological Review*, **98**(2), 224-253.

Mosley, R.W. (2007) 'Customer experience, organisational culture and the employer brand', *Brand Management*, **15**(2), 123-134.

Negroni, C. (2011) 'Tracking your Wi-Fi trail', *The New York Times*, 22 March, B5.

Oliver, R., Rust, R. and Varki, S. (1997) 'Customer delight: Foundations, findings and managerial insight', *Journal of Retailing*, **73**, 311-336.

Palmatier, R.W., Burke, C.B., Bechkoff, J.R. and Kardes, F.R. (2009) 'The role of gratitude in relationship marketing', *Journal of Marketing*, **73**, 1-18.

Pawle, J. and Cooper, P. (2006) 'Measuring emotion - Lovemarks, the future beyond brands', *Journal of Advertising Research*, **46**(1), 38-48.

Phillips, L. (2008). 'The plan for Olympic standard customer service', *People Management*. Accessed 17 October 2011 from http://www.peoplemanagement.co.uk/ pm/articles/2008/10/the-plan-for-olympic-standard-customer-service.htm

Phillips, L. (2008). 'London "will host most diverse Olympics ever"', *People Management*. Accessed 10/17/2011 from http://www.peoplemanagement.co.uk/pm/ articles/2008/10/london-will-host-most-diverse-olympics-ever.htm

Pine, B. J. II and Gilmore, J. H. (1998) 'Welcome to the experience economy', *Harvard Business Review*, **76**(4), 97–108.

Roberts, K. (2004) *Lovemarks: The Future Beyond Brands*, New York: Powerhouse Books.

Smith, A.M. (2006) 'A cross-cultural perspective on the role of emotion in negative service encounters', *The Service Industries Journal*, **26**(7), 709-726.

Sprague, B. (2009) 'Customer service is crucial in a downturn', *Bloomberg Businessweek*. Accessed 11/29/2011 from http://www.businessweek.com

Triandis, H. (1994) *Culture and Social Behaviour*, New York: McGraw-Hill.

Triandis, H. (1995) *Individualism and Collectivism*, Boulder, CO: Westview Press.

Triandis, H. (2001)'Individualism and collectivism: Past, present and future', In D. Matsumoto (Ed.), *Handbook of Culture and Psychology* (pp. 35-50). New York: Oxford University Press.

Walls, A., Okumus, F., Wang, Y. and Kwun, D. J-W.(2011)'Understanding the consumer experience: An exploratory study of luxury hotels', *Journal of Hospitality Marketing & Management*, **20**(2), 166-197.

Wang, E. S-T. (2009) 'Displayed emotions to patronage intention: consumer response to contact personal performance', *The Service Industries Journal*, **29**(3), 317-329.

Waites, R. (2011) 'Why is service still so bad in the UK?' *BBC News Magazine*. Accessed 25 May 2011 from http://www.bbc.co.uk/news/magazine-12123463

Wardrop, M. (2010). 'Golden rules: How to avoid insulting the 2012 tourists'. *The Daily Telegraph*, 11 August, p. 7.

Wilkes, D. (2010). 'Don't mention the war! The Visit Britain guide to tourist etiquette'. Accessed 11 May 2011 from http://www.dailymail.co.uk/travel/article-1302075/Visit-Britain-releases-guide-tourism-etiquette.html

Woods, D. (2011). 'LOCOG appoints customer service training provider for London 2012 Olympic Games', *HR Magazine*. Accessed 10/17/2011 from http://www.hrmagazine.co.uk/hro/news/1019746/locog-appoints-training-provider-staff-london-2012-olympic-games

Zeithaml, V. A., Bitner, M. J., Gremler, D., Mahaffey, T. and Hiltz, B. (2007) *Services Marketing: Integrating Customer Focus Across the Firm*, Canadian Edition, New York: McGraw-Hill.

Zeithaml, V.A., Berry, L.A. and Parasuraman, A. (1993) 'The nature and determinants of customer expectations of service', *Journal of Academy of Marketing Science*, **21**(1), 1-12.

 Scan here to get the hyperlinks in this chapter

3

4 Developing and Maintaining a Service Culture

With a name like Sharp, it goes without saying that Isadore 'Issy' Sharp has some sound business acumen. It has been his Golden Rule that has given Four Seasons a remarkable record of customer service excellence for half a century. In his quest to be tops for service, Sharp's modus operandi is to 'treat others as you wish to be treated yourself' and this considerate culture has permeated all levels of Four Seasons' personnel.

After a background in architecture and construction, Sharp identified a niche in the hospitality industry: stressing quality service in mid-size properties with luxurious appurtenances. He had studied architecture

Isadore Sharp. Photo courtesy of Four Seasons Hotels and Resorts

at Ryerson and worked with his father in Max Sharp & Son, the family renovation business. Then in 1960, he branched out to form Four Seasons Hotels, with a motel in downtown Toronto opening for business in 1961. The family element remained at Four Seasons, with Sharp at the helm and his wife, Rosalie Wise Sharp, the lead interior designer.

Aided by seasoned hotelier, Ian Munroe, Sharp was the first to introduce shampoo in bathrooms as well as value-added extras, such as 24-hour room service, bathrobes, laundry service, two-line phones, a desk, shoe repair and 24-hour secretarial service. His benchmark for excellence back then was London's Dorchester Hotel which inspired him to go one step further with the Four Seasons Inn on the Park in 1970. Winning 'hotel of the year', it was London's first modern hotel, even incorporating air conditioning in order to satisfy international visitors.

It is consistency that has paid off for Four Seasons which has benefited from the staunch leadership and unswerving vision of Sharp. His philosophy has always been that service is more important than fixtures and fittings. The Four Seasons' website ascribes its success to Sharp's Golden Rule: 'The reason for our success is no secret. It comes down to one single principle that transcends time and geography, religion and culture. It's the Golden Rule – the simple idea that if you treat people well, the way you would like to be treated, they will do the same.'

But this was no business plan, according to Sharp. It was instead a moral thread that has lasted from the outset, remaining steadfast through all his expansion plans. One of the reasons for this consistency was the early decision to manage only mid-sized luxury hotels. This is the company's first pillar: 'We will only operate medium-sized hotels of exceptional quality with an objective to be the best,' Sharp emphasizes. He has kept true to his word and, having no other business diversification, has ensured a sturdy brand. The second Four Seasons' core value is about service. 'True luxury will be defined not by architecture or décor, but by service. So we must make the quality of our service our distinguishing feature and a competitive advantage.' Sharp has made a science out of anticipating peoples' needs. Third comes the company's world renowned culture, based on the simple premise of the Golden Rule, which guides employees' actions towards its guests, business partners and with each other. The fourth is brand, reflecting a decision to manage rather than own its hotels: 'We will grow as a management company and build a brand name synonymous with quality'. This credo has always been accompanied by external quality control audits resulting in nearly 300 operating standards which are under regular assessment.

At Four Seasons, recruiting staff is primarily a personality search. Interviews take place over four sessions with in-depth behavioral assessments. Sharp believes that attitude is more important than experience in the first place as he can provide polished training once he has the right type of highly motivated employee. The interviews look for body posture, eye contact, communication skills, attitude to service, self-esteem, word choice, interaction with public. He looks for 'naturals' who can provide innate rather than scripted service. When the Four Seasons Hotel New York opened, only 400 staff were chosen out of 30,000 original applicants. Sharp's input doesn't stop at hiring, though. Attempting to increase longevity of employees, he promotes career planning within the company, employee benefits such as complimentary room nights, retirement plans and awards for those who go beyond the call of duty. Empowering his staff has paid off as on average his senior executives stay 25 years with Four Seasons.

What Sharp's personal service culture has garnered for him in business terms is an increasing customer base of repeat guests who perceived greater value for money because of all the thoughtful extra touches – such as the full concierge services, valet services, 24-hour room service, twice daily housekeeping, overnight valet service. Sharp astutely discovered exactly the right ratio between hotel size, price and amenities offered in order to provide a luxurious experience with the highest possible standards of service and additional amenities – meaning the customer would be willing to pay more, come back again and recommend it to friends.

Since its first motor hotel opened in Canada back in 1961, Four Seasons has expanded to employ around 36,000 staff with 88 hotels in 35 countries plus a division for residential property management. The group has been given many awards, including more Five Diamond AAA Awards each year for the past decade than any other hotel company. In 2004, after 11 consecutive years of being one of *Fortune* magazine's top 100 companies to work for in the USA, it was inducted into the magazine's Hall of Fame, earning the Great Place to Work® Respect Award two years later. Also in 2006, the special 30th anniversary edition of the *Robb Report* celebrated Four Seasons as one of 'the most exclusive brands of all time,' ranking alongside Rolls-Royce, Cartier, Louis Vuitton and Château Lafite Rothschild. Four Seasons properties are consistently named as top hotels by *Condé Nast Traveler, Gallivanter's Guide* and *Andrew Harper's Hideaway Report, Travel & Leisure* and *Institutional Investor*.

Sharp himself was the recipient of the American Lodging Investment Summit's Lifetime Achievement Award 2005. He won the Canadian Hotel Industry Icon Award the same year and has received three honorary doctorates. Now in his eighties, he has already paved the way for Four Seasons to perpetuate after his retirement. Rather than keep the company public, the board of directors sold to Bill Gates' Cascade Investment LLC, Prince Al-Waleed bin Talal's Kingdom Hotels International and the Sharp family in 2007 for a reported $3.7 billion. The new owners' combined wealth of more than $75 billion should ensure the company continues to grow in the way Sharp has planned. Currently as Chairman, Sharp stayed on initially as CEO until the appointment of Kathleen Taylor in 2010 as President and CEO. 'Four Seasons today is a brand that people equate with exceptional experiences and the lifelong memories that come with them,' says Issy on the company website. 'The business decisions we've made over the past five decades ensure that Four Seasons will continue to hold this esteemed position for decades to come.'

Sources

Jackson and Naipaul (2008); www.fourseasons.com/about_us/awards_and_accolades. html; http://www.fourseasons.com/about_four_seasons/service-culture/; correspondence with Rozvita Gabric, Administrative Assistant, PR, Four Seasons Hotels and Resorts, 24 August 2012.

Internal marketing

The spotlight on Isadore Sharp and the Four Seasons Hotels and Resorts shows the critical importance of developing a service culture in order to enable superior customer service. Having a service culture is one part of internal marketing, the focus of this chapter. Internal marketing was introduced in Chapter 1 as an integral part of the services marketing triangle (see Figure 1.2), and can be defined as marketing aimed internally, targeted at a company's own employees. Internal marketing takes place through the fulfilling of promises. Promises are easy to make, but unless, like at the Four Seasons, employees are recruited, trained, equipped with tools and appropriate internal systems, and rewarded for good service, the promises may not be kept. Internal marketing was first proposed in the 1970s (Berry, Hensel and Burke, 1976) as a way to deliver consistently high service quality, but despite the rapidly growing literature on internal marketing, very few organizations actually apply the concept in practice. One of the main problems is that a single unified concept of what is meant by internal marketing does not exist. Lack of investment in internal marketing may also be the result of corporate distraction. Companies that are busy trying to boost revenues and cut costs may not see why they should spend money on employees, thus missing the point that these are the very people who ultimately deliver the brand promises the company makes.

However, there is growing awareness that an effective internal marketing program will have a positive effect on service quality, customer satisfaction and loyalty, and eventually profits. One study of the hotel sector in Turkey found a significant positive relationship between internal marketing and dimensions of hotel performance such as occupancy ratio, customer loyalty, profitability, and service quality (Turkoz and Akyol, 2008). Figure 4.1 illustrates the link between internal marketing and profits.

Figure 4.1: The link between internal marketing and profits

The main objective of internal marketing is to enable employees to deliver satisfying products to guests. For the tourism and hospitality sector, this takes place through a four-step process: establishment of a service culture; development of a marketing approach to human resource management; dissemination of marketing information to employees; and implementation of a reward and recognition system.

Establishment of a service culture

Organizational culture refers to the unwritten policies and guidelines, to what has been formally decreed, and to what actually takes place in a company. It is the pattern of shared values and beliefs that helps individuals understand organizational functioning and thus provides them with norms for behavior in the business. In the past few decades, researchers have begun to analyze the linkage between culture and the marketing of services. Due to the unique characteristics of services (i.e., intangibility, inseparability of production and consumption, perishability, and heterogeneity), the nature of the culture of a service organization is particularly important and worthy of attention.

Marketing culture refers to the unwritten policies and guidelines that provide employees with behavioral norms, to the importance the organization as a whole places on the marketing function, and to the manner in which marketing activities are executed. Since service quality is one dimension of marketing culture, it follows that the kind of marketing culture an organization has would be particularly important for a service organization, as the simultaneous delivery and receipt of services brings the provider and customer physically and psychologically close. Research has shown a strong positive relationship between the kind of marketing culture a service organization has and its profitability and degree of marketing effectiveness (Webster, 1995). A strong service culture will also assist in retaining good employees (Moncarz, Zhao and Kay, 2008).

A service culture is a culture that supports customer service through policies, procedures, reward systems, and actions. An internal marketing program flows out of a service culture. A services marketing program is doomed to failure if its organizational culture does not support servicing the customer. Such a program requires a strong commitment from management. If management expects employees to have a positive attitude toward customers, management must have a positive attitude toward the customer and the employees. All organizational leaders are crucial in transmitting and preserving the culture (Ford and Heaton, 2001). The spotlight at the beginning of this chapter shows how Four Season's service culture is driven by Chairman and CEO Isadore Sharp, but there are numerous examples in this book of similar inspirational leaders; Walt Disney, Jonathan Tisch, Bruce Poon Tip, Clive Beddoe, Richard Branson, Andrew Dunn and Cliff Roberts. For companies without a strong service culture, the change to a customer-oriented system may require changes in hiring, training, reward systems, and customer complaint resolution, as well as empowerment of employees. It requires that managers spend time talking to both customers and customer-contact employees.

Benchmark tourism and hospitality organizations spend considerable time and money teaching a culture value system so that when a situation with a customer arises that is not discussed in the training manual or can't be done by the book, the employee who has learned the culture will know how to do the right thing at that moment, will want to do the right thing, and will be empowered to do so by the organization (Ford and Heaton, 2001). Disney indoctrinates all new employees in the culture as soon as they arrive. It puts all newcomers through a 'traditions' course that details the company's history with customer service and how it is the backbone of Disney. Southwest Airlines created a 'Culture Committee' whose responsibility is to perpetuate the Southwest spirit. Members promote the company's unique, caring culture to fellow employees, appearing anywhere, at any time, to lend a helping hand. The case study at the end of this chapter shows not only how WestJet fosters a caring culture, but also how protecting that culture is the number one focus for the airline as it grows its labor force.

Establishing a service culture may be easier in some parts of the world. In Japan, for example, a high standard of customer service is the norm. The Japanese word for 'customer' translates as 'the invited' or 'guest', showing the status they give to their customers. At the Peninsula Tokyo, Malcolm Thompson, the hotel's general manager, says the hotel has been successful by incorporating deep Japanese hospitality into its model. 'In other parts of the world, I would have to train staff on how to behave toward guests,' Thompson says. 'Here, that's the kind of knowledge every Japanese employee already possesses on an almost instinctive level.' The formality of Japanese culture takes a subtle yet distinctive form at the hotel. Upon seeing a guest returning from a run, a doorman outside radios in so that just as he crosses the threshold, the runner is greeted with a bottle of water and a hand towel. 'That's omotenashi,' Thompson explains, 'a kind of hospitality that involves anticipating what your guest needs' (Downey, 2012).

The importance of empowerment

Turning potentially dissatisfied guests into satisfied guests is a major challenge for tourism and hospitality organizations, and empowering employees to go the extra mile in satisfying guests is recognized as one of the most powerful tools available to a service organization. Empowerment is the act of giving employees the authority to identify and solve guest problems or complaints on the spot, and to make improvements in the work processes when necessary. Often this will mean decentralizing decision-making and flattening organization charts in order to give more power to the front-line employees who directly serve customers. It also means that managers must have greater levels of trust in their subordinates and must respect their judgment.

Empowerment is regarded as an essential aspect of internal marketing, and as essential for the operationalization of Gronroos's interactive marketing concept, a part of the services marketing triangle introduced in Chapter 1. For interactive marketing to occur, front-line employees need to be empowered – that is, they require a degree of control over the service task performance in order to be responsive to customer needs and to be able to perform service recovery. However, the degree of empowerment is contingent on the complexity and variability of customer needs and the degree of task complexity. Also, empowerment does not suit all employees because of the extra responsibility that it inevitably entails. The end of chapter case study highlights how WestJet staff members are empowered to think outside of the box and go the extra mile to provide customers with exceptional service.

Advocates of empowerment claim some impressive benefits to tourism and hospitality operators who introduce empowerment to their organizations. For example, research in the restaurant sector has shown that empowerment and job satisfaction have a significant impact on customers' perception of service quality (Gazzoli, Hancer and Park, 2010). However, traditional organizations can create problems for themselves by engendering feelings of disempowerment. Employee empowerment requires by definition that managers withhold from directly controlling employees during service delivery (Klidas, van den Berg and Wilderom, 2007). Table 4.1 summarizes these benefits and problems.

Table 4.1: Empowerment and disempowerment in tourism and hospitality operations (Source: Based on Lashley, 1995, pp. 28).

Benefits of Empowerment	Drawbacks of Disempowerment
More responsive service	Limited authority to meet service needs
Complaints dealt with quickly	Complaints dealt with slowly
Greater customer satisfaction	Higher level of costs in generating new customers
More repeat business	Fewer loyal customers
Well-motivated staff	Poor motivation and low morale
Less turnover of staff	High turnover of staff
Increased productivity	Low productivity
Lower labor costs	Low wages but high labor costs
Increased profits	Low profits

Some researchers have found that empowerment is often more likely to mean greater employee responsibility for decisions which impact on the immediate circumstances of their job, rather than greater involvement in wider workplace decision-making. Hales and Klidas (1998), for example, studied five-star hotels in Amsterdam, and found little 'empowerment' in practice. What there was amounted to increased responsibility rather than greater choice over how work was done or more voice in organizational decisions, and that supporting forms of recruitment, training and remuneration were mostly absent. A similar study of luxury hotels in New Delhi found very few hotels that had formal empowerment training (Mohsin and Kumar, 2010). Ro and Chen (2010) suggest that to implement a successful empowerment program, service organizations should have appropriate organizational supporting systems including service training, service rewards and service communication. They found from their research on theme park employees, that employee's customer orientation is an important antecedent of their perceived empowerment. In other words, the more employees describe themselves as customer oriented, the more they felt confident about their job performance and meaningfulness of their jobs.

The case study at the end of the chapter shows that for WestJet, empowerment is more than a buzzword because it wants its front-line staff to be able to make the right decision in any given situation. In an empowerment culture, staff are encouraged and rewarded for thinking outside of the box and for going the extra mile to provide exceptional customer service. In December 2008, during a particularly fierce snowstorm that caused flight delays and cancellations from one coast to the other, WestJet employees were seen giving out pizzas to stranded passengers. Of course, staff members were empowered (and rewarded) for doing this, but rumour had it that they also gave pizza to Air Canada passengers. This was a fabulous publicity stunt, as Air Canada employees were probably not empowered to spend money in this way. WestJet spent $2 million that week to help stranded passengers (Wilson, 2008).

Development of a marketing approach to human resource management

A marketing approach to human resources management (HRM) involves the use of marketing techniques to attract and retain employees. As the tourism and hospitality industry grows, employers need to think creatively about attracting qualified employees. EasyJet, the UK-based low-cost airline, recently added a 'come and work for us' plea to the address that greets passengers boarding its planes. The airline employs over 2000 cabin crew across Europe, and this was an attempt to recruit staff by saving money on advertising. Taking a marketing approach to HRM also means using marketing research techniques to understand the employee market. Different employee segments look for different benefits, and it is important to understand what benefits will attract employees. Advertising for staff can then be developed with prospective employees in mind, building a positive image of the company for present and future employees and customers. Four Seasons invests a huge amount of time and funds in finding the right people. When they opened Four Seasons Hotel Mumbai – their first property in India – 34,000 people applied, resulting in 15,000 interviews, to hire 450 people – one out of every 75 who applied. In Baltimore, it was one out of 16.

Marketing can help by working with the human resources (HR) department to identify the key elements in employee motivation, including the effect of incentives and the development of training and improvement programs. Marketing can help most of all with research, working with HR to determine, internally, what can be done to improve the delivery of 'customer-facing' people and to help understand what motivates employees, channel partners, and customer-service representatives. If marketers are good at understanding customers, consumers, and end-users of products and services, they should be able to lend those talents to HR to help them understand internal marketing conducted by internal marketers.

Such a marketing approach to developing positions and benefits helps to attract and retain good employees. Companies should ensure that they recruit employees who are highly motivated, customer-oriented, and sales-minded because changing employee attitudes and behaviors is more difficult and costly once the employees have been recruited. Employees also need the right type and level of training to perform their jobs. This can help to reduce ambiguity surrounding their role and can help employees to meet the needs of customers more effectively. There is a clear link between training and levels of customer service. Publix Super Markets, a popular grocery chain in the Southeast of the US, estimates that it spends nearly $3000 training each employee before they begin work (Business Week, 2007), perhaps indicating why the company is continuously ranked in the top 20 American companies for excellent customer service by *Business Week* magazine. The average spent on training in the US is just over $1000 per employee.

More and more managers are trying to tap into the psyche of employees as the continuous turnover of staff takes its toll on the industry. Employee turnover in the hospitality industry is often double that of other industries (Harris et al, 2011). Turnover in EasyJet, mentioned above, for example, is about 18-20% annually. Some managers are finding that giving increased responsibility is improving retention and performance, a strategy that has proved successful for both WestJet and the Renaissance Hong Kong, companies profiled in this chapter. Fairmont also offers employee exchange programs to boost staff loyalty. It is not, however, just entry-level positions that are difficult to keep filled. Turnover among hospitality industry sales and marketing professionals is at almost 25%. A National Restaurant Association poll of more than 400 foodservice managers also found that about one-quarter of the respondents intended to leave their positions in the near future, with at least half of those planning to depart the foodservice business entirely (Sutherland, 2002).

According to Jon Katzenbach, author of *Why Pride Matters More Than Money*, feelings of pride can motivate people to excel far more effectively than money or position (Katzenbach, 2003). He says that institutions such as Southwest Airlines and Marriott International, which manage to sustain the emotional commitment of a large proportion of their employees over good times and bad, seldom rely on monetary incentives. Instead, they find ways to instill institution-building pride in what people do, in why and how they do it, and in those with whom they do it. Pride builders accomplish this by (a) setting aspirations that touch emotions, (b) pursuing a meaningful purpose, (c) cultivating personal relationships of respect, (d) becoming a person of high character, and (e) injecting humor along the way. For the Sheraton Suites Calgary Eau Claire (see Chapter 7), instilling pride in employees is a key motivator.

Continuous training can also help improve employee morale and reduce turnover of employees. The Canadian Tourism Human Resource Council (CTHRC) provides human resource development solutions for the tourism industry in

Canada, and in 2002 it introduced the *Performance First HR Tool Kit*, a pragmatic guide to human resource management. The kit (which includes a manual and CD) provides the 'ready-made tools' needed to recruit, select, hire, train, coach, and manage employees effectively. Several customizable, user-friendly templates and forms are available in the kit, including application forms, interview evaluations, job-offer letters, training plans, and employee manuals suited to the position. In Singapore, an unusual training program for taxi drivers is improving the service offered to tourists. Hundreds of taxi drivers have qualified as tourist guides, having spent more than 80 hours training over a three-month period. After sitting a written exam and taking practical assessments, drivers who make the grade are awarded a special Taxi Tourist Guide License (Telegraph Travel, 2004). Seok Chin Poh of the Singapore Tourism Board, which helped set up the scheme, said: 'We are seeing a growth in independent travelers from Europe visiting Singapore who want to explore at their own pace but still benefit from the knowledge of a guide. The scheme offers visitors a refreshing and interesting alternative to touring Singapore'.

Snapshot: Igniting the spirit to serve at the Renaissance Harbour View Hotel Hong Kong

Photo courtesy of Renaissance Harbour View Hotel Hong Kong

Hong Kong has long been known as an international business hub, frequented by wealthy businessmen and tourists with the requisite high-end hotels, restaurants and retail. Naturally there is considerable competition among companies for the plentiful pool of visitors and so hotels rely on a variety of differentials to attract and keep their clientele.

Karl Hudson is the Multi Property Vice President and General Manager for the Renaissance Harbour View Hotel – a Marriott property in Hong Kong. He brings in outside experts to enhance customer service training at the five-star hotel which houses 808 rooms and 49 suites over 42 floors. Bob Brown and Cynthia Goins 'provide the icing on the cake' says Hudson.

As well as working as a seminar leader and management consultant for restaurants and hotels, Brown is a leading keynote speaker and author. His book, *Little Brown Book of Restaurant Success*, is an international bestseller which outlines the strategies, tools and techniques he advocates to high-powered customers such as Disney, Ritz Carlton and Hilton as well as Marriott. He was influenced in his early days while working in top restaurants in the US. Cynthia Goins' firm, CJ Goins & Associates, has been working in hospitality for over 30 years. Their mandate is 'passionately exceeding expectations' in order to differentiate a destination with wow factors and emotional connections with customers.

These service experts help his team 'develop the real passion and spirit to serve'. Frontline ambassadors review each day's arrivals in advance, check on any previous comments and react accordingly. 'For example, if a particular female repeat guest needs more recognition – she needs to be given more face – therefore she is met by a senior manager and escorted to her room,' says Hudson. If any of the arrivals are Platinum members, they will receive their guaranteed room type, access to the Club Lounge and a Platinum gift – all intended to make them feel special.

Wow factors for Renaissance clients include cold bottled water in their valet-parked cars on hot days and coat hangers placed in their cars to hang up jackets. It's like having 'Mom' look after you. If there is a group booking, staff members make efforts to find out about favorite snacks, the boss's beverage of choice and any birthdays in the party – for which they provide cakes. It is not just the managers who can implement this. All front line associates – who Hudson calls 'high guest contact personnel' – are empowered as ambassadors. These extras are all covered by the hospitality budget as well as within the training budget.

Although this kind of hospitality is pre-planned, there is also considerable flexibility for ambassadors to react spontaneously to a guest's needs. 'The structure is formed from the corporate guidelines and the internal and external training. We then empower ambassadors to make decisions according to the specific needs of each guest,' Hudson explains. As well as job satisfaction, frontline ambassadors who provide the little extras for their guests are rewarded with monthly 'Spirit to Serve' certificates at the quarterly 'Town Hall Meetings'. 'Gifts are also given to the top performers, who are lauded in the daily meetings, plus photos in the heart of house areas and a personal note from the General Manager,' Hudson adds.

Careful customer research via Guest Satisfaction Surveys (GSS) has led to these honed hospitality garnishes. Hudson also works with Brand Karma which analyses online postings from social media as well as Trip Advisor, online travel agents and blogs. The website offers 'Simple and Free Social Media Monitoring for Hotels'. Continually on the lookout for innovative ways to wow customers, Hudson says they also look to airlines and other hotels for inspiration as well as newsletters such as ehotelier.com. 'Yes, we sit in the lobbies of other hotels and observe whilst drinking tea,' Hudson quips.

The Renaissance customer service training is also designed to help counteract and prevent problems. Good damage limitation can even turn a complaint into a compliment. For example, a room was flooded once after a bathroom leak. The American customer who was a hotel loyalty card member asked to speak to the manager. None of his belongings were damaged but the incident made him late for an appointment and he was avidly taking photos of the leak in case of future legal proceedings. He was also threatening not to pay the previous night's room charge and moving to another hotel. However, when he was offered an upgrade to Club Lounge access he accepted the offer. 'He eventually apologized for his bad temper earlier and said he would pay for the room charge of last night. He also wrote a note before he left the hotel to the Guest Service Manager for the great assistance,' says Hudson. He stresses, however, that surprising and cosseting guests is routine for all customers and not just for those who experience a problem.

Repeat elite loyalty members are particularly appreciated at the Renaissance. 'Their stays are more personalized with handwritten notes from the General Manager, escorted to their room without having to check in at Front Desk, given practical gifts, upgraded to the best room possible, and flexibility accorded for check out time,' says Hudson.

The Renaissance brand has developed three 'Live Renaissance Values' which are 'Intriguing, Indigenous and Independent'. 'To sum it up, when a guest goes back to a Marriott they expect to find that everything is the same as their last visit. When a guest returns to a Renaissance they expect to find something wonderfully new. The guests have different desires. Renaissance guests are discoverers,' Hudson explains. Staff members purvey these values by engaging with clientele and touching emotions through common interests, giving the guests stories to take back home with them. They are trained to 'watch, listen and ACT', seeking clues from the guest. Emphasis is placed on anticipating needs. For example, says Hudson, if a guest is reading a map at breakfast time then assist them and recommend off the beaten track discoveries revolving around savor, sip, shop and see. They will then be armed with wow stories to return home with rather than the cookie cutter tourist guide activities. Although aware of cultural differences between different nationalities staying at the Renaissance, Hudson believes that differences are even more specific than ethnicity. 'Each individual from each culture is also different. You need the skills to quickly evaluate and ascertain what the guest needs,' he insists.

Service consistency is furthered through Mystery Shopping. This is intended to 'determine the real status of emotional engagement of ambassadors with guests,' says Hudson. 'Then we conduct training based on that hotel's needs – training which should cover the importance of first impressions, body language, use of guest names, offering active assistance and thanking the guest.' He maintains that attention to this kind of detail leads to a 'higher intent to return, higher average rate and higher profitability – it increases the value proposition'.

Sources

Personal interview with Karl Hudson, 3 November 2011;

http://www.marriott.com/hotels/travel/hkghv-renaissance-harbour-view-hotel-hong-kong/

http://www.bobbrownss.com/

http://cjgoins.com/

Dissemination of marketing information to employees

Managers need to pay significant attention to the communication of marketing (and other organizational) strategies and objectives to employees, so that they understand their own role and importance in the implementation of the strategies and in the achievement of the objectives. Research evidence suggests that the frequency, quality, and accuracy of downward communication moderates employee role ambiguity and hence increases job satisfaction. Communication with employees can be one-to-one. When managers take the time to go out and connect with staff it can make a big difference, and actually lead to lower turnover of staff (Izzo, 2008; Moncarz, Zhao and Kay, 2008).

Other communication mechanisms may come in the form of company meetings, training sessions, newsletters, emails, annual reports, or videotapes. Fairmont distributes a bi-monthly newsletter in each hotel as well as a company-wide newsletter to keep staff up to date on new company procedures. Southwest Airlines has a blog called 'Nuts about Southwest' which addresses employees concerns, relays information about changes in the company, and tries to boost employee morale (see Figure 4.2). Recent posts celebrated Southwest's history by showing old pictures of the airports that Southwest operates out of and pictures of the evolution of Southwest's air fleet. The blogs are also used to show how Southwest is connected to current events. For example, posts in 2010 followed an employee who went to Vancouver for the Winter Olympic Games.

Unfortunately, many companies exclude customer-contact employees from the communication cycle. The director of marketing may tell managers and supervisors about upcoming promotional campaigns, but some managers may feel that employees do not need to have this information. However, it is important that staff is informed about marketing promotions. They should hear about promotions and new products from management, not from external advertisements meant for customers. Changes in the service delivery process should also be communicated. In fact, all action steps in the marketing plan should include internal marketing. For example, when a company introduces a new mass media campaign, the implementation should include actions to inform employees about the campaign. Because service advertising and personal selling promise what people *do*, frequent and effective communication across functions – horizontal communication – is critical. If internal communication is poor, perceived service quality is at risk. If company advertising and other promises are developed without input from operations, contact personnel may not be able to deliver service that matches the image portrayed in marketing efforts.

4

Figure 4.2: Southwest use a blog to communicate with employees and customers (Source: http://www.blogsouthwest.com/).

Implementation of a reward and recognition system

For employees to perform effectively, it is important that they know how they are doing, so communication must be designed to give them feedback on their performance. At the Sheraton Suites Eau Claire in Calgary, every effort is made to recognize the achievement of employees and to ensure that they are happy and proud of their jobs (see Chapter 7). In a Canadian survey, almost 90% of employees reported that 'being made to feel like a valued employee is important in motivating them to achieve company goals' (Galt, 2003). The survey was conducted by Bob Macdonald, president of Maritz Canada. Macdonald argues that in order to feed an employee's energy level and overall desire to perform, organizations need to communicate clearly performance objectives, as well as provide relevant training, feedback, and recognition in the form of non-cash rewards. However, the rewards should be tailored to the interests of the employees they are designed to motivate. Group excursions are popular with employees in the 18-to-29 age groups, while older employees prefer personal trips. More men than women, for some reason, appreciate getting 'company-logo merchandise' as a reward. For some, the ideal reward is the gift of a personal chef for the evening, and for others time off with pay is the perfect reward.

Some companies recognize superior performance with reward points that can be redeemed for an array of gifts. At the high end, the rewards can range from airline tickets to big-screen televisions. Sometimes recognition alone is enough. Macdonald says that 73% of the surveyed employees reported that receiving 'recognition as top performer' was important. Furthermore, most employees want regular feedback. Macdonald found in his survey that only 15% of employees said that their companies offer that extra something for a job well done. He suggests that most employers do not offer non-monetary rewards because they are concerned about the cost or are not sure what their employees would value. Macdonald says that as the labor market tightens, retention of top performers will become an issue for employers. He adds that employees have made clear, in repeated surveys, that money is important - but it takes more than money to engage them in their jobs.

Finally, if tourism and hospitality companies don't look after their employees, they may garner some unwanted publicity. A growing number of workers are exiting their jobs in an extravagant manner that is catching the attention of the media (Petrecca, 2011). In August 2011, Joey DeFrancesco quit his job at a Providence hotel in an incredibly outlandish fashion. He sneaked members of a brass band into the hotel and had them strike up a lively Serbian folk song as he turned in his resignation letter. He then posted the whole episode on YouTube where it was viewed over three million times. DeFrancesco wanted to highlight the poor working conditions of the hotel, which he said included little respect for employees. The previous year, Steven Slater, a JetBlue flight attendant, exited his job in a different manner: by flying down the emergency chute of a jet – with a beer from the galley in hand. Again, the incident attracted considerable attention.

Case Study: WestJet Airlines: Fostering a caring culture

Photo courtesy of WestJet Airlines

WestJet Airlines is a company that has, so far, beaten the odds to become a favorite of both travel agents and consumers in Canada. It is, after all, the airline that boards passengers by sock color or zodiac sign; concocts promotions that enable passengers with names like 'Love' and 'Heart' to fly free on Valentine's Day; and has seen gate agents break out flutes to entertain stranded passengers during an ice storm. And compared to rigid, often humorless Air Canada, WestJet earns raves from the travel trade. 'They'll do almost anything for you,' one Ontario agent gushed to *Canadian Travel Press*. In fact, WestJet has placed first in 'Canada's Most Admired Corporate Cultures' by Waterstone Human Capital for three consecutive years.

WestJet's Manager of Public Relations, Robert Palmer joined the company in 2008. In the first three months of employment he posed as Elvis for Las Vegas flights on three different occasions, earning himself the company's informal 'bobble head' award. The trophy is actually fashioned after Bob Cummings, Executive VP for Sales and Marketing. 'We always put an Elvis in the boarding lounge and on the flight – I've done it five times altogether now. It's a quirky thing we do,' Palmer explains. The company also has more formal awards such as the Kudos program whereby satisfied customers can send a kudos by internet and, even if they don't have the employees name, WestJet will track down the recipient. Traditionally, WestJet has celebrated service achievements with the President's Award at the annual Christmas party. 'With almost 8500 WestJetters now, we recognize the importance of internal service quality, too. It is as important as external service because, if we are not treating each other well, it cannot help but eventually reflect in the way we work with external customers,' says Palmer.

Pride in product is intrinsic to WestJet's success. 'We have won a lot of awards for our guest experience – which is different than customer service – and received a lot of praise and accolades about our people. This is justifiably something to be proud of, to be so successful in very difficult times,' says Palmer. WestJet continues to be one of the most profitable airlines in the world despite its relatively small size. Employees are dubbed WestJetters and attract attention wherever they go: 'If it comes out at a party or somewhere that you work for WestJet, what happens is quite remarkable – everyone has a WestJet story and they take pleasure in seeking you out to tell you their story. 90% of the time it is about an agent who went beyond the call of duty.'

He attributes WestJetters' pride in their company also to their sense of ownership and aligned value system. 'They really are owners, over 85% of people who work for WestJet own shares,' he explains. 'They can devote up to 20% of their pay check and the company matches it share for share.' There is also a profit share twice annually which Palmer says further instills vested interest in employees.

WestJet, which was founded in 1996, now provides low-cost, scheduled and charter flights to over 71 destinations in 13 countries – airports in Canada, USA, Mexico and the Caribbean, transporting around 45,000 passengers per day on an average of 450 flights. Based out of a new $100 milllion building near Calgary International Airport, it employs more than 8500 non-unionized staff to serve approximately 15 million passengers per year. Palmer explains the link between WestJet's culture and customer service: 'We have a number of sayings that illustrate that link. Probably the most important one is if you take care of your people, your people take care of guests and that takes care of your business. We call all our passengers guests, which is also somewhat unique to us.'

Empowerment is fundamental to WestJet's spontaneity. 'Obviously we have our share of policies and procedures because, of course, it is a very highly regulated industry – but we think people on the frontline should be empowered to make extraordinary decisions to solve problems whether that is calling someone a taxi cab to get home and back quickly because they forgot their passport. Little things like that – those are the things other airlines and service industries might have to go to a supervisor to undertake. We don't think that is necessary,' says Palmer. He calculates that employees will make the right decisions 98% of the time, providing a much better, more streamlined experience for guests.

WestJet has evolved to become more of a hybrid model within the airline industry. It is moving away from the no-frills, discount airline reputation with the addition of live seat-back satellite TV at every seat and pay-per-view movies as well as buy-on-board services. It also boasts one of the most modern fleets of all aircraft in North America with the average age of its fleet of Boeing 737 Next Generation jets being only four years.

But as the company grows, how will the personal and lighthearted service culture persist? 'What won't go away is our focus on the guest and on our people,' Palmer avows. WestJet has been consistently profitable even while other airlines fail, recording only a slight loss in 2004. As such, it attracts more than 1000 unsolicited resumes every week. Palmer says the company's value system is as strong now with 8500 staff as it was back in 1996 when they had only three planes and a team of 200 people. 'We look at our new incoming WestJetters and at our existing employees. We hire for attitude and train for skill for all employees – with the exception of our pilots and mechanics, of course,' says Palmer who is determined that the culture will not get diluted with increasing volume of employees and passengers. WestJet puts considerable effort and money into its CARE department – the acronym for Create A Remarkable Experience – which is charge of internal celebrations. 'They are event planners to a large extent who help to keep the culture alive,' says Palmer. The CARE department holds over 250 events across Canada which range from small pizza parties to Christmas and profit sharing events.

Sources

Interview with Robert Palmer, 14 November 2011; Jang and Grant (2006); Baginski (2002); Fitzpatrick, P. (2001); Quinn, P. (2001); Welner and Briggs (2002).

4

References

Anon (2004) 'Singapore cabbies wheel out the knowledge', *Telegraph Travel*, 31 July, p4.

Baginski, M. (2002) 'WestJet celebrates sixth anniversary'. Accessed 02/26/2002 from http://www.canadatourism.com/en/ctc/ctx/ctx-news/search/newsbydateform.cfm

Berry, L. L., Hensel, J. S. and Burke, M.C. (1976) 'Improving retailer capability for effective consumerism response', *Journal of Retailing*, **52**(3), 3–14.

Business Week (2007) 'Customer Service Champs'. Accessed 01/30/2012 from http://images.businessweek.com/ss/07/02/0222_top25/index_01.htm

Downey, T. (2012) 'Made better in Japan,' *Wall Street Journal*, January 27. Accessed 01/30/2012 from http://online.wsj.com/article/SB100014240529702045424045771572 90201608630.html

Fitzpatrick, P. (2001). 'Wacky WestJet's winning ways'. *National Post*, p. C1

Ford, R.C. and Heaton, C.P. (2001) 'Lessons from hospitality that can serve anyone', *Organizational Dynamics*, **30**(1), 30-47.

Galt, V. (2003) 'Can't pay more? Try some little extras', *The Globe and Mail*, 12 Feb., p. C2.

Gazzoli, G., Hancer, M. and Park, Y. (2010) 'The role and effect of job satisfaction and empowerment on customers' perception of service quality: A study in the restaurant industry', *Journal of Hospitality & Tourism Research*, **34**(1), 56-77.

Hales, C. and Klidas, A. (1998) 'Empowerment in five-star hotels: Choice, voice or rhetoric?', *International Journal of Contemporary Hospitality Management*, **10**(3), 88-95.

Harris, C., Tregidga, H. and Williamson, D. (2011) 'Cinderella in Babylon: The representation of housekeeping and housekeepers in the UK television series *Hotel Babylon*,' *Hospitality & Society*, **1**(1), 47-65.

Izzo, J. (2008) 'In your face – far more effective', *Globe & Mail*, 15 August, p. C1.

Jackson, L and Naipaul, S. (2008) 'Isadore Sharp & Four Seasons Hotels and Resorts: Redefining luxury and building a sustained brand', *Journal of Hospitality and Tourism Education*, **20**(2), 44-50.

Jang, B., & Grant, T. (2006, October 17) 'Fuller planes, cost cuts propel airlines', *Globe & Mail*, B12

Katzenbach, J. (2003) *Why Pride Matters More Than Money*, New York: Crown Business.

Klidas, A., van den Berg, P.T. and Wilderom, C.P.M. (2007) 'Managing employee empowerment in luxury hotels in Europe', *International Journal of Service Industry Management*, **18**(1), 70-88.

Lashley, C. (1995) 'Towards an understanding of employee empowerment in hospitality services', *International Journal of Contemporary Hospitality Management*, **7**(1), 27-32.

Mohsin, A. and Kumar, B. (2010)'Empowerment education and practice in luxury hotels of New Delhi, India', *Journal of Hospitality & Tourism Education*, **22**(4), 43-50.

Moncarz, E., Zhao, J. and Kay, C. (2008) 'An exploratory study of US lodging properties' organizational practices on employee turnover and retention', *International Journal of Contemporary Hospitality Management*, **21**(4), 437-458.

Petrecca, L. (2011) 'Quirky quitting techniques mark some job departures', *USA Today*, 15 November, p. B1-2.

Quinn, P. (2001) 'Success stories.Flying in the face of adversity', *Financial Post*, p. E1

Ro, H. and Chen, P-J. (2010) 'Empowerment in hospitality organizations: Customer orientation and organizational support', *International Journal of Hospitality Management*, **30**, 422-428.

Sutherland, S. (2002) 'Hospitality trends', *Alberta Venture*, **6**(4), 49–53.

Turkoz, I. and Akyol, A. (2008) 'Internal marketing and hotel performance', *Anatolia*, **19**(1), 149-177.

Webster, C. (1995) 'Marketing culture and marketing effectiveness in service firms', *The Journal of Services Marketing*, **9**(2), 6–22.

Welner, C., & Briggs, D. (2002) 'Reaching for the skies', *Alberta Venture*, **6**(5), 26–27;

WestJet annual information form, 20 March 2002.

Wilson, B. (2008) 'WestJet to passengers – merry Christmas', *Aviation Week*, 28 December. Accessed 31 July 2011 from http://www.aviationweek.com

 Scan here to get the hyperlinks in this chapter

5 Managing Service Encounters

Marcos and cheerleaders: Photo courtesy of Ten Travel

Running a business and incentive travel agency in Tenerife – a Spanish-owned island off the northwest coast of Africa – involves daily customer service dilemmas for Marcos Van Aken. As conference manager for Ten Travel, part of Red Carpet Destination Management Service, he is in charge of both wooing businesses and keeping delegates happy during their visits. Owned by John Lucas, the company began 35 years ago with a package holiday focus but quickly diversified into the business group and incentive travel market. 'Business and incentive travel require a very high level of specialization. We segmented into that and, slowly but surely, we were approached by various cruise companies, too. We aim for the top end of the market,' explains Van Aken, who, although born in Tenerife, studied for his Masters degree in Hotel Management at the University of Surrey, England.

Van Aken spends a considerable amount of his time solving problems for customers. A dilemma presented itself when a German company wanted red carpet treatment for their clients at the airport. 'They insisted on them leaving the plane and getting on to the coach without touching a suitcase,' Van Aken remembers. Although he appreciated the desire to offer this kind of top end service, he marveled at the amount of paperwork, lobbying and money it required to make it happen. 'I can understand why the client wanted that: he wanted to offer the top end of service, to get unloaded at the cocktail area straight away with drinks ready, and while they were having a cocktail, the luggage would be delivered to their rooms.' Van Aken thinks that this type of service is what quality is all about, making something difficult happen smoothly.

Although Ten Travel employs multiple staff members and regular tour guides, the key accounts are Van Aken's personal responsibility. As middle man between tourism and business industries, he is in a prime position to elevate service standards in Tenerife. Part of his job is to make sure that the service levels seen on inspection visits are translated literally to the galas and conferences when guests eventually arrive. He has the perfect multi-cultural background for this, with a Dutch mother and Spanish father, British and German schooling, a year traveling in South America and experience in the hotel industry. 'That's my edge,' he says. 'I speak five languages which gives me the means to reach the Dutch market as well as UK, German and Spanish businesses and, what's more, I've been around, I've had experience of the world.'

Before joining Ten Travel in 2003, Van Aken worked in hotel management where he was exposed regularly to the minutiae of conferences and business events. He believes in providing a wow factor for his clients who often have a limited conception of what Tenerife is all about. 'Most of the time they think it is 99 % sun and beach,' he says. Surprising his clients mainly consists of taking them away from the coast to inland destinations with mountain biking and hiking in diverse landscapes and national parks. He tries to go beyond the usual tourist trip to Tenerife's volcanic park at Mt Teide. 'We go up in the cable car and then on to a lodge where you stay overnight. Then there's a two-hour walk at four o'clock in the morning to make it to the top for sunrise. That's the kind of thing that will take people over the edge and say wow that was different,' he explains.

As well as organizing anything from dolphin and whale-watching, to kayaking and quad biking, Ten Travel arranges inter-island itineraries. He also has a stable of dedicated local guides and experts to draw from both for tours and for presentations. 'Employing the right people who have both knowledge and experience and who really care about the island is key. They emanate a warmth, having been in tourism all their lives.' However, Van Aken has noticed a trend in not overloading the schedules of delegates too much: 'People need time to breathe. They are often so burnt out when they come away that they don't want to be running around the whole time. I find they are incorporating free time strategically – which is not necessarily good for my business – but it certainly is better for them to come away rested.'

Loyalty to the company has been achieved by looking after staff and suppliers despite the economic recession. 'In the crisis, we decided to carry on paying exactly what we paid before, unlike many other businesses on the islands,' says Van Aken. 'Sometimes it has meant not cashing in on the last payments from the group ourselves but everyone else has been paid. Admittedly you need cash flow to do that and not everyone has access to that. But strategically we decided that and it has paid off as suppliers will bend over backwards for us.' This pays off particularly when Ten Travel faces an emergency. Recently two clients sustained severe leg injuries during a sporty tournament on a remote beach. The area was not usually accessed by ambulance but when the emergency services got the call from Van Aken, they pulled out all the stops, negotiating four-wheel drive ambulances on to the dunes.

Service is not all about what the client actually experiences on his visit. It is sometimes entirely behind the scenes. 'After winning over the client, from then on it is all in the planning and it is the nitty gritty details that really count. The client enjoying the trip is oblivious of the behind-the-scenes battles that have been going on,' Van Aken explains. Sticking to budget is another important area for service quality. Ten Travel has to quote accurately for business travel events around 18 months in advance. If Van Aken later finds the client wants some more expensive services than originally expected, he is unable to increase his estimate. 'I have to try and find a margin elsewhere,' he says. Service recovery is also crucial to Ten Travel's sustained reputation. With six full-time staff in Tenerife plus one in Lanzarote and another in Gran Canaria, Ten Travel can afford the personal touch. 'Everything is just a telephone call away and I think that is our edge,' says Van Aken. He also knows the limits to the volumes they can handle, adding on extra days before and after each event for preparing and later dismantling all the special facilities. 'We need people who can handle that sort of pressure,' he says.

Source: Interview with Marcos Van Aken, 12 July 2011.

The employee role in delivering service

The opening spotlight highlights the critical importance of 'service encounters', defined as 'the dyadic interaction between a customer and a service provider' (Surprenant and Solomon, 1987, pg. 87). Marcos Van Aken of Ten Travel specializes in personalized and customized service for his clients, and has developed strong business relationships because of this attention to detail. The majority of research examining social interactions in commercial service settings has focused on such exchanges between consumers and frontline employees (e.g. Gremler and Gwinner, 2000; Parasuraman, Zeithaml and Berry, 1988). This is particularly the case within tourism and hospitality settings, including hotels (Hartline and Jones, 1996), restaurants (Lin and Mattila, 2010), and tour groups (Conze, Bieger, Laesser and Riklin, 2010). As 'service encounters are first and foremost social encounters'

(McCallum and Harrison, 1985, p. 35), it follows that consumers derive important social benefits, which include friendship, personal recognition, and enjoyable connections with service providers, particularly in high-contact, customized personal services (Gwinner et al, 1998). Companies can also derive corresponding benefits, as the opening spotlight illustrates.

The importance of frontline employees in the provision of customer service was recognized in Chapter 1 and captured in the people element of the services marketing mix as well as the interactive marketing activity depicted in the services marketing triangle. Interactive marketing occurs in the 'moment of truth' when the customer interacts with the organization and the service is produced and consumed. From the customer's point of view, the most vivid impression of service occurs in the service encounter or the moment of truth. It is in these encounters that customers receive a snapshot of the organization's service quality, and each encounter contributes to the customer's overall satisfaction and willingness to do business with the organization again. Table 5.1 lists 15 'moment of truth' customer service techniques that the authors of this book use in customer service training seminars.

Table 5.1: Fifteen customer service techniques for delivering great service at the moment of truth (Source: Based on Timm, 2008)

Technique	Description
1) Promptly greet all customers	The word 'promptly' is key here. Nobody likes to be ignored or made to wait. Greet the customer as though they were a guest in your own home
2) Use appropriate icebreakers	Break the ice with safe conversation starters such as the weather. Then build rapport based on common interests
3) Compliment freely and sincerely	Customers love to be complimented – even if they know it may not be truly genuine. Research shows that even fragrant flattery can generate positive feelings and lead to customer loyalty
4) Call customers by their name (if known)	People love nothing more than the sound of their own name. So use it if you know it but be sensitive to the use of the customer's first or last name. Be careful not to become overfamiliar too quickly
5) Make and maintain eye contact with customers	Eye contact creates a bond between you and your customer. There are three "I's" to eye contact: 'Intimidation', 'Intimacy', and 'Involvement'. You are looking for 'Involvement' in a customer service setting
6) Ask for feedback	You need to know how you are getting on, so continuously ask the customer for feedback. You want to know as soon as possible if there are any problems in the service delivery
7) Listen carefully	Good listeners: tilt face towards channel of information; look at the other person; react to the speaker by sending out nonverbal signals; stop talking and use receptive language; and concentrate on what the speaker is saying
8) Use effective service vocabulary	Don't say: 'I don't know', 'We're really busy', 'That's not my department', 'There's nothing I can do', 'It's company policy'. Use positive phrases instead: 'Let me find out for you' for example. 'Please', 'thank you' and 'you're welcome' are powerful words for building customer rapport and loyalty.

9) Smile freely and often	Customer satisfaction dramatically increases with a genuine smile. Customers often indicate that they feel valued when they receive a smile. Customer loyalty, retention, and profits all fall in line with the rest of the interaction once the tone is set and continued with a smile
10) Appropriately touch customers when possible (handshake, pat on the back, etc).	Physical touch is a powerful form of communication. According to one restaurant study, one single gesture increased waiters' and waitresses' tips by an average of 36%: they physically touched the patrons at some point during the meal. Of course, you have to be careful about who and where you touch (a handshake is usually safe)
11) Enjoy people and their diversity	Avoid the tendency to judge; accept diversity for the quality it brings to our lives. Work on verbal discipline and avoid saying anything negative or judgmental about customers – or anyone!
12) Have a good attitude about your job	Also, you will benefit from having a positive attitude about life. Optimists live 8-9 years longer than pessimists according to the book Authentic Happiness!
13) Keep your workplace clean and attractive	Customers notice subtle things such as cleanliness, so it is important to create a strong first impression by keeping the workplace attractive to the eye
14) Dress and groom yourself appropriately	The way a person dresses goes a long way to creating a first impression. So determine what level of professionalism you want to convey to your customers, and dress appropriately
15) Maintain a good body posture	Posture involves the way you position your body. By standing or sitting with an erect posture, walking confidently, or assuming a relaxed, open posture, you can appear to be attentive, confident and ready to assist.

Parasuraman et al (1985) have showed that consumers judge service quality by using the same general criteria, regardless of the type of service. This criteria can be summarized in five dimensions: assurance, empathy, reliability, responsiveness, and tangibles. All of these dimensions will be influenced directly by frontline employees. Delivering the service as promised – reliability – is often totally within the control of frontline employees. These employees can also directly influence perceptions of responsiveness through their personal willingness to help customers. The assurance dimension of service quality is highly dependent on the ability of frontline employees to communicate their credibility and to inspire trust and confidence. Empathy implies that employees will pay attention, listen, adapt, and be flexible in delivering what individual customers need. Finally, employee appearance, body language and dress are all important aspects of the tangible dimension of service quality (see Table 5.1). Chapter 6 will explain in more detail how these dimensions are measured in a service setting.

For frontline employees to be consistently empathetic, responsive, friendly, courteous, etc. towards customers often requires huge amounts of 'emotional labor', a term coined by Arlie Hochschild (1983) to refer to labor that goes beyond the physical or mental skills required to deliver quality service. It means making eye contact, delivering smiles, showing sincere interest and engaging in friendly conversation with people who are essentially strangers. It may also require employees to supress real feelings if they are not feeling well or just having a bad day. Successful service companies carefully select people who can handle emotional stress, and then train them in the necessary skills to cope with emotional labor, such as listening and problem solving skills. The next section takes a more in-depth look at customer service training.

Customer service training

As discussed in Chapter 1, there is a consensus – certainly in the Western world – that customer service standards are falling, and organizations are keenly aware of their continued failure to meet minimum customer service expectations. A survey by Novations, a Boston-based consultancy, revealed that 64% of human resource executives believe there is a greater need for more customer service training compared with 24% who reported no increase needed (Laff, 2007). There is a widespread recognition that service oriented firms, such as those in the hospitality sector, are reluctant to invest in training initiatives (Beeton and Graetz, 2001). Small firms, in particular, are wary of investing time, finance and other resources in training, despite the evidence that shows a strong relationship between training and employee retention. A recent study in Australia found that attitudes towards training, together with length of industry experience and prior attendance in training activities are the strongest predictors of customer service training uptake for organizations in the hospitality sector (Butcher et al, 2009).

Training for a service-oriented culture will require more than a single program or class. Even before customer service training, new hires should have an initial training session that sets the tone for the employee's experience and begins to build a foundation for service. As discussed in Chapter 4, benchmark tourism and hospitality organizations spend considerable time and money teaching a culture value system (Ford and Heaton, 2001). Once the value system is taught, training can be more specific. At The Broadmoor Resort in Colorado Springs, for example, every new restaurant employee attends a two-day orientation program, followed by a workshop series covering how to answer a phone, greet a guest, properly serve wine, bus a table, and so on. This is followed by specific customer service training. At The Broadmoor, there are 16 standards common to all employees based on five-star, five-diamond standards (Simons, 2005). These standards like 'use the guest's name', always say 'I will find out', and never say 'I don't know', and 'walk a guest to his or her requested location', specifically define what exceptional service means. These standards are reinforced through classes, contests and recognition programs.

Ritz Carlton employees are also trained based on certain specific standards. Each new recruit to the company receives a high level of continuous training and feedback, and is introduced to the Ritz Carlton Gold Standards. Printed on a card that every employee carries around, the Gold Standards illustrate the company's credo, the employee promise and rules for behavior towards guests and fellow members of staff. These rules explain, for example, the exact vocabulary that should be used to greet guests and guidance on personal appearance. Further, they form a social contract between the institution and everyone that works there. The credo is summed up simply as 'We are ladies and gentlemen serving ladies and gentlemen.'

Training needs to be ongoing in order to avoid apathy on the part of employees. Tenerife, has been a top European destination for over 50 years, but has suffered from its share of tourism tiredness. 'Tourist assassins – terroristes de touristes – we call it,' says Marcos Van Aken from Ten Travel (see spotlight above). But Van Aken believes such apathy can be counteracted with an emphasis upon customer service training with motivation from mid and top management. As a hotel manager, he performed training exercises with bellboys who had been complaining about diminishing tips. He himself role-played as the bellboy, demonstrating how to show guests how to work the elevator, point out amenities in the hotel and rooms, draw curtains and explain how safes worked, etc. When the bellboys remained unconvinced of his tactics, he then stood in as a bellboy himself and proved his point with pocketfuls of tips by the end of the day. 'They realized that it is all about surprising people,' he says.

Many service providers look externally for customer service training. The snapshot on the Renaissance Harbour View Hotel in Chapter 4 explained how the hotel recruits outside experts to enhance customer service training at the five-star hotel. Hotels in Alberta, Canada, use WorldHost programs and workshops to elevate their service culture. WorldHost was responsible for training frontline volunteers for the Vancouver Olympics and the London Olympic and Paralympic Games (see snapshot in Chapter 3). Working across Canada and also internationally with over 500 certified trainers, WorldHost has also been involved with customer service training in Alberta for Coast Hotels and Resorts in Edmonton and Jasper and also for the Sandman chain. Treva Gardner, Human Resources Manager for Sandman Hotels and Suites, says around 500 Sandman employees have been trained using the WorldHost program since 2005. 'We use WorldHost as our basic customer service training tool, in addition to our own training,' says Gardner. 'It gives the team a grounding in common sense, and helps give them additional skills in listening and problem solving.' She says that customer loyalty, achieved through great customer service, is intrinsic to their business. The course encourages staff to think outside the box, ensuring guests the best experience. While not being able to pin a dollar amount on repeat customers, she says they are Sandman's 'brand cheer leaders'.

One often neglected area of customer service training is how to serve an ethnically and social diverse customer base. Different cultures have different concepts of appropriate dress, hygiene, family, punctuality, and how to address members of the same and opposite sex, so training is necessary to ensure that standards of service are delivered in a uniformed but cultural sensitive manner. In the 'Connections that Make a Difference' program, described in the snapshot below, employees were trained in the personal skills necessary to deal with a variety of cultures. In one exercise, trainees would be shown various hand gestures and asked what they mean. One of the pictures would have someone holding out a palm, which in most cultures would mean a sign to stop or a wave or even a thank you. However, in Greece, the gesture – known as the *moutza* – is deeply insulting. The offensiveness dates back to the days when chained criminals would be paraded around town and have cinders (moutzos) and excrement wiped in their faces as a form of public humiliation (McCrum, 2008). The closer you put your hand to someone's face, the more threatening it is considered.

The snapshot below describes how an increasing number of international airports are sending employess on customer service training courses. Even in France, where air travel is not normally associated with a pleasant experience, Charles de Gaulle airport, Europe's second-largest airport, is sending its employees to charm school in order to improve the passenger experience. By March 2012, more than 5000 airport staff had atended a so-called University of Service that opened in 2011, aimed at improving attention and responsiveness to passengers' needs (Clark, 2012).

Snapshot: Calgary International Airport: Connections that Make a Difference

Calgary International Airport, courtesy of Marek Ślusarczyk

It has been universally recognized by tourism authorities that airports are often the first and last impression tourists have of a country or city and, as such, can make or break the experience. Consumers globally are raising expectations for service and quality and airports have had to raise their standards to compete for passengers. The American Association of Airports has produced an on-site training workshop to help employees 'understand the skills, attitudes and behaviors necessary for reaching excellence in service delivery'. This workshop moved away from traditional greetings and towards personal attitudes and insights. It stressed 'the importance of customer service to the overall mission of the airport', identifying the employee's role within the big picture. It was a one-day workshop with team problem-solving, personal action and experiential learning activities.

Other airports have decided to conduct their own training programs for employees. Miami International airport, for example, hired the services of the Disney Institute to improve its staff customer service skills. The Florida-based training company, which specialises in coaching executives and frontline workers, is now teaching the airport's terminal operations employees – including retail staff – staff relations, leadership practices, team-building and communication skills. Miami airport's media relations manager, Greg Chin said 'This is just one of many customer service initiatives we're doing. We're hoping it generates a new thinking, a culture change here at the airport that is more accommodating to travellers. Most airports provide the same service, but what distinguishes good airports from great airports is the customer service they provide.'

In 2008 Calgary International Airport (YYC) started a program called 'Connections that Make a Difference' to bring their customer service up to par. In the past Vancouver, Edmonton and Ottawa airports had all been awarded customer service accolades but Calgary had not. Instituted by Peggy Blacklock for the Calgary Airport Authority, the customer service training course has impacted frontline service providers ranging across the board from the retired 'White Hat' meeters and greeters to the traditionally surly immigration and customs officials.

Blacklock employed a customer service consultant from the University of Calgary as part of the project as well as a local film maker for the training video. In a newsletter, she explained to her employees that 'Connections that Make a Difference' are: 'the interactions you have every day with people – passengers, co-workers, family, friends. Whether the connections you make with people are positive or negative is entirely up to you. The only way that the Calgary International Airport can make a difference in the lives of people is through you – our Airport People!'

The day-long training course blends key messages about creating positive experiences, surprising customers and gaining pride in the workplace. Using video and interactive techniques, airport staff are given a new outlook on diverse customer service techniques including how to say 'no' to a passenger in a positive way and treating everyone in the airport with value and respect. Time is devoted to understanding the passenger's frame of reference. Above all the program stresses that each staff member 'is YYC' and it is their airport. It underlines 'moments of truth when what you communicate will be what people think of YYC'. It encourages teamwork between the very disparate entities at work within the airport and how to stay motivated when co-workers don't share the same commitment. Finally, there is coaching on service recovery. Blacklock stresses that while educational, the sessions are also interesting and even entertaining for the staff. 'All participants are asked and encouraged to provide service and facility improvement suggestions,' she adds, and many of their ideas have subsequently been adopted. Some of the Authority's key offerings now include a competitive total rewards program, ongoing professional development, opportunities to give back to the community, and a unique work environment.

One of the innovative lessons in Calgary Airport's training program invokes the 'Law of the Garbage Truck'. Some people are 'like garbage trucks', full of personal frustration, anger, disappointment and rage. When they need a place to dump it, they let rip at some poor service provider. Trainers counseled the staff not to take this personally, but to recognize it as a 'garbage truck' situation, saying 'Don't pick up their garbage and spread it to other people in your life, whether at work, at home, or to people you don't even know on the streets'. Instead the Mantra is 'Love the people who treat you right and forgive and pray for the ones who don't'. Not all passengers are garbage trucks, but naturally there are many fraught customers at airports. They could be lost, disoriented, worried about missing a flight, having problems understanding signage or even not really wanting to leave loved ones behind. Alternatively, they could have just been delayed, missed connections, stranded, missed meetings or events, had a terrible, bumpy flight or a bad experience in the air. This can lead to some high emotions. So participants are advised on how to deal with highly-charged situations, through role-play and video examples.

In 2011 YYC surpassed 12.7 million annual passengers, tended by around 15,000 employees. Its adoption of customer service initiatives has led to some fruitful results in the past few years. It was named on Mediacorp Canada Inc's Alberta's Top 50 Employers list for 2009 and 2011. This designation recognizes Alberta's employers that lead their industries in offering exceptional places to work. 'It is thanks to our incredible staff that we are successful on the local and global network stage. YYC is among the best airports in the world,' said Cynthia Tremblay, Senior Director of Human Resources for the Calgary Airport Authority, in an interview for Travel Alberta. 'We are focused on continually benchmarking our great employment offerings to ensure they meet the needs of our current and future staff. These are the tools that enable us to attract and retain the dedicated people that work hard every day at making YYC the best airport in the country, and we are pleased to be recognized for that commitment'. And, by 2011 Calgary Airport was showing up in the international awards charts, winning third place for Customer Service Initiatives in the ACI Excellence in Airport Marketing and Communications Contest.

Sources: Anon (2011); Airports Council International (2007); Airport Customer Service; Muldowney (2008); Calgary Airport Authority Media Center.

The customer role in delivering service

Customer participation is often inevitable in service delivery and co-creation, as services are actions or performances, typically produced and consumed simultaneously. The importance of customers in successful service delivery is clear if service performances are looked at as a form of drama (Zeithaml et al, 2007; Pine and Gilmore, 1998). The drama metaphor for services suggests the reciprocal, interactive role of employees (actors) and consumers (audience) in creating the service experience. The service actors and audience are surrounded by the service setting or the servicescape (discussed in Chapter 8). The level of customer participation varies across services. At a theatre featuring a murder mystery stage play, there is a very low level of participation from customers, whereas in an interactive murder mystery evening hosted in a private house, customers are co-creators of the service.

Customers can play three major roles in service delivery (Zeithaml et al, 2007). The first is as productive resources. Customers can often be considered as 'partial employees' as their contribution may enhance an organization's productivity, in addition to increasing their own satisfaction (Bowen, 1986). WestJet, for example (see Chapter 4), depends on customers to perform critical service roles for themselves, such as self check-in, carrying their own bags, getting their own food, and self-seating. Another role customers can play is that of contributor to their own satisfaction. In services such as healthcare, education, personal fitness and weight loss, the service outcome is highly dependent on customer participation. Customers contribute to quality service delivery when they ask questions, take responsibility for their own satisfaction, and complain when there is a service failure. A final role played by service customers is that of potential competitor. Whether to produce a service for themselves (internal exchange) or have someone else provide the service for them (external exchange) is a common dilemma for consumers. Such dilemmas may occur in services like childcare, house cleaning, yearly tax returns, or car repair.

■ Customer-to-customer (C2C) interactions

Consumer satisfaction is frequently influenced by other people, and as service consumption often takes place in the presence of other customers, customer-to-customer (C2C) interactions can have a substantial impact on consumption experiences. Positive interactions among consumers, in a variety of service settings, have been shown to be important to both consumers and companies, and research shows that managerially facilitated positive customer-to-customer interactions enhance consumer satisfaction and enjoyment (Levy, Hudson and Getz, 2011). Table 5.2 contains a summary of past research on this topic.

Table 5.2: Consumer-to-consumer interaction studies in the marketing, tourism and hospitality literature (**Source:** Levy, Hudson and Getz, 2011).

Methodology	Type of service	Setting	Individual factors	Situational factors	Reasons for C-to-C interaction	Outcomes	Authored work
Surveys, interviews	Utilitarian (retail)	Gardening Shop	Extroversion, age	Service failures, servicescape, duration, waiting lines	Risk reduction, display knowledge, information seeking, social contact making	Increased enjoyment, social involvement, improved purchases, increased knowledge	Parker and Ward (2000)
Observation, interviews, shopping with informants		Retail stores	Gender, age	Similarity, servicescape	Information seeking, pro-social behavior		McGrath and Otnes (1995)
Field experiment		Ladies clothing store			Information seeking, risk reduction, product knowledge, credibility of advice	Satisfaction, likelihood to purchase	Harris, Davies, and Baron (1997)
Surveys		IKEA	Gender, age, social tendencies/ gregariousness			Enjoyment	Harris, Baron and Radcliffe (1995)
Surveys, interviews		Do It Yourself (DIY) Superstore	Willingness to provide information, ability to provide information		Information seeking, advice		Harris, Baron and Davies (1999)
Surveys		Hair Salon	Gender	Servicescape		Firm satisfaction, firm loyalty, firm word of mouth	Moore, Moore, and Capella (2005)
Ethnography	Utilitarian and hedonistsic	Rail Travel	Willingness to engage (gregariousness)	Service failure	Risk/anxiety reduction, supply of social interaction, pro-social behavior	Defuse dissatisfaction	Harris and Baron (2004)

Methodology	Type of service	Setting	Individual factors	Situational factors	Reasons for C-to-C interaction	Outcomes	Authored work
Surveys		Fitness Center			Sense of belonging, social contact making	Purchase intention, frequency of usage, intention to recommend	Guenzi and Pelloni (2004)
Surveys		Professional association meeting	Previous experience		Social contact making, networking	Value of firm offering, intention to recommend, conference value, intention to return	Gruen, Osmonbekov, and Czaplewski (2007)
Critical incident technique	Hedonistic	Theme Park	Gregariousness/friendliness, culture, relationship status, education, income, age	Waiting lines (servicescape), conversational time units (duration)	Social contact making, pro-social behavior, incidental	Satisfaction	Grove and Fisk (1997)
Personal interviews, surveys		Restaurant			Social needs	Satisfaction, willingness to pay	Andersson and Mossberg (2004)
Focus groups, mail surveys		Restaurant and bowling centre	Age, gender, gregariousness			Satisfaction	Martin (1996)
Lab experiment		Restaurant	Mood, involvement, perceived control, prior expectations, personal values		Incidental	Perceived incompatibility	Raajpoot and Sharma (2006)
Surveys		Tour Groups	Age, gender, relationship		Social contact making, pro-social behavior, incidental	Evaluation of fellow customers, satisfaction	Wu (2007)
Surveys		Cruise Travel			Relaxation, learning	Vacation satisfaction	Huang and Hsu (2010)

5

C2C interactions have been successfully fostered and managed for strategic gain by a number of firms. For instance, consumer goods producers, such as Harley Davidson, Jeep, Apple and Saturn, have all managed to build very successful consumer clubs and/or brand communities (Muniz and O'Guinn, 2001). These brand communities have been shown to lead to higher levels of consumer identification and involvement (Muniz and O'Guinn, 2001), and manufacturers who actively manage their brand communities are seen to enjoy an increase in market share, sales, and commitment on the part of consumers (McAlexander, Schouten and Koenig, 2002).

Companies can also enhance the quality of life of consumers by facilitating social interactions among their clientele. As the traditional sense of community continues to deteriorate due to an emphasis on individual rather than collective experiences (Putnam, 1995), consumers are increasingly turning to marketplace environments to supplement social relationships. Parker and Harris (1999) maintain that 78% of all spontaneous conversations among strangers take place in commercial service environments. Often, these settings are considered 'third spaces', which are places away from home and work that help foster a sense of community (Oldenburg, 1999). Places such as coffee shops, laundromats, and restaurants are increasingly sought by consumers to satisfy social needs for belonging and membership (Aubert-Gamet and Cova, 1999; Muniz and O'Guinn, 2001).

Marketing academics have long argued for managerial involvement in facilitating C2C interactions. In their exploration of managerial roles to enhance customer compatibility, Pranter and Martin (1991) suggest that service providers can be 'cheerleaders' and introduce customers to each other, in the hopes of achieving a sense of belonging and togetherness among consumers. Harris et al (2000) called for staff recruitment, training and empowerment with specific aims for encouraging conversations between consumers. Grove and Fisk (1997) suggested that organizations should attempt to 'warm up [their] audiences' (p. 79) as entertainers do, to encourage consumers to be in the right frame of mind, which would result in positive C2C relationships. Martin and Clark (1996) encourage firms to target similar consumers, form consumer groups, and maintain control over the physical and social environments where consumers interact. In the leisure context, Horner (2003) opines that hospitality companies should encourage C2C interactions 'to form groups of people with a shared understanding based on customer demand' (p. 19).

Studies in this topic area (see Table 5.2) have found positive relationships between consumer interactions and key marketing outcomes such as firm satisfaction (Andersson and Mossberg, 2004; Harris et al, 1997; Wu, 2007), vacation satisfaction (Huang and Hsu, 2010), enjoyment (Harris et al, 1995; Parker and Ward, 2000), intention to return and word of mouth referral (Gruen, Osmonbekov and Czaplewski, 2007; Moore, Moore and Capella, 2005). In an exploratory study of the multidimensional nature of dining, Andersson and Mossberg (2004) surveyed customers on their actual and ideal restaurant experiences and found that other customers positively contribute to satisfaction with the restaurant. Within the Taiwanese tour group context, Wu (2007) reported that the evaluation of fellow tour group members was a significant determinant of traveler satisfaction, with positive C2C interactions (e.g. conversations, shaking hands, opening doors) serving as a major influencer of these evaluations.   Utilizing an online panel survey to American cruise passengers, Huang and Hsu (2010) discovered that the quality, not quantity, of C2C interaction influences cruise vacation satisfaction. Levy et al (2011) employed a field experimental methodology utilizing four half-day cultural heritage tours to examine consumer-to-consumer interactions within the group travel context. Their findings demonstrate that managerially facilitated C2C interactions significantly increase tour member satisfaction and enjoyment.

■ Enhancing customer participation

The overall goals of a customer participation strategy will typically be to increase organizational productivity and customer satisfaction while simultaneously decreasing uncertainty due to unpredictable customer actions (Zeithaml et al, 2007). Figure 5.1 illustrates the three main strategies companies might use for enhancing customer participation.

Figure 5.1: Strategies for enhancing customer participation (Source: Based on Zeithaml et al, 2007, pp. 345)

The first strategy involves defining exactly what the customer's job is going to be in the service delivery process. The service may require only the customer's presence such as a theatre or bus transportation, or it may need certain levels of customer input, as it would at a health and wellness resort, for example. In the last few years, airlines have given more control to passengers at airports in order to save money and improve service levels. The International Air Transport Association (IATA), for example, has introduced a *Fast Travel* initiative that consists of five projects designed to offer a range of self-service options for passengers.

The initiative is expected to save up to $2.1 billion annually across the industry. The five areas with more self-service options are:

1 *Bags ready-to-go*: Enabling passengers to deliver their bags tagged and ready for acceptance by an airline check-in agent or a self-service bag drop.

2 *Document scanning*: Allowing passengers to scan their travel documents at kiosks for onward transmission to government agencies and automatic verification against travel data requirements, so they can avoid going to a check-in desk to complete required travel document checks

3 *Flight re-booking*: Allowing passengers to get proactively rebooked and obtain a new boarding pass via a self-service channel such as kiosks in case of delays or cancellations, avoiding long lines

4 *Self-boarding*: Allowing passengers to self-scan their boarding token to gain entry to the aircraft, potentially using automated boarding gates like in a train or metro station

5 *Bag recovery*: Allowing passengers to report a missing bag via a self-service channel instead of waiting in line at a baggage claim service counter.

Once the customer's role is clearly defined, strategies for managing customers can mimic to some degree the efforts aimed at service employees. The 'right' customers need to be recruited, educated, and rewarded in performing their roles effectively. For IATA's *Fast Track* initiative to be successful, passengers will therefore need to be informed as to why and how they should participate in the new self-service options. Chris Goater, IATA's Communications Manager said: 'The attraction of the Fast Travel program is that it represents a win for airports, airlines and passengers. Airports have more flexibility in using existing infrastructure to meet current needs, as self-service facilities take up less space. Airports and airlines can also enhance throughput and better manage passenger flows at peak times. Airlines have the opportunity to enhance the passenger experience, reduce costs and delays. Passengers can have more choice, convenience and control throughout their journey' (Ghee, 2010).

The final strategy for enhancing customer participation is the effective management of the customer mix. As mentioned earlier in this chapter, consumer satisfaction is frequently influenced by other people, and as service consumption often takes place in the presence of other customers, customer-to-customer interactions can have a substantial impact on consumption experiences. Managerially facilitated customer-to-customer interactions can therefore significantly increase customer satisfaction and enjoyment. The process of managing multiple and sometimes conflicting segments is known as compatibility management, and some organizations approach this by attracting largely homogenous groups of customers through careful positioning and segmentation strategies. The Ritz-Carlton or Four Seasons, for example, attract mainly upscale travelers, whereas budget hotels like those under the Red Roof Inn franchise, attract a more cost-conscious, value-seeking guest.

Case study: People Power at Fairmont Hotels & Resorts

Fairmonht Banff Springs Hotel: Photo courtesy of Fairmont Hotels & Resorts

Fairmont Hotels and Resorts is a good example of a company that aims its marketing efforts toward its employees. Fairmont is one of the largest luxury hotel management companies in North America and has achieved great success since the brand was established in 1907. The company now operates 63 hotels in 16 countries with a total of 26,700 rooms and 30,000 employees. The company sees internal marketing as critical in achieving guest satisfaction, and consequently Fairmont is world-renowned for its excellent guest service. The company measures the success or failure of its internal marketing programs through employee turnover rate which is much lower than industry averages. Staff loyalty in turn encourages customer loyalty; repeat guests make up approximately 60% of Fairmont's business.

Jenny Dunbar is Fairmont's Regional Director for Public Relations, Mountain Region, based in Banff, Alberta, Canada. 'Customers tell us that the strongest attribute of Fairmont is the people. Fairmont engages in service with guests – it is not just a transactional interface,' she says. Fairmont knows that it is important to segment the employee market as well as the guest market, and to develop a marketing mix to attract the best staff for its company. Attracting self-motivated, results-oriented staff for Fairmont is key to its employee marketing mix, which is why it has an extensive recruiting and hiring process to select the best employees to interact with its guests. Once hired, the employee participates in a mandatory two-day orientation offered by the Fairmont Learning Organization (FLO).

New recruits learn Fairmont's service culture (policies, procedures, reward systems, and actions) and organizational culture (mission, vision, values, and history of the company) – creating both staff loyalty and, as a result of their commitment, guest loyalty. 'Ultimately customer and guest loyalty programs can only be successful if they resonate as a true value proposition to the guest. An organization must "live its brand" internally as much as externally,' says Dunbar.

Empowerment is about turning the traditional organizational structure upside down, with the customers and employees at the top of the structure and management at the bottom. Management and employees now work to serve the guest, versus serving the CEO or 'boss'. Focusing on the needs and wants of the customer and granting employees the power to achieve the ultimate guest service creates an atmosphere in which employees are not afraid to tell supervisors of a mistake in order to rectify it and satisfy the guest. The company-wide emphasis is on giving each employee – at both the corporate and the property levels – the tools, training, authority, and support they need in order to make informed decisions and take appropriate actions to deliver the highest level of service excellence to Fairmont guests. The goal is to empower employees to create customized experiences that make lifetime memories for guests – what Fairmont calls 'wow' experiences. The following are examples, provided by Dunbar, of how Fairmont staff 'turned moments into memories' during 2011:

Kathryn turned Moments into Memories for our Young Guests by 'treating each and every guest as a unique individual'

This evening we had a young girl of 6yrs old on our floor that was searching high and low for a 'princess' in the hotel. So our very own Kathryn quietly slipped into her costume and surprised this little girl 'Ava' in the lounge. She was speechless and absolutely thrilled. Pictures were taken and Ava's evening was made.

Ajay turned Moments into Memories for our Guests by 'resolving guests problems and never saying "no" without offering an alternative', and 'being an ambassador for My Brand, My Hotel, My Community and My Colleagues'

Ajay has been doing an amazing job running the evening housekeeping shift. On top of organizing the team, improving communication with other departments and personally attending to any guest concerns he still finds time to offer personalized service to our guests. A great example of this is an encounter he had with a guest this past week. He received a call of a guest having challenges operating their phone. He went to the room and tried trouble shooting the problem with numerous options but could not get the phone operating properly. The guest had a family emergency back home and Ajay could tell she was distressed. He offered her his personal cell phone to make a long distance call to her family. Although this seems like a small gesture, this put our guests mind at ease and was a creative solution.

Going the extra mile to satisfy customers is part of Fairmont's 'Service Promise' which Francisco Gomez (Regional Vice President, Canada's Western Mountain Region and General Manager, The Fairmont Banff Springs) says is 'a mindset, not a skill set'. Fairmont's focus is on anticipating needs in order to facilitate them. Employees carry with them a pocket size 'Service Promise' which outlines Fairmont's mission to create enduring memories for guests through engaging service and authentic local experiences. The emphasis is on training staff as ambassadors for the brand, making guests feel valued and unique and turning negative situations into positive experiences by offering innovative alternatives. This is summed up in the acronym RITE: Respect, Integrity, Teamwork and Empowerment.

Employee reward and recognition programs are an important part of the process of internal marketing. Once Fairmont has attracted and recruited the right employees, attention is focused on keeping employees satisfied and motivated to continue to impress the guest. Benefits and perks are important factors in compensating employees. Substantial discounts of up to 50% off food, beverages, and hotel rates are offered as employee incentives to encourage them to use these products/services, thus facilitating first-hand knowledge. Employees are part of the product, and encouraging them to be excited about Fairmont hotels and services will in turn make the customer more excited. Fairmont also has a number of recognition awards that are presented throughout the year. These benefits and awards market the company to the employees and install a positive attitude within the workplace. Internal communication at Fairmont is also taken seriously. A bi-monthly newsletter is distributed in each specific hotel, and a company-wide newsletter, *The Dialogue*, keeps staff up to date on new company procedures.

Sources

Interview with Jenny Dunbar, 2011; Interview with Mike Taylor, 2011; Cohen (2001); Liddle (2002); Mueller (2000); The Fairmont Learning Organization (2001).

References

Airports Council International (2007) 'Airport Service Quality Awards 2007'. Accessed 10/03/2008 from http://www.airports.org/cda/aci_common/display/main/aci_content07

Airport Customer Service, Accessed 02/28/2008 from http://www.aaae.org/products/200

Andersson, T. D. and Mossberg, L. (2004) 'The dining experience: Do restaurants satisfy customer needs?' *Food Service Technology*, 4(4), 171-177.

Anon (2011) 'The Calgary Airport Authority is 'tops' on Alberta's Top 50 List', *Travel Alberta News*. From http://industry.travelalberta.com/News/News%20Archive/News%20Article.aspx?id=%7B74FB84C7-9DCC-4B09-9436-1B7B536076E3%7D accessed 08/11/2011

Aubert-Gamet, V. and Cova, B. (1999) 'Servicescapes: From modern non-places to postmodern common places', *Journal of Business Research*, **44**, 37-45.

Beeton, S. and Graetz, B. (2001) 'Small business small-minded? Training attitudes and needs of the tourism and hospitality industry', *The International Journal of Tourism Research*, **3**(2), 105-113.

Bowen, D.E. (1986) 'Managing customers as human resources in service organizations', *Human Resource Management*, **25**(3), 371-383.

Butcher, K., Sparks, B. and McColl-Kennedy, J. (2009) 'Predictors of customer service training in hospitality firms', *International Journal of Hospitality Management*, **28**, 389-396.

Calgary Airport Authority Media Center, Accessed 07/11/2011 from http://www.yyc.com/Default.aspx?cid=162&lang=1

Clark, N. (2012) 'Charles de Gaulle airport hopes to win traffic with smiles and shorter lines', *The New York Times*, 30 March, B5.

Cohen, S. (2001). 'Concierges go the extra mile to make visitors' stays memorable', *TheBusiness Journal*, **19**(50), 24.

Conze, O., Bieger, T., Laesser, C. and Riklin, T. (2010) 'Relationship intention as a mediator between relational benefits and customer loyalty in the tour operator industry', *Journal of Travel and Tourism Marketing*, **27**(1), 51-62.

Cova, B.(1997) 'Community and consumption: Towards a definition of the "linking value" of product or services', *European Journal of Marketing*, **31**(3/4), 297-316.

Cova, B. and Cova, V. (2002) 'Tribal marketing: The tribalisation of society and its impact on the conduct of marketing', *European Journal of Marketing*, **36**(5/6), 595-620.

Czepiel, J. A. (1990) 'Service encounters and service relationships: Implications for research', *Journal of Business Research*, **20**, 13-21.

Fairmont Learning Organization (2001) 'MyFairmontServiceplus Training Binder'.

Ford, R.C. and Heaton, C.P. (2001) 'Lessons from hospitality that can serve anyone', *Organizational Dynamics*, **30**(1), 30-47.

Ghee, R. (2010) 'IATA sets ambitious Fast Travel target following successful 2010', *Futuretravelexperience.com*. from http://www.futuretravelexperience.com/2011/04/iata-sets-ambitious-fast-travel-target-following-successful-2010/#, accessed 11/24/2011

Gremler, D. D. and Gwinner, K. P. (2000) 'Customer-employee rapport in service relationships', *Journal of Service Research*, **3**(1), 82-104.

Grove, S. J. and Fisk, R. P. (1997) 'The impact of other customers on service experiences: A critical incident examination of getting along', *Journal of Retailing*, **73**(1), 63-85.

Gruen, T.W., Osmonbekov, T. and A.J. Czaplewski (2007) 'Customer-to-customer exchange: Its MOA antecedents and its impact on value creation and loyalty,' *Journal of the Academy of Marketing Science*, **35**(4), 537-549.

Gwinner, K. P., Gremler, D. D. and Bitner, M. J. (1998) 'Relational benefits in service industries: The customer's perspective', *Journal of the Academy of Marketing Science,* **26**(2), 101-144.

Harris, K., Baron, S. and Parker, C. (2000) 'Understanding the consumer experience: It's good to talk', *Journal of Marketing Management,* **16**(1-3), 111-127.

Harris, K., Baron, S. and Ratcliffe, J. (1995) 'Customers as oral participants in a service setting', *Journal of Services Marketing,* **9**(4), 64-76.

Harris, K., Davies, B. and Baron, S. (1997) 'Conversations during purchase consideration: Sales assistants and customers', *The International Review of Retail, Distribution and Consumer Research,* **7**(3), 173-190.

Hartline, M. D. and Jones, K. C. (1996) 'Employee performance cues in a hotel service environment: Influence on perceived service quality, value, and word-of-mouth intentions', *Journal of Business Research,* **35**(3), 207-215.

Hochschild, A. (1983) *The Managed Heart: Commercialization of Human Feeling,* Berkeley: University of California Press.

Horner, S. (2003) 'Relationship marketing in hospitality – developing friends for life?', *Hospitality Review,* **5**(3), 19-25.

Huang, J. and Hsu, C. H. C. (2010) 'The impact of customer-to-customer interaction on cruise experience and vacation satisfaction', *Journal of Travel Research,* **49**(1), 79-92.

Lemon, K. N., Rust, R. T. and Zeithaml, V. T. (2001) 'What drives customer equity', *Marketing Management,* **10** (Spring), 20-25.

Levy, S., Hudson, S. and Getz, D. (2011) 'A field experimental investigation of managerially facilitated consumer-to-consumer interaction', *Journal of Travel & Tourism Marketing,* **28**(6), 656-674.

Liddle, A. J. (2002) 'Regional powerhouse chains', *Nations Restaurant News,* **36**(4), 100–102.

Lin, I. Y. and Mattila, A. S. (2010) 'Restaurant servicescape, service encounter, and perceived congruency on customers' emotions and satisfaction', *Journal of Hospitality Marketing and Management,* **19**(8), 819-841.

Lynn, A. and Lynn, M. (2003) 'Experiments and quasi-experiments: Methods for evaluating marketing options', *Cornell Hotel and Restaurant Administration Quarterly,* **44**(2), 75-84.

Martin, C. L. (1996) 'Consumer-to-consumer relationships: Satisfaction with other consumers' public behavior', *Journal of Consumer Affairs,* **30**(1), 146-168.

Martin, C. L. and Clark, T. (1996) 'Networks of customer-to-customer relationship in marketing: Conceptual foundations and implications', In D. Iacobucci (Ed.), *Networks in marketing* (pp.342-366). London: Sage Publications.

Martin, C. L. and Pranter, C. A. (1989) 'Compatibility management: Customer-to-customer relationships in service environments', *Journal of Services Marketing,* **3**(3), 5-15.

McAlexander, J. H., Schouten, J. W. and Koenig, H. F. (2002) 'Building brand community', *Journal of Marketing*, **66** (January), 38-54.

McCallum, J. R. and Harrison, W. (1985) 'Interdependence in the service encounter', In J. A. Czepiel and M. R. Soloman (Eds.), *The service encounter: Managing employee/customer interaction in service businesses* (pp. 35-48). Lexington, MA: Lexington Books.

McCrum, M. (2008) *Going Dutch in Beijing. The International Guide to Doing the Right Thing*, London: Profile Books Ltd.

Moore, M., Moore, M. L. and Capella, M. (2005) 'The impact of customer-to-customer interactions in a high personal contact service setting', *Journal of Services Marketing*, **19**(7), 482-491.

Muldowney, C (2008), 'Finding the Solution to Airport Customer Service', *Madison Magazine*. Accessed 04/28/2008 from http://www.madisonmagazine.com/article.php?xstate=view

Mueller, S. (2000). 'How do you set your hotel apart from others?', *The Business Journal*, **17**(51), 44.

Muniz Jr., A. M. and O'Guinn, T. C. (2001) 'Brand community', *Journal of Consumer Research*, **27** (March), 412-432.

Oldenburg, R. (1999) *The Great Good Place*, New York: Marlowe and Company.

Parasuraman, A., Zeithaml, V. A. and Berry, L.L. (1985) 'A conceptual model of service quality and its implications for future research', *Journal of Marketing*, **49**(4), 41–50.

Parasuraman, A., Zeithaml, V. A. and Berry, L. L. (1988) 'SERVQUAL: A multiple-item scale for measuring consumer perceptions of service quality', *Journal of Retailing*, **64**(1), 12-40.

Parker, C. and Harris, K. (1999) 'Investigating the antecedents of customer-to-customer interaction', In A. Menon and A. Sharma (Eds.). *American marketing association winter educators' conference proceedings, vol. 10* (pp.248-249). Chicago: American Marketing Association.

Parker, C. and Ward, P. (2000) 'An analysis of role adoptions and scripts during customer-to-customer encounters', *European Journal of Marketing*, **34**(3/4), 341-358.

Pine, B. J. II and Gilmore, J. H. (1998) 'Welcome to the experience economy', *Harvard Business Review*, **76**(4), 97–108.

Putnam, R. D. (1995) 'Bowling alone: America's declining social capital', *Journal of Democracy*, **6**(1), 65-78.

Simons, K. (2005) 'Exceptional customer service requires training all employees', *H&MM*, 20 June, 10 & 17.

Surprenant, C. F. and Solomon, M. R. (1987) 'Predictability and personalization in the service encounter', *Journal of Marketing*, **51**(April), 86-96.

Timm, P.R. (2008) *Customer Service: Career Success Through Customer Loyalty*, Upper Saddle River, N.J.: Pearson Education.

Wu, C. (2007) 'The impact of customer-to-customer interaction and customer homogeneity on customer satisfaction in tourism service – the service encounter perspective', *Tourism Management*, **28**, 1518-1528.

Zeithaml, V. A., Bitner, M. J., Gremler, D., Mahaffey, T. and Hiltz, B. (2007) *Services Marketing: Integrating Customer Focus Across the Firm*, Canadian Edition. New York: McGraw-Hill.

 Scan here to get the hyperlinks in this chapter

5

 **6** # The Importance of Market Research

Charlie Locke (left) and Sandy Best (right). Photo courtesy of Lake Louise

Sandy Best has been in the hospitality business since the 1970s. Starting out running chalets in French ski resorts, he is now Director of Public Relations for Lake Louise and Director of the newly renovated Great Divide Lodge.

Best is passionate about every little detail in his work whether it is staff training, daily operations, customer contact or service recovery. 'You know why I am good at it, it's because I love what I do,' he says. 'If you don't believe you have the best product on the planet, the guests won't believe it.'

One of the areas to which he devotes significant research – and great attention – is media. He encourages and conducts numerous media visits as well as travel industry fam trips every year at Lake Louise, Alberta – arguably Canada's most famous ski resort. 'It's the most cost-effective form of marketing you can do,' he explains. 'If you look at dollar per column length, if I had to buy that, it would be ten times what it costs to look after the media.'

One of his party tricks for visiting journalists is to greet them in their own language. 'I speak reasonable Mandarin so the Chinese are always amazed when I say hello and welcome. I can welcome almost every nationality in their language,' he says.

Lake Louise hosts the Winterstart World Cup every year, attracting skiing VIPs and media from all over the world. Best's job is to provide them with a seamless experience to take back to their readers, listeners and fans. 'We had an executive producer and VP from Channel 9 here recently and they said they would only call *me* when they come back to the Rockies because I totally understand what they are about.' He does his research before a press visit so that he can be ready with interesting and unique sound bites rather than just rolling out the usual press kit full of turgid statistics.

Best has noticed that many other ski resorts do not employ seasoned marketers and ski lovers as their press coordinators: 'Many resorts employ 25 to 30 year olds who don't even ski for media contact,' he says. 'I get very angry when journalists don't get treated as if they are valued.' One of the big differences in Best's red carpet treatment for journalists is to introduce them to Charlie Locke, Lake Louise's owner. 'Journalists are always impressed by this, they comment "so the owner will come and talk to me". They are surprised as this is not the case with other resorts,' says Best. Most ski hill owners delegate media duties to their fam trip organizers and various specialists around the resort.

Best's work does not stop at media and industry, though. He is also responsible for customer service for fee-paying visitors and for staff training and motivation. He considers customer service the lynchpin of operations for both the ski hill and for his hotel: 'Customer service makes pay days possible, the rest is bullshit,' he jokes.

One of the difficulties faced by ski hills world over is line-ups. There are various peak periods during a ski season when waiting in line is inevitable. Best has a contingency plan for this. 'People don't mind standing in a line as long as they are recognized. In the old days when we had lines Charlie would go out and give out chocolate. If people see you do something about a problem 99.9 % of people are fine with it.'

He carries this theory over to his daily work where he thrives on face-to-face communication in and around the ski lodge and at his hotel. He works in a challenging industry where the operational staff are often young, fresh out of college and mainly there for the skiing and nightlife rather than a career. And he has noted changes in the way they tend to communicate. 'The culture has changed,' he says. 'I see people under 30 in tourism,

6

supposedly the leaders of tomorrow, sitting at a table and texting each other. They just can't communicate face to face,' he laments.

Despite this, he inspires his employees with enthusiasm for people contact, leading by example. 'Good generals lead from the front not from behind. They see me being nice to people, caring about things, wiping tables, and picking up litter.' He has also helped implement a new 'service with no boundaries' system for employees to deal with service issues. Staff are empowered to solve problems and also compensate for them: 'For example, if a washroom has no toilet paper, the staff solve the issue but if, as the customer, you are still really pissed off, the staff member offers you lunch in return. We train them to do that.'

Best has found that employees feel good about their work when they are empowered in this way. The extra money spent is well worth the good PR that service recovery engenders. In the era of instant communication through all the far-reaching tentacles of social media, Best deems it cheaper to solve a problem instantly than to let it escalate into something more serious by leaving it until a guest gets home.

Despite initial concerns from 'the money people', Best says that the new 'service with no boundaries' system is working well. It is monitored weekly, he adds, as a learning tool for management: 'If the bottom of the totem pole rots out, the management hit the ground hard and fast because they fall from higher up,' he explains.

Another way that service quality is monitored at Lake Louise is via an 'excellence card'. Customers can nominate a particular member of staff and management can do the same within their own staff pool. Employees are recognized at parties each month with prizes. At the end of the season, an overall winner is honoured with a trip to Charlie Locke's house in Hawaii and $1000 spending money. Loyalty is also valued and every staff member who comes back for a second season is given a pay rise. As a former ski bum himself, Best recognizes the major motivation for his staff: skiing or snowboarding. So, accordingly, he gives everyone a 'ride break' during the day so they can remember exactly why they are at Lake Louise.

His market research also extends to product, trying to provide a better all-round service than the competition. 'It's not just other ski hills, my competition is the all-inclusive holiday,' he says. In answer to the deals tourists are used to enjoying at resorts and on cruises, he offers a reasonably-priced meal plan at the 1926 Great Divide Lodge – something which is unusual in ski lodges. For $129 in the 2011/12 season, guests got a cooked breakfast, accommodation, ski ticket and dinner. After extensive renovations, the lodge features sauna, fitness facility, quiet reading room, bar, upmarket dining room, outdoor firepits, wireless internet and shuttles to and from the ski hill, which is also a hiking and wildlife reserve in the summer. 'It's the only place in the National Park where tourists can get a room under $100 during summer high season,' says Best.

People who work at ski hills are always asked the same question: 'But what do you do in the summer?' Best, as usual, has an enviable answer: he operates his own hotel and restaurant in Tonga in the South Pacific with his wife, Cathy Best. And the Prime Minister of Tonga employs him regularly as a tourist consultant to help improve service elsewhere on the islands.

So, why doesn't everyone do customer service as well as Best? According to his wife, it is because it is an innate skill and not a learned one: 'Other people just don't come by it naturally. The problem a lot of companies face is hiring people with education but not with belief,' she concludes.

Sources

Personal interview with Sandy and Cathy Best, 12/14/2011; www.skilouise.com/vacations/west_louise_lodge_vacation.php; www.skilouise.com; www.vavauvilla.com/

An introduction to research in tourism and hospitality

6

The focus of market research is on the analysis of markets (Kinnear et al, 1993), and it is a critical marketing function. Unfortunately, in the tourism and hospitality sector, many smaller organizations feel that 'real' market research is a costly and time-consuming luxury only available to large companies that have professional research staff, sophisticated computers, and almost unlimited budgets. Other organizations see market research as something to be undertaken when a major event is about to occur – the introduction of a new product, the acquisition of a new property, or a change in target markets. Its value at these junctures is recognized, but its ability to contribute to an organization's success on a day-to-day basis is often overlooked. Another common problem in the tourism industry is that organizations are not making full use of the information that already exists and is easily accessed. Sometimes information is available and studies are done, but the results are either ignored or not fully considered in the final decision-making process. The opening spotlight profiles a Director of Public Relations, Sandy Best, who understands the significance of doing advanced research before his customers (the media) arrive at his facility.

Applied research in tourism and hospitality can be grouped into eight categories: research on consumers; research on products and services; research on pricing; research on place and distribution; research on promotion; research on competition; research on the operating environment; and research on a destination. Table 6.1 lists some of the typical research programs undertaken within these categories.

Table 6.1: Applied research in the tourism and hospitality sector.

Research on consumers
- Identifying existing markets
- Identifying potential markets
- Identifying lapsed consumers
- Testing customer loyalty
- Developing detailed consumer profiles
- Identifying general trends in demographics and psychographics
- Identifying changes in attitudes and behavior patterns (generally)
- Identifying changes in attitudes and behavior patterns (product specific)

Research on products & services
- Measuring attitudes towards existing products or services
- Identifying potential new products which may be at the end of their product life cycle
- Identifying products that are considered acceptable substitutes/alternatives
- Evaluating competitor's products
- Evaluating consumer attitudes toward décor, presentation and packaging
- Evaluating consumer attitudes about combinations of products and services (bundles of product attributes)

Research on pricing
- Identifying attitudes towards prices
- Testing attitudes towards packages and individual pricing
- Identifying costs
- Identifying costing policies of competitors
- Testing alternative pricing strategies
- Testing payment processes (credit cards, electronic funds transfer, etc.)

Research on place & distribution
- Identifying attitudes towards location
- Identifying attitudes toward buildings/premises
- Identifying attitudes on virtual sites
- Identifying potential demand for product or services at other locations
- Identifying cooperative opportunities for distribution of information or services

Research on promotion
- Testing and comparing media options
- Testing alternative messages
- Testing competitor's messages and their effectiveness
- Testing new communications options (internet, email, web pages social media)
- Identifying cooperative opportunities
- Measuring advertising and promotion effectiveness

Research on the competition
- Measuring awareness
- Measuring usage

- Identifying levels of customer loyalty
- Identifying competitors' strengths and weaknesses
- Identifying specific competitive advantages (locations, suppliers, etc.)
- Identifying cooperative opportunities
- Observing levels of customer service

Research on the operating environment
- Economic trends
- Social trends
- Environmental issues
- Political climate and trends
- Technological development and their impact

Research on a destination
- Measuring residents attitudes
- Benchmarking
- Measuring customer loyalty
- Identifying tourism activities
- Identifying spending patterns
- Branding research

6

Consumer research is one type of applied research that is of particular interest to those interested in the study of customer service. As the table suggests, there may be a number of objectives in carrying out consumer research, and one is to measure customer loyalty. As the end-of-chapter case study points out, Enterprise Rent-A-Car have found from research that 'completely satisfied' customers were three times more likely to rent with Enterprise than those who were 'somewhat satisfied', so it is important to gauge customer satisfaction on an ongoing bases. In the golf sector, the National Golf Foundation (NGF) in the U.S. undertakes research on behalf of its members, and one of its programs, the 'Voice-of-Customer Operating Model' (VOCOM) enables facilities to analyze, track and monitor customer behavior to develop one-to-one relationships with customers and increase profitability. As part of this program, NGF measures customer loyalty for participating golf facilities, developing a Loyalty Index. Customer Loyalty Awards are given each year to managers of high-performing facilities.

One common way of measuring customer loyalty is calculating a Net Promoter Score for consumers. Researchers ask one question: 'How likely are you to recommend this product or service to a friend or colleague?' When offered a scale of 0 to 10, the responses will fall in to three categories: promoters (those rating the service a 9 or 10), who are loyal fans; passives (the 7s and 8s); and detractors (those giving scores of 0-6). By taking the percentage of promoters and deducting the percentage of detractors, executives can determine a metric known as Net Promoter Score (NPS).

Another important type of applied research is competitor intelligence. If a company wants to keep track of competition, it requires a clear understanding of who the competition is, as well as knowledge of how the company is doing in comparison to the competitors. Competitor intelligence is available through a variety of sources, including competitors' annual reports, local tourism authorities and state tourism departments, magazine articles, speeches, media releases, brochures, and advertisements. While some information is willingly shared, to get a true picture of how the competition is doing, a firm often needs to undertake research. The form of this research varies from business to business. For a tourist attraction or food operation, it could be as simple as counting the number of cars in the parking lot at various times, or actually going into the facility to see how busy it is. For a hotel, it might mean checking room availability at particular times or watching for advertisements of special offers and discounts. For tour operators, it may involve counting the number of competing coaches at major destinations and collecting tour brochures and schedules. Participant observation is also often used to gather competitor intelligence. For example, executives of airlines might travel with competitors, or hotel managers might check in to competitor hotels. These are effective ways of gathering valuable knowledge for research purposes. The snapshot later in this chapter focuses on this type of data gathering.

More recently, the practice of benchmarking has received attention from tourism market researchers. Benchmarking is essentially a management technique that allows companies to compare how well they are performing relative to their competitors and is fairly common in the hotel sector (Kozak and Rimmington, 1999). Benchmarking initiatives might include collecting guest satisfaction scores. For Sheraton Hotels and Resorts, profiled in Chapter 7, measuring guest satisfaction is a crucial part of marketing research, and plays an important role in internal marketing. Guest satisfaction scores (GSS) are closely monitored, and results are shared with all hotels and all employees. To measure satisfaction, Sheraton Hotels has commissioned NFO Worldwide Group to send out a questionnaire to every customer who stays in a Sheraton property in North America.

Restaurants are also using benchmarking to measure service performance against competitors. Min and Min (2011) developed a series of benchmarks for the fast-food sector to help them monitor their service-delivery processes, identify relative weaknesses, and take corrective actions for continuous service improvements using an analytic hierarchy process. As shown in Figure 6.1, the top level of the hierarchy represents the ultimate goal of determining the best-practice fast-food restaurant. At the second level of the hierarchy are five distinct service criteria, generally considered important in measuring fast-food restaurant service quality: service image, menu selection, location, accessibility and drawing power. The attributes belonging to one of the five service criteria were connected to the bottom level of the hierarchy represented by six fast-food restaurants under evaluation.

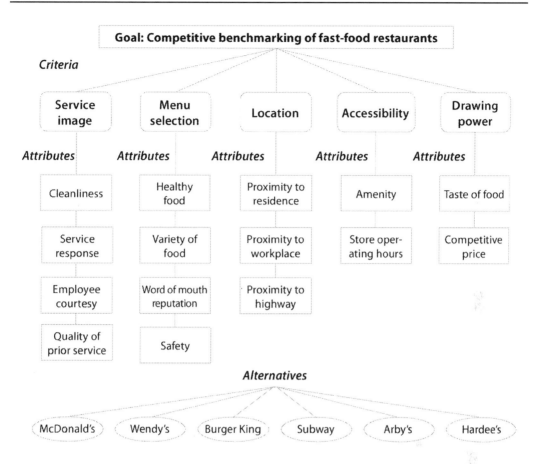

Figure 6.1: A hierarchy of benchmarking fast-food restaurants (Source: Adapted from Min and Min, 2010, p. 290)

Attractions can also benefit from benchmarking against competitors. A recent study of visitor attractions by *Which?* (2011) asked 3001 members of the public online for their views on the UK tourist attractions they visited between May 2009 and May 2011. The survey measured satisfaction ratings for theme parks, museums and art galleries, wildlife attractions, and historic properties and gardens. The study measured perceptions of a number of criteria such as value for money, length of crowds and food services, but visitors were also asked to give a 'customer score' out of 100 based on overall satisfaction and the likelihood to recommend to others. Those customer scores are presented in Table 6.2. London's free museums and art galleries top the table while visitors were less impressed with attractions in Blackpool. Perhaps surprising is the ranking of Madame Tussauds in London, but clearly value for money is important to consumers: a family of four would have had to pay about $140 to enter the wax museum in 2011, compared to nothing at the V&A Museum!

Table 6.2: Benchmarking the UK's top 20 visitor attractions

Visitor Attraction Name	Customer Score (out of 100)	Rank
Victoria & Albert (V&A) Museum	81	1
National Gallery	80	2
Science Museum	79	3
British Museum	79	4
Natural History Museum	79	5
Chester Museum	78	6
Alton Towers	75	7
Thorpe Park	73	8
Edinburgh Castle	72	9
Tower of London	72	10
Legoland, Windsor	72	11
Eden Project	70	12
Tate Modern	69	13
Warwick Castle	69	14
London Zoo	69	15
York Minster	67	16
Madame Tussauds	64	17
London Eye	64	18
Blackpool Tower and Circus	58	19
Pleasure Beach Blackpool	58	20

The Gaps model of service quality

As discussed in Chapter 3, the issue of understanding needs and expectations is an important part of the quest for customer satisfaction. The Gaps model of service quality (see Figure 6.2) provides a method of graphically illustrating these needs and expectations (Parasuraman, Zeithaml and Berry, 1985). This conceptual model enables a structured thought process for evaluating and designing in customer satisfaction. The model begins with expected service as viewed by the customer. Every customer has certain expectations about a service, which may come from word of mouth, personal needs, group needs, past experience, and/ or external communications. When the service is delivered and the customers' expectations are exceeded, the customers perceive the quality as relatively high. When their expectations have not been met, they perceive the quality as relatively low. Thus, as stated above, customer satisfaction can be defined as the difference between what the customer expects and the perceived quality of what is actually delivered. Often there is a gap between expected service and the actual service as perceived by the customer, and in the model, this is gap 5. The magnitude of this gap is driven by four other possible gaps, each of which denotes failure in some aspect of service delivery. The five gaps are discussed below.

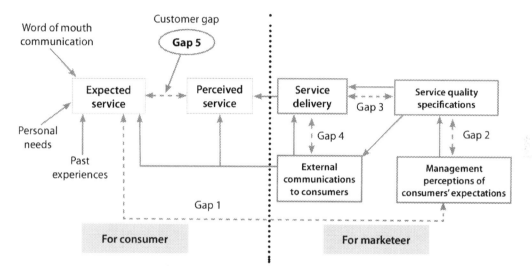

Figure 6.2: The Gaps model of service quality (Source: Parasuraman, Zeithaml, and Berry, 1985)

Gap 1: The difference between the customer's expectations of service and management's perception of those expectations

Many reasons exist for managers not being aware of what customers expect: they may not interact directly with customers, may be unwilling to ask about expectations, or may be unprepared to address them. The four key factors responsible for gap 1 are the service provider's inadequate marketing research orientation, lack of upward communication, insufficient relationship focus, and inadequate service recovery. The importance of both relationship marketing and service recovery are discussed later in this book. By building stronger relationships, understanding customer needs over time, and implementing recovery strategies when things go wrong, gap 1 – the customer expectations gap – can be minimized.

Gap 2: The difference between the management's perception of customer expectations and the way that these perceptions are then translated into specifications or processes

Gap 2 occurs when managers know what their customers want but are unable or unwilling to develop systems that will deliver it. Some of the reasons that have been given for gap 2 are poor service design, absence of customer-defined standards, and inappropriate physical evidence and servicescape. One of the most important ways to avoid gap 2 is to design services clearly, without over-simplification, incompleteness, subjectivity, or bias. To do this, tools are needed to ensure that new and existing services are developed and improved in as careful a manner as possible. Service blueprinting is often used as an implementation tool to address the challenges of designing and specifying intangible service processes (see Chapter 3). Service organizations must also explore the importance of physical evidence, the variety of roles it plays, and strategies for effectively designing physical evidence and the servicescape to meet customer expectations (see Chapter 8 for a discussion of the servicescape).

Gap 3: The difference between management's specifications of service and the actual service that is delivered to the customer

Even when guidelines exist for performing services well and treating customers correctly, high-quality performance is not a certainty. Research on customer experience has identified many of the critical inhibitors to closing gap 3. These include employees who do not clearly understand the roles they are to play in the company, employees who see conflict between customers and company management, the wrong employees, inadequate technology, inappropriate compensation and recognition, and lack of empowerment and teamwork. To deliver better service performance, these human resource issues must be addressed across functions. A second cause of gap 3 is the challenge involved in delivering service through intermediaries such as travel agents or franchisees. It is a huge task for organizations to attain service excellence and consistency in the presence of intermediaries who represent them, interact with their customers, and yet are not under their direct control. Other variables in gap 3 include the customers – who may not understand their roles and responsibilities and may negatively affect each other – and the failure to match supply and demand. Because services are perishable and cannot be inventoried, service companies frequently face situations of over- or under-demand. Marketing strategies for managing supply and demand should be used to reduce gap 3.

Gap 4: The difference between the delivery of the service and external communications about the service

Gap 4 is created when promises do not match performance. Broken promises can occur for many reasons: over-promising in advertising or personal selling, inadequate coordination between operations and marketing, and differences in policies and procedures across service outlets. There are also less obvious ways in which external communications influence customers' service quality assessments. Service companies frequently fail to capitalize on opportunities to educate customers in using services appropriately. They also frequently fail to manage customer expectations of what they will receive in service transactions and relationships. Therefore, in addition to improving service delivery, companies must also manage all communications to customers, so that inflated promises do not lead to overly high expectations. Many companies profiled in this book—such as Canadian Mountain Holidays and WestJet— make it a policy to 'under-promise and over-deliver.' Unfortunately, there are too many examples of companies that do just the opposite. Aeroplan, Air Canada's frequent flyer program, for example, promises free flights for loyal customers. However, the reality is that those free flights are very difficult to book, and there is also a booking fee. Only one attempt in five to book a flight using accumulated mileage is successful (Cohen, 2002). This difference between what is promised and what is delivered can cause customer frustration, perhaps driving the customer to the competition.

Gap 5: The difference between customer's expectations and perceptions

The central focus of the gaps model is gap 5, the customer gap: the difference between the service a customer expects and the service the customer perceives that he or she receives. Firms need to close this gap in order to satisfy customers and to build long-term relationships with them. To close this all-important customer gap, the four other gaps – the provider gaps – need to be closed.

Measuring service quality

■ Importance–Performance Analysis (IPA)

Importance–Performance Analysis (IPA) is one of many research instruments that have been developed over the years to analyze the concepts of quality and consumer satisfaction in the service industry. IPA is a procedure that shows both the relative *importance* of various attributes and the *performance* of the company, product, or destination under study in providing these attributes. Its use has important marketing and management implications for decision makers, and one of the major benefits of using IPA is the identification of areas for service quality improvements. Results are displayed graphically on a two-dimensional grid, and through a simple visual analysis of this matrix, policy makers can identify areas where the resources and programs need to be concentrated. Introduced over 20 years ago (Martilla and James, 1977), IPA is well documented in the literature.

Figure 6.3 shows the importance and performance mean scores of ski attributes from a study in Switzerland (Hudson and Shephard, 1998). The action grid identifies where each of the attributes falls in terms of the four quadrants, with examples pinpointed in each quadrant. In this variation, the largest number of attributes (42%) was plotted into the 'Concentrate Here' area of the action grid. Respondents rated these attributes high in importance but low in performance. These attributes included the majority of services on the ski slopes, comfortable beds, value for money in bars and restaurants, and the prices in the ski shops.

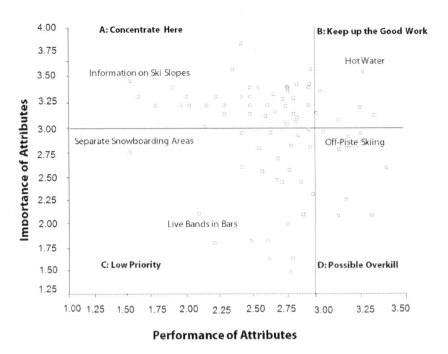

Figure 6.3: Importance–performance grid with attribute ratings for a ski destination (Source: Hudson and Shephard, 1998).

■   SERVQUAL

Another popular research instruments often used analyze consumer satisfaction in the service industry is SERVQUAL, an instrument developed by Parasuraman, Zeithaml, and Berry (1985), which is used to measure the difference between consumers' expectations and perceptions of service quality. Exploratory research conducted in 1985 showed that consumers judge service quality by using the same general criteria, regardless of the type of service. Parasuraman et al capture these criteria using a scale composed of 22 items designed to load on five dimensions reflecting service quality. The dimensions, introduced in Chapter 5, are assurance, empathy, reliability, responsiveness, and tangibles. Each item is used twice: first, to determine customers' expectations about companies in general, within the service category being investigated; second, to measure perceptions of performance of a particular company, within this same service category. These evaluations are collected using a seven-point Likert scale. According to the authors, the service quality is determined as the difference between customers' expectations and perceptions. A simple way of tracking performance using this gap is shown in Figure 6.4. Both expectations and service perceptions are plotted on the graph and the gap between them shows the shortfall in service quality. The diagram depicted shows the results of a study that evaluated the various stages of a package holiday as perceived by British tourists.

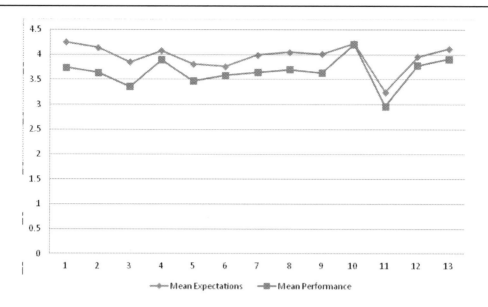

X-Axis Key: various stages of the holiday experience

1. Brochure
2. Waiting to go
3. Journey
4. Meeting the representative
5. Transfer to accommodation

6. Arrival accommodation
7. Accommodation
8. Welcome
9. Resort activities
10. Skiing/snowboarding

11. Company magazine
12. Departure
13. Transfer to airport

Figure 6.4: Tracking service quality (Source: Adapted from Hudson, Hudson and Miller, 2004)

SERVQUAL has been adapted to serve different industry sectors. For the lodging industry, Knutson et al (1990) created LODGSERV based on the five dimensions of service quality identified in SERVQUAL but made up of 26 lodging-specific items. DINESERV is another variation drafted from the lessons learned in developing and refining LODGSERV (Stevens et al, 1995). It is an instrument specific to the restaurant industry, with 29 items that measure the five dimensions of service quality. Table 6.3 contains the questions that would be asked during a DINESERV interview with a customer. Respondents would be asked to indicate their position on each of the 29 statements by assigning a number from seven (strongly agree) to one (strongly disagree). The first ten questions measure perceptions of tangibles, 11-15 reliability, 16-18 responsiveness, 19-24 assurance, and 25-29 empathy.

Table 6.3: A typical DINESERV interview

The restaurant	
1	Has visually attractive parking areas and building exteriors
2	Has a visually attractive dining area
3	Has staff members who are clean, neat, and appropriately dressed
4	Has a décor in keeping with its image and price range
5	Has menu that is easily readable

6	Has a visually attractive menu that reflects the restaurants' image
7	Has a dining area that is comfortable and easy to move around in
8	Has rest rooms that are thoroughly clean
9	Has dining areas that are thoroughly clean
10	Has comfortable seats in the dining room
11	Serves you in the time promised
12	Quickly corrects anything that is wrong
13	Is dependable and consistent
14	Provides an accurate guest check
15	Serves your food exactly as you ordered it
16	During busy time, has employees shift to help each other maintain speed and quality of service
17	Provides prompt and quick service
18	Gives extra effort to handle your questions completely
19	Has employees who can answer your questions completely
20	Makes you feel comfortable and confident in your dealings with them
21	Has personnel who are both able and willing to give your information about menu items, their ingredients, and methods of preparation
22	Makes you feel personally safe
23	Has personnel who seem well trained, competent, and experienced
24	Seems to give employees support so that they can do their jobs well
25	Has employees who are sensitive to your individual needs and wants, rather than always relying on policies and procedures
26	Makes you feel special
27	Anticipates your individual needs and wants
28	Has employees who are sympathetic and reassuring if something is wrong
29	Seems to have the customers' best interests at heart

■ Comment cards

The customer comment card is a common source of customer feedback employed at the time of the service experience, and is a useful tool for measuring service quality. Customer comment cards represent a performance-based measure of the perception of service outcomes. They do play an important role in assessing consumer satisfaction, and if managed well, the feedback received from comment cards can be used as a diagnostic tool for improving service and encouraging patronage (Keith and Simmers, 2011). But poor card availability and problematic return methods often contribute to ineffective evaluation, and typical comment cards do not assess all the five service quality dimensions established in the SERQUAL instrument (Wisner and Corney, 1997).

However, some researchers have suggested that comment cards are actually more effective than SERVQUAL or Importance-Performance Analysis (Cronin and Taylor, 1994; Yuksel and Rimmington, 1998). They argue that the mere fact of asking respondents to mark their perceptions of performance already leads them to compare mentally their perceptions and their expectations. In other words, the estimation of perceptions might already include a 'perception minus expectation' mental process. They suggest that performance on its own, or SERVPERF (which stands for 'service performance'), is the measure that best explains total quality.

Hotel managers find comment cards very useful. At The Sanctuary on Kiawah Island, South Carolina, guests are encouraged to complete a comment card and rate their satisfaction with the services they received. The card is left in the hotel room for the guests to fill in, but also has an attached pre-paid postage if the guest wants to complete it and send it from home. Every guest then receives a follow-up email from Bill Lacey, the hotel manager, with a link to an electronic version of the comment. 'If guests prefer to talk to me about their experiences, then I will follow up with a telephone call,' Lacey says. 'We are always looking to improve.'

Mystery shopping

Mystery shopping, the name given to participant observation in the commercial sector, has become a common market research technique in tourism and hospitality. In the services context, mystery shopping provides information about the service experience as it unfolds, and helps to develop a richer knowledge of the experiential nature of services. Table 6.4 summarizes the various advantages and disadvantages of using this method of participative observation.

One example of such a study is that by Boote and Mathews (1999), who were employed by Whitbread PLC to develop guidelines for the siting of middle-market restaurant outlets. Part of their research involved participant observation of customers at lunchtime and in the evenings, so as to identify whether the actual clientele matched the intended market segment. Another example of mystery shopping in action comes from the Canary Islands, where the Lopesan Group, profiled in Chapter 1, employs an outside company to conduct its mystery shopping. Researchers come in twice a month during dinner service when they also surveys guests, getting a 50-60% response rate. The results of these audits and surveys are used to enhance customer service and also to evaluate and reward managers and staff. 'Based on university research, we started to analyze feedback about service by computer,' explains Pablo Lorenzo, Lopesan's quality control manager. 'We now aggregate the issues and create a top 10 problem list across the chain and also a top 50 for each hotel – including things such as service, language issues, etc. We then talk to managers from each section in each hotel to try to deal with these problems and negotiate how to improve both the top 10 and the top 50, creating at least three projects to work on during internal meetings.' There is a fund to help solve these problems and Lopesan gives incentives to managers who are able to get out of the top 10. A good solution in one hotel can then be applied across other hotels in the chain, making it more cost-effective if they have had to invest in the solution.

Table 6.4: Advantages/disadvantages of covert participative observation or mystery shopping.

Advantages

- Offers deep insights into feelings and motivations behind service/practice (Palmer, 2000)
- Experience is natural and not contrived for the sake of the observer (Bootte and Mathews, 1999)
- Serves as a management tool for improving standards in customer service by providing actionable recommendations (Erstad, 1998; Cramp, 1994)
- Ideal for investigating services (Crano and Brewer, 1986; Grove and Fisk, 1992)
- Serves as a management tool for enhancing human resource management (Erstad, 1998)

Disadvantages

- Raises ethical issues by observing people without their knowledge (Jorgenesen, 1989)
- Based on assumptions that need to be made explicit and addressed (Savage, 2000)
- Information collected may be biased as a result of arbitrary or careless selection of observation periods, or the observers own prejudices (Smith, 1995)
- In the long term, advantages for improving customer service can wear off if not integrated with other measures of service delivery process (Wilson, 1998)
- Can be very costly and time-consuming (Grove and Fisk, 1992)

Snapshot: Checking out the competition

Glassdrumman Lodge, Northern Ireland: Photo courtesy of Ben Hall, Glassdrumman Lodge

Every business needs to know what its industry rivals are up to in order to stay current, be competitively priced and even ahead of the game. This can involve discreet mystery shopping with visits to local establishments and also checking out websites and social media for destinations further afield. For those serious about being the best in their industry, though, the search for new ideas and customer service excellence can go further than the hotels in the same town to other countries and even other industries.

Todd Felsen, General Manager of the Cheyenne Mountain Resort in Colorado Springs, visits both neighboring hotels and hotels nationwide to gain insight on the competition. 'We do many "blind" visits of other properties and we also conduct business meetings off-site at competitors,' he says. 'Both ways give us great insight. When we meet with our competitive set personnel, the focus is more on destination objectives and lifting the entire region.'

Other hoteliers are doing the same kind of field research. When Michael Papierno travels he is always on the lookout for areas other hotels are excelling in: 'If it something that I can do myself with my team, I will bring it to them and implement it right away,' he says. Papierno, General Manager of Viana Hotel and Spa in Westbury NY, also notes any negative situations and looks at these from the guest's perspective. 'I say to myself, "Is my team doing the same thing?" If so, I change it and start training those individuals that might be providing the bad experience,' he explains.

Tim Peters, Senior General Manager of The Nautical Beachfront Resort in Lake Havasu City AZ, visits local competition monthly, specifically looking for nuances on staff interaction with guests. 'I am looking for changes in sense of arrival, communication to guests whether by a personal concierge or via information boards, etc.,' he says. Peters is also vigilant about checking out the competition in different locations whenever he finds himself in resort destinations. 'You can never learn enough and I am always looking for ways to bring new ideas back to my resort that I may not find in my immediate market,' he says. 'Someone is always coming up with new ideas to improve the guest experience and your competition or similar hotels and resorts can provide some great direction in this area. You can never be too old to learn new things from just about anyone.'

Managers at the Renaissance Harbour View Hotel in Hong Kong will often visit other hotels for inspiration. 'We sit in the lobbies of other hotels and observe whilst drinking tea,' jokes Multi-properties VP and General Manager, Karl Hudson. His co-managers regularly visit rival hotels to see what they are doing well. 'By drinking tea, my meaning is that we are spending money and not taking up potential revenue-generating space of our competitors,' he explains. The service focus at Renaissance is on surprising and delighting the guest, therefore it is up to management to devise ever more creative ways to do this.

Social media is another useful tool for hoteliers to check on the competition. Hudson uses Brand Karma for tools and tips on how to leverage social media to improve his five-star hotel's hospitality and service ratings and keep customers coming back. Brand Karma aspires to take the hard work out of collecting and analyzing social media data so that hoteliers can then get on with acting upon the collective results. The Renaissance goes one step further by employing two professional customer service consultants, Bob Brown and Cynthia Goins to help 'provide the icing on the cake'. Wow factors for Renaissance clients include cold bottled water in their valet-parked cars on hot days and coat hangers placed in their cars to hang up jackets. It's like having 'Mom' look after you. If there is a group booking, staff members make efforts to find out about favourite snacks, the boss's beverage of choice and any birthdays in the party – for which they provide cakes. It is not just the managers who can implement this. All frontline staff – who Hudson calls 'high guest contact personnel' – are empowered to be ambassadors.

For Bill Lacey, Hotel Manager at The Sanctuary on Kiawah Island, South Carolina, checking out the competition is not so easy. 'When I worked for the bigger groups, we would get regular updates on what other hotels in the franchise were up to, and we would implement any new ideas or services that we liked the sound of. But with an isolated private hotel it is more difficult to keep up to date with trends and to find out what the competition is doing,' he says. Lacey relies heavily, therefore, on the internet and social media to source new ideas, and his managers regularly send him articles on any hotel doing something new. 'We also look at publications and magazines, and I ask my management team to come up with two new ideas every quarter. But I do still keep my eyes open when I stay in another hotel,' he says. 'I was just at the Ritz Carlton in Charlotte, and I had a good look around.'

The Ritz Carlton provides the inspiration for service innovation for another hospitality entrepreneur. Ben Hall runs the Glassdrumman Lodge in Northern Ireland with his family. Nestled in the foothills of the majestic Mourne Mountains, the original property, in the form of a farm, was purchased by the Hall family in 1980, and five years later was converted into a 10-bedroom country house to accommodate golfers, walkers and holidaymakers alike. After more than 25 years of guests, from leading politicians to iconic sports personalities, the Hall families' single aim remains to create an enjoyable environment for relaxation and reflection, with good food and great service. Ben likes to visit hotels like the Ritz Carlton that have a reputation for top-notch customer service training, and consistent high standards. He then takes back ideas that the family can adapt with an individualized spin. 'We don't want our customer service to appear systematic,' he says. 'We prefer it to come across as a genuine personalized relationship between our staff and the guests.'

Sources

Lamberg (2011); Interview with Bill Lacey, 20 January 2012; Correspondence with Karl Hudson, 2011; Interview with Ben Hall, 25 June 2012.

■ Critical incidents studies

The critical incident technique (CIT) is a qualitative interview procedure in which customers are asked to provide verbatim stories about satisfying and dissatisfying service encounters they have experienced. This may be done one-to-one or in a focus group. The use of CIT techniques has been reported in hotels, restaurants, airlines and amusement parks (Gremler, 2004), and these studies have explored a wide range of service topics such as consumer evaluation of services, service failure and recovery, employee and customer participation in service delivery, and service experience. CIT has four main benefits (Zeithaml et al, 2007). First, data collected from the respondent's own perspective are usually vivid because they are expressed in the customers' own words and reflect their true thoughts. Second, the method provides sound information about the way the company and its employees behave and react, thereby making the research easy to translate into action. Third, like most qualitative methods, the research is particularly useful when the service is new and very little other information exists. Finally, the method is useful for assessing perceptions of customers from different cultures because it allows respondents to share their perceptions rather than answer research-defined questions.

6

■ Lost customer research

This type of research involves deliberately seeking customers who have dropped the company's service to inquire about their reasons for leaving. The research can identify failure points and common problems in the service, but also be used for calculating the cost of lost customers. Many companies are committing substantial resources for the purposes of retaining customers and keeping them happy, but few have effective processes and programs in place to evaluate why customers leave. Recently, a national chain of entertainment properties employed research company NBRI to explore why revenues had been steadily declining over the previous 18 months, although new customers were being added on a steady basis. NBRI recommended the use of its standard customer loss review survey. It was believed that surveying former customers would provide more pointed data than might be obtained from present customers. NBRI found that the root cause driving down customer's intent to return, customer loyalty, and customer satisfaction, along with 68 % of all survey items, was 'wait time'. Clearly, wait time was of utmost importance and needed to be minimized in every area of the business affecting the customer. Following NBRI recommendations, swift interventions to the root cause alone were put into place which directly, positively impacted revenues, and reversed the trend of the previous months.

■ Online research

A relatively new way of conducting research is the use of electronic surveys that ask consumers questions and immediately record and tabulate the results.

Data-collecting electronic equipment might be placed in a hotel lobby, mall, or other high-traffic location – for example, Whistler Resort collects data from its skiers using electronic devices placed up and down the main street. Alternatively, respondents may be asked to complete a survey online. Internet-based survey methodology is gaining increasing popularity. Meliá Hotels International engaged marketing consultants Market Metrix to move their infrequent paper questionnaire data collection method online in order to increase sample size and data reliability. Every guest is now invited to participate to better represent the entire guest experience every day. Customer input is available instantly, not only to the head office, but also to the GM and front-line staff at every property. It is now possible to use customer feedback for instant service recovery as well as long-term service improvement. Meliá's own customer feedback is compared with relevant industry benchmarks in the local markets where they compete in order to ensure that competitive standards are met and guest value remains high.

Virtual focus groups are also becoming more common. Online 'chat' sessions, in which one to dozens of pre-recruited respondents type in responses to a guided online discussion, can be used effectively to bring together participants from virtually anywhere to discuss experiences with a service, or provide feedback on products. While virtual focus groups will not always be able to replace in-person interviews, the time- and cost-saving benefits of such groups make them a very useful tool for researchers – especially for gathering website feedback with participants when they are using the Internet. Companies are also using virtual worlds to gather useful consumer feedback. Starwood Hotels and Resorts used Second Life, an online world with a thriving virtual economy, as a three-dimensional test bed for its new chain of hotels called Aloft. The company created an elaborate digital prototype for the new chain not just to promote the venture, but also to give its designers feedback from prospective guests before the first real hotel opened in 2008.

A number of companies are leveraging social media in order to unearth consumer insights that will help their businesses. The activity has been called crowdsourcing and is discussed in Chapter 9. Crowdsourcing-led innovation means opening the door to allow customers, employees, or the general public at large into the innovation process to help improve products, services or marketing efforts.

Virgin Atlantic Airways, for example, monitors social media opportunity to gather insights to drive continual incremental improvements in its service. For example, in response to online-community suggestions, it launched a system to arrange taxi sharing on arrival with passengers from the same flight. The Renaissance Harbour View Hotel in Hong Kong, profiled in Chapter 4, works with an outside consultant, Brand Karma, which analyses online postings from social media as well as Trip Advisor, online travel agents and blogs.

Common research errors

There are many potential pitfalls in conducting research; the most common four errors are discussed here.

1. Not including enough qualitative information

As mentioned earlier in the chapter, qualitative research can be particularly useful for launching a new service or product. EuroDisney in France got off to a poor start partly due to a lack of in-depth, qualitative research. A key problem was a lack of sufficient understanding of the potential customer. Researchers failed to understand domestic tourists and those traveling from other parts of Europe. For example, the original ban on alcohol at the park had to be lifted due to public demand as no self-respecting French person could contemplate lunch without a glass of wine. Pets also had to be accommodated as the French routinely take dogs and even cats on their road holidays. Other errors were made in the way visitors booked their Disney vacations. Reservations started out as direct bookings made by telephone or by Internet. This alienated British tourists who usually book holidays via travel agencies. Disney also expected European tourists to change their travel habits for their park. Traditionally French tourists travel in August during a one-month vacation period when factories and offices shut down and the British take two weeks sometime between the end of July and the first week of September. Disney predicted erroneously that both nationalities would take their children out of school for shorter periods outside of the main vacation periods.

2. An improper use of sophisticated statistical analysis

It is possible for a multitude of errors to creep into the research process if collection, tabulation, and analysis are not done properly. In today's environment, tabulation is likely to take place on the computer; a number of excellent packages are available for this purpose. However, statistical conclusions must be interpreted in terms of the best action or policy for the organization to follow. This reduction of the interpretation to recommendations is one of the most difficult tasks in the research process. Hotels will often use statistical reports on which to base decision-making. Shaun Durant, General Manager of the Residence Inn by Marriott in Florence, South Carolina, relies heavily on the services of Smith Travel Research (STR). 'Smith Travel Research offers a great tool called the STAR report that is utilized by a number of hotels to analyze industry trends. With this report we can easily compare occupancy percent and average daily rates across our competitive set,' he says.

3. Failure to have a sample that is representative of the population

A sample is a segment of the population selected to represent the population as a whole. Ideally, the sample should be representative, so that the researcher can make accurate estimates of the thoughts and behaviors of the larger population. The Sheraton Suites Calgary Eau Claire, profiled in Chapter 7, mainly targets the business traveler, so it is important to get feedback from this segment when they stay during the business week. Every Wednesday, the hotel holds a weekly cocktail party. Four or five managers are on hand to greet the guests, and it is a unique opportunity for business travellers to meet hotel managers and get to know them. The meetings are an opportunity for managers to build relationships, gain more knowledge about guest preferences, and listen to any concerns, so that they can ultimately improve customer service.

4. Problems with interpretation

The task of interpretation is not an easy job – rather it requires a great skill and dexterity on the part of the researcher. One should always remember that even if the data are properly collected and analyzed, wrong interpretation would lead to inaccurate conclusions. When measuring service quality, for example, even if the perceptions format (SERVPERF) offers the most predictive power – a finding that has consistently emerged in the literature – it offers little diagnostic potential and, indeed, may result in inappropriate priorities being established. From a managerial perspective, it would seem important to track trends of the extent to which expectations are met over time as well as trends in performance. The use of difference scores gives managers a better understanding of whether increasing expectations or diminishing performance might be responsible for declining service quality and customer satisfaction. An examination of minimum expectations may also be fruitful. Similarly, disregarding importance may mean losing useful insights. Without considering attribute importance, one has no indication of the relative importance that respondents attach to particular aspects of service performance.

Effective use of market research in decision making

There is little doubt that in an industry as dynamic and expansive as tourism, research must play a critical role in its development. Not only should research be undertaken by every organization, whether large or small, to assist in the task of practical decision-making at a strategic level, but it should also be acknowledged as important at the academic level for its shedding of valuable light on the development of tourism on a global basis. For research to be worthwhile, it has to be acted upon. A good example of a company successfully using the results of marketing research is the Marriott Corporation (Lovelock and Wirtz, 2007). When they were designing a new chain of hotels for business travelers (which eventually became known as Courtyard by Marriott) they sampled 601 consumers using a sophisticated technique known as conjoint analysis, which asks respondents to make trade-offs between different groupings of attributes. The objective was to determine which mix of attributes at specific prices offers them the highest degree of utility, so they were asked to indicate on a five-point scale how likely they were to stay at a hotel with certain features, given a specific room price per night. Features included room fixtures, food-related services, leisure facilities and other services.

The research yielded detailed guidelines for the selection of almost 200 features and service elements, representing those attributes that provided the highest utility for the customers in the target segments, at prices they were willing to pay. Using these inputs, the design team was able to meet the specified price while retaining the features most desired by the target market. After testing the concept under real-world conditions, the company subsequently developed a large chain that filled a gap in the market with a product that represented the best balance between the price customers were prepared to pay and the physical and service features they most desired.

Research is never an exact science, but it can reduce the margins of error to which hunches on their own are subject. The feasibility study, for example, is an essential prerequisite to any new project, whether it is the launch of a new company, the introduction of a new logo, or the development of a new product. Above all, the success of research will be contingent on three conditions:

1 Sufficient resources must be allocated to do the job properly, both in terms of time and money.

2 Managers must be willing to believe the results of the research when they become available, even if they conflict with the management's own preconceived views.

3 The results should be used. All too frequently, research is commissioned in order to avoid making an immediate decision. Expensively commissioned research is then left to gather dust in a drawer instead of being used to enable managers to make better decisions on the future direction of the company's strategy.

6

Case Study: Enterprise Rent-A-Car: Driving complete customer satisfaction

Ryan Levin and Jon Shortsleeve, Customer Service representatives at Enterprise Rent-A-Car in Charlotte Airport, North Carolina

The world's largest car rental company, Enterprise Holdings Inc., has been heavily engaged in market research since the 1990s. Founded back in 1957 by Jack Taylor, the St Louis, Missouri-based business has grown from a seven-car one-man-band to a $14.1 billion company in 2011 with 68,000 staff. Adding Alamo and National to its flagship Enterprise Rent-A-Car brand in 2007, it now has more than 6000 neighborhood and airport locations in North America and Europe and is part of a global strategic alliance with Europcar. With a fleet of 1.2 million vehicles, Enterprise Holdings owns and operates more leased and rental cars and trucks than any other company.

This success is in part due to its customer service philosophy that hinges on complete satisfaction. When the founder's son, Andy Taylor took over in the early 1990s as President and CEO, he worked to expand upon his father's mantra of taking care of customers and employees first, to develop lifelong relationships for a strong business infrastructure.

In July 1994 Taylor implemented a revolutionary research program with a simple customer satisfaction survey. However, the results of this initial Enterprise Service Quality index – or ESQi – were disappointing with a mere 25% response rate. This first survey did indicate, nevertheless, a big disparity between the best and worst performing regions for Enterprise. So, the next survey was reduced to just two questions put to customers by telephone and the method was refined to compare branch to branch rather than regions. Results were collected and analyzed quarterly from then on.

From the outset, data analysis revealed that 'completely satisfied' customers were three times more likely to rent with Enterprise than those who were 'somewhat satisfied'. Further investigation revealed that there were three different areas causing the lack of satisfaction: 1) attitude and helpfulness of staff; 2) speed of transaction; and 3) cleanliness of the car. Enterprise was then able to make improvements in these areas and also rank each branch based on their percentage of 'completely satisfied' clients. High ranking was dubbed 'Top Box'.

Promotions for local and regional managers were based thereafter on rankings above the corporate average. This incentivized staff and the resulting customer satisfaction went up from 60% in 1994 to around 80% in 2011. Enterprise also made service quality improvements by implementing a 'Cycle of Service' training program as well as 'The Vote' – a system of constructive criticism. Employees at each branch have to rank each other in their customer service quality with explanations for their choices. Results are published for every staff member at each branch and awards are given to the top performers. Service improvements included better screening of new hires based on communication skills; knowing the customer's name; aiming for total customer satisfaction from phone to pick-up to car return; never using industry jargon; and providing unsolicited help.

Alan Levine is Vice President/General Manager at Enterprise Holdings Inc. in the Miami/Fort Lauderdale area, and he acknowledges the significance of customer service in the organization. 'Customer service is vitally important to our success. In fact, it is the foundation that Enterprise is built on. We pride ourselves on earning repeat business, whether it's from the consumer or the referral source, and none of that would occur without a high level of customer service and satisfaction.' In new hire training classes, the company spends a significant portion of time discussing the culture and how customer service is a way of life for Enterprise. 'To emphasize the importance of customer service, we discuss initiatives such as our cycle of service and the three critical questions that are key to the Enterprise Service Quality Index (ESQi),' says Levine.

The ESQi enables Enterprise to publish ranked results for 6000 or so branches in a few days ensuring a quick response throughout the branches. Enterprise also conducts 'Brand Integrity Audits' whereby a network of assessors visits branches to evaluate customer service, brand image, facilities, wait times, vehicle cleanliness and condition. 'If you do not achieve an ESQi at or above the Group or Corporate level you are not even eligible for promotion!' says Levine.

Levine says that his employees are constantly reminded that they are empowered to handle any potential concerns to ensure the customer leaves the office completely satisfied. He gives some examples of employees in Florida going 'above and beyond' to satisfy customers. 'There was a management trainee in South Florida who helped a customer who had reserved a full-size car for a holiday weekend, not realizing the vehicle was not large enough for five adults and a child. After an extensive search, our employee located a large SUV at a location 30 minutes away – but the customer and family had somewhere to be in 15 minutes. So our management trainee took the family to their planned event and later delivered the SUV to them. In northern Florida, a branch manager got an urgent call from a commercial aviation operator about a passenger who had suffered cardiac arrest and needed to be rushed to a hospital. It was Sunday, when our branches are closed, but the branch manager arranged for a minivan to be delivered to the airport within an hour to transport the patient and his family to the hospital.'

Enterprise Rent-A-Car was named by J.D. Power and Associates as number one in customer satisfaction in the car rental industry for seven years up to 2011. In the 2010 North American airport car rental survey, Enterprise Holdings took three of the top four rankings. Enterprise Rent-A-Car ranked highest, National second and Alamo fourth. The company has been repeatedly named by *BusinessWeek* magazine on its annual list of 'Customer Service Champs.' In 2011 Enterprise won *Budget Travel* magazine's Readers' Choice Award as the best rental car company for customer service worldwide. National won *Executive Travel* magazine's 'Leading Edge Awards.'

Sources

Correspondence with Alan Levine and Ned Maniscalco, Enterprise Holdings, September 2012; Smith (2012); Reichheld and Allen (2004); Enterprise Holdings, Inc. Company Profile; Fiscal 2011 Highlights and Inaugural Sustainability Report; www.enterprise.co.uk; www.enterpriseholdings.com_

References

Boote, J. and Mathews, A. (1999) 'Saying is one thing; doing is another: The role of observation in marketing research', *Qualitative Market Research: An International Journal*, **2**(1), 15-21.

Cohen, A. (2002, January 8) 'Mileage junkies feed their habit', *Financial Times*, p. 10.

Cronin, J. and Taylor, S. (1994) 'SERVPERF versus SERVQUAL: Reconciling performance based and perceptions-minus-expectations measurement of service quality', *Journal of Marketing*, **58**(1), 125-131.

Enterprise Holdings, Inc. Company Profile, 14 Dec 2010. Accessed from http://www.datamonitor.com/

Gremler, D. D. (2004) 'The critical incident technique in service research', *Journal of Service Research*, **7**, 65-89.

Hudson, S. and Shephard, G. (1998) 'Measuring service quality at tourist destinations: An application of Importance–Performance Analysis to an Alpine ski resort', *Journal of Travel and Tourism Marketing*, **7**(3), 61-77.

Hudson, S., Hudson, P. and Miller, G. A. (2004) 'The Measurement of Service Quality in the UK Tour Operating Sector: A Methodological Comparison', *Journal of Travel Research*, **42**(3), 305-312.

Keith, N.K. and Simmers, C. S. (2011) 'Measuring service quality perceptions of restaurant experiences: The disparity between comment cards and DINESERV', *Journal of Foodservice Business Research*, **14**(1), 20-32.

Kinnear, T., Taylor, J., Johnson, L. and Armstrong, R. (1993) *Australian Marketing Research*, Sydney, Australia: McGraw-Hill.

Knutson, B., Stevens, P., Wullaert, C., Patton, M. and Yokoyama, F. (1990) 'LODSERV: A service quality index for the lodging industry', *Hospitality Research Journal*, **14**(2), 277-284.

Kozak, M. and Rimmington, M. (1999) 'Measuring tourist destination competitiveness: Conceptual considerations and empirical findings', *Hospitality Management*, **18** 273-83.

Lamberg, E. (2011) 'Checking-in to check-out the competition', *Hotel Interactive*, 18 November. Accessed 12 January 2012 from http://www.hotelinteractive.com/article.aspx?articleID=22859

Lovelock, C. and Wirtz, J. (2007) *Services Marketing: People, Technology, Strategy*, 6th edition, New Jersey, USA: Prentice Hall International.

Martilla, J. A. and James, J. C. (1977) 'Importance–Performance Analysis', *Journal of Marketing*, **41**(1), 13-17.

Min, H. and Min, H. (2011) 'Benchmarking the service quality of fast-food restaurant franchises in the USA: A longitudinal study, *Benchmarking: An International Journal*, **18**(2), 282-300.

Parasuraman, A., Zeithaml, V. A. and Berry, L. L. (1985) 'A conceptual model of service quality and its implications for future research', *Journal of Marketing*, **49**(4), 41-50.

Reichheld, F. F. and Allen, J. (2004) 'One number to grow', *Insights*, Bain & Com. Accessed 01/30/2012 from http://www.bain.com/publications/articles/one-number-to-grow-newsletter.aspx

Smith, S. S. (2012) 'The Car-Rental Enterprise of CEO Andy Taylor', *Investor's Business Daily*. Accessed 01/30/2012 from http://news.investors.com/Article.aspx?id=598722&ibdbot-1&p=3

Stevens, P., Knutson, B. and Patton, M. (1995) 'DINESERV: A tool for measuring service quality in restaurants', *Cornell Hotel and Restaurant Administration Quarterly*, **12**(2), 25-37.

Which? (2011) 'Top 20 visitor attractions rated', *Which? Magazine*, August, 60-64.

6

Wisner, J. D. and Corney, W. J. (1997) 'An empirical study of customer comment card quality and design characteristics', *International Journal of Contemporary Hospitality Management*, **9**(3), 110-115.

Yuksel, A. and Rimmington, M. (1998) 'Customer-satisfaction measurement', *Cornell Hotel and Restaurant Administration Quarterly*, **39**(6), 31-46.

Zeithaml, V. A., Bitner, M. J., Gremler, D., Mahaffey, T. and Hiltz, B. (2007) *Services Marketing: Integrating Customer Focus Across the Firm*, Canadian Edition. New York: McGraw-Hill.

 Scan here to get the hyperlinks in this chapter

Building and Maintaining Customer Relationships

John O'Connor with his new Wine for Dudes vehicle (Photo courtesy of John O'Connor)

Wine for Dudes is the brainchild of John O'Connor who set up his wine tour company in Margaret River, Western Australia back in 2003. As well as typical wine tours, he includes wine-blending in his itineraries as well as beer, cheese, venison and olive oil tastings.

The entrepreneurial company has been given many different business and enterprise awards for its innovative concept, service and marketing. Its approach is chatty, cheeky and light-hearted rather than the more snobbish ambience of traditional wine tasting. The idea is to make wine accessible to everyone – a daily quaff as in the Mediterranean rather than a special occasion drink.

As well as comprehensive information about its own tours and events – and virtual tours – the Wine for Dudes website provides a full service with information and photos for nearby accommodation plus all the necessary websites, email contacts and phone numbers. This is done with a view to creating the best possible all-round experience for the tourist beyond the actual Wine for Dudes tours. For Owner/Operator O'Connor, it is this type of complete customer service which is key to business success: 'Customer service is King! We rely on word of mouth as the most cost-effective form of marketing so we need our customers talking about positive experiences to friends and other travelers.'

O'Connor does his research personally: 'From personalized phone calls and email responses, I build a relationship with customers not only providing tour information, but also information about transport, accommodation, restaurants, bars, activities and the surf report, depending on an individual's needs.' Facebook is another means of both promoting the company's products and gaining valuable insight into the customer. He uses a quarterly newsletter to reach out to 9000 people who have been added to the company database through social networking. It's a 'low cost tool', he says, and a great way to provide news about the company and information about the region.

Recognizing the value of groups, O'Connor offers customized tours for families or groups of friends including scenic options and child-friendly venues. He makes a point of really getting to know his customers: 'If we have any customers with a birthday, I surprise them with a cake and candles. We go the extra yard making restaurant bookings, assisting parents with children and suggestions about the region's attractions.' He's even played golf and gone surfing with customers after one his tours. If a customer likes a particular wine at a tasting, O'Connor arranges nationwide freight. He also provides free photos from each tour which he posts on the website for clients to download free of charge.

Repeat customers are also important for Wine for Dudes and O'Connor encourages them to provide their own input to create new itineraries so they don't cover the same ground as on previous tours. The company produces a wide range of merchandise from hoodies to stubby holders (beer bottle holders) and uses these as gifts to repeaters. 'We give out "Dudes Dollars", our own currency for their next trip,' says O'Connor. 'And three-time customers enter our hall of fame and receive a free Wine for Dudes t-shirt.'

Much of O'Connor's market research comes from a daily wine quiz – the 'Dudes of Fortune Quiz Challenge'. Although ostensibly a fun competition with prizes, it also doubles as a customer feedback form. 'It's for comments, demographics, how they heard about us, any repeat customers and email collection,' says O'Connor. 'We then send out a thank you email with a link to the day's photo gallery on our website as well as links to our Facebook page and the Trip Advisor review site.' The company also uses Facebook for posting regional photos, promoting other local businesses, favourite places in the area and events. They are experimenting with Twitter, too.

Service recovery can pose a communication challenge if there is ever a problem leading to a customer complaint. 'With dependence on text messages and voice mail, which isn't always 100% reliable as coverage is limited in our country area, issues can arise,' says O'Connor. However, the nature of his business can lead to a successful conclusion: 'With our game, wine is often part of the solution!' Staff members have the discretion to handle problem situations on the ground and are able to change an itinerary on the spot to suit a customer's needs. 'When it comes to a discerning customer who becomes disgruntled it is often a case of "wine heals all wounds",' says O'Connor. He makes a point of following up any problems after the customer has gone home with a phone call and email: 'It is much better to have happy customers bouncing around in Cyberspace than disgruntled ones.'

Sources

Personal Interview with John O'Connor, 7 February 2012; http://www.winefordudes.com/

Relationship marketing

Relationship marketing is a form of marketing that attracts customers, retains them, and enhances their satisfaction (Berry, 1983). Historically, tourism and hospitality marketers have put more emphasis on attracting new customers, but in the last few decades, the idea of nurturing the individual relationships with current and past customers has received greater attention. Most marketers now accept that it is less expensive to attract repeat customers than to create new ones, and this is the basic concept behind relationship marketing. The key outcome of all relationship marketing efforts is to make individual customers feel unique and to make them believe that the organization has singled them out for special attention. The opening case demonstrated how Australian John O'Connor, owner of Wine for Dudes, takes such customization and personalization very seriously in his efforts to build relationships with customers.

The impetus for relationship marketing came from a number of studies demonstrating a dramatic increase in profits from small increases in customer retention rates (Reichheld and Sasser, 1990). Other studies by consultants like McKinsey have shown that repeat customers generate over twice as much gross income as new customers. Improvements in technology and innovation in loyalty programs have made it much easier to deliver on the promise of greater profitability from reduced customer attrition. But in order to build relationships with customers, there are a number of steps that companies need to follow, as suggested in the customer relationship management model (Figure 7.1).

Step 1
• **Construct a database:** transactions, customer contacts, descriptive information, and response to marketing stimuli

Step 2
• **Analysis:** Define segments and understand behavior

Step 3
• **Customer Selection:** *Which customers to target ?*

Step 4
• **Cutomer Targeting**

Step 5
• **Implement Relationship Marketing**

Figure 7.1: Customer Relationship Management Model (Source: Based on Winer, 2001).

The first step is the construction of a customer database, which should include information about transactions, customer contacts, descriptive information about the customer, and response to marketing stimuli. British tour operator Thomson Holidays, enlisted the assistance of travel agents in building its database. They collected descriptive information and data on trips taken, which allowed them to calculate the profit on a per customer trip basis. The data needs to be analyzed with the intent to define customer segments and understand their current and future profitability to the firm (or the Lifetime Customer Value as discussed in Chapter 2). The next step is to consider which customers to target before rolling out the company's relationship marketing programs.

British Airways used data from its Executive Club loyalty scheme to segment its European customer base and identify, among others, a high value segment that generates substantial margin through a low volume of premium class bookings. Analysis of the data also revealed that these people were flying a significant number of times each year in premium classes using alternative airlines. A 'Customer Value Management' strategy was developed to 'steal' a greater share of their wallet, with tailored communications across Europe. The result was an increase in flying behavior among this group of consumers with British Airways that generated an incremental revenue of 10:1 for the associated campaigns and an increase in customer value by a factor of three (Tullo, 2008).

Retention strategies

There are four different levels of retention strategies that encourage relationship marketing: financial bonds, social bonds, customization bonds, and structural bonds (Zeithaml and Bitner, 2000). These are illustrated in Figure 7.2.

At level 1, the customer is tied to the organization primarily through financial incentives – often in the form of lower prices for greater volume purchases or lower prices for customers who have been with the company for a long time. Frequent flyer programs are a good example of such retention strategies. In other cases, firms aim to retain customers by simply offering loyal customers the assurance of stable prices, or at least smaller price increases than those paid by new customers. The opening case showed how Wine for Dudes gives out 'Dudes Dollars', as currency for future trips. Other types of retention strategies that depend primarily on financial rewards are focused on bundling and cross-selling of services.

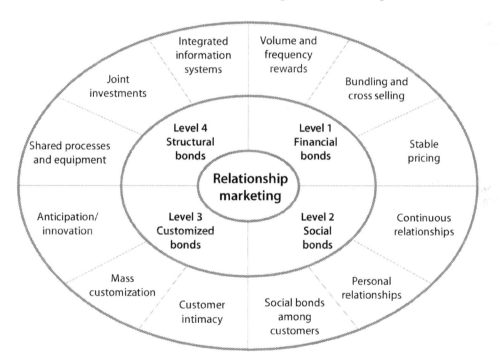

Figure 7.2: Levels of retention strategies for relationship marketing (Source: Adapted from Zeithaml and Bitner, 2000)

Level 2 strategies bind customers to the business through more than just financial incentives. Marketers using this retention strategy build long-term relationships through social and interpersonal, as well as financial bonds. Services are customized to fit individual needs, and marketers find ways of staying in touch with their customers, thereby developing social bonds with them. Social, interpersonal bonds are common among professional service providers and their clients, as well as among personal care providers and clients. Sometimes relationships are formed with the organization due to the social relationships that develop among customers rather than between customers and the service provider. For example, people who vacation at the same place during the same weeks every year build bonds with others who vacation there at the same time. Chapter 5 discussed the importance of customer-to-customer (C-to-C) interactions, which have been successfully fostered and managed for strategic gain by a number of firms. For instance, consumer goods producers, such as Harley Davidson, Jeep, Apple and Saturn, have all managed to build very successful consumer clubs and/ or brand communities.

Fairmont Resorts & Hotels has developed an Internet-based, 'Everyone's an Original' program in order to encourage customer-to-customer interactions and ultimately loyalty. The program is a platform for guests to share their experiences through social media options such as Facebook and Twitter. This forum contains contests and special promotions, and visitors are encouraged to join the Fairmont President's Club (with complimentary membership) which is a recognition program designed with individual travel preferences, passions and interests in mind. Members' benefits start on arrival at a Fairmont property with a special private reception desk offering express check-in and check-out. Membership also includes free high-speed Internet and local phone calls, Fairmont Fit, complimentary golf clubs and retail and spa discounts.

Level 3 strategies involve more than social ties and financial incentives, and two commonly used terms fit within the customization bonds approach: mass customization and customer intimacy. Both of these strategies suggest that customer loyalty can be encouraged through intimate knowledge of individual customers and through the development of one-to-one solutions that fit the individual customer's needs. Anticipation of needs facilitates the development of such bonds. The Ritz-Carlton, for example, maintains a computerized guest history profile of thousands of individual repeat guests. When guests visit any Ritz-Carlton, members of staff already know about their likes and dislikes. Casinos also maintain sophisticated databases of guest preferences, as well as their wagering habits. The snapshot profiling the Sheraton Suites Eau Claire shows how the hotel takes care of preferences before the guest arrives. A guest relations officer is employed for the sole purpose of coordinating the 'It's Our Pleasure' program, and a room is not ready for a guest until this officer has ensured all preferences are taken care of. Previous research has shown that hotel guests perceive personalization, familiarization, and social bonding to be very influential in the relationship formation process (Scanlon and McPhail, 2000).

Level 4 strategies are the most difficult to imitate and involve structural as well as financial, social, and customization bonds between the customer and the firm. Often structural bonds are created by providing the client with customized services that are technology-based and that serve to make the customer more productive. An example would be a reservations system installed in a travel agency by a tour operator. The agent is therefore structurally bound to that operator in its operations.

Loyalty programs in tourism and hospitality

Loyalty programs have become extremely common in the tourism and hospitality sector, especially in the US where such programs have 662.3 million members – 32% of US loyalty program membership. Table 7.1 shows the growth in memberships between 2008 and 2010 in various tourism and hospitality sectors.

Table 7.1: Tourism and hospitality loyalty program memberships in the US, 2008-2010 (Source: Based on Hlavinka and Sullivan, 2011)

Industry sector	2008 memberships	2010 memberships	Growth 2008-10
Airline	277, 410,000	324,900,000	17%
Hotel	161,896,000	176,800,000	9%
Car rental & cruise	13,500,000	17,760,000	32%
Gaming	106,043,000	133,040,000	26%
Restaurant	8,377,000	9,790,000	17%
Total	**567,226,000**	**662,290,000**	**17%**

7

Airlines have been making changes in their frequent flyer programs, increasingly giving their best rewards not just to passengers who fly the most, but who also pay the highest fares. United, Southwest, JetBlue and Virgin America, all reward passengers who spend more (Levere, 2011). Airlines are trying to make sure that the financial benefits they offer elite passengers are commensurate with the revenues and profitability that these travelers generate. Another evolution in loyalty programs for airlines is the growing influence of the issuers of carriers' co-branded credit cards. The issuers pay carriers for miles awarded to cardholders, making them an increasingly significant source of airline's income.

In fact, one of the most dominant trends of loyalty programs in general is the coalition model. Businesses in various industries have turned single-brand loyalty programs into corporate-wide programs across different brands, partnering with other businesses in order to offer customers added value. For example, airlines are partnering with hotels, rental cars, restaurants as well as credit card companies and offering loyal customers more opportunities to earn points and benefits. Yoo and Bai (2007) have found that the value creation from these strategic alliances has a key influence on loyalty.

Table 7.1 shows a 9% growth in hotel loyalty program memberships between 2008 and 2010, which is a solid gain in such a mature industry. According to Colloquy (2011), increased activity in social media and more experiential benefits contributed to this growth, as did the use of data to customize rewards on a global scale. The use of these programs to lure guests has led hotel brand owners like

Starwood and Hilton to match each other and ratchet up benefits. Programs for the highest frequency guests routinely include complimentary meals and free wireless Internet access. Hotel owners, who usually sign management contracts or franchise agreements with the brand companies, pay a fee – roughly 5% of the room price – to cover costs for the loyalty programs (Berzon, 2012). The smaller hotel brands and individual boutique hotels have begun to join together to create their own loyalty programs with perks that reflect the personalized service and local flair that independent hotels tend to offer (Higgins, 2011). In March 2011, Global Hotel Alliance rolled out a loyalty program, GHA Discovery, that rewards frequent guests with insider experiences instead of points. Examples include wine tastings at a local vineyard with the hotel's sommelier and a hot air balloon ride over Egyptian ruins.

In the three other sectors identified in Table 7.1, significant gains in memberships were made in car rental & cruise (32%), and gaming sectors (26%). The more competitive and fragmented restaurant industry meanwhile, saw a 17% increase in memberships, as chains like T.G.I. Friday's and Starbucks followed the example set by the airlines. Chicago-based Lettuce Entertain You Enterprises (LEYE), a multi-concept operator whose restaurants include Shaw's Crabhouse, Maggiano's and Wildfire, has 130,000 guests enrolled in its frequent diner program. Brent Carter, Frequent Diner manager says, 'From the time they enter the program, and progressively thereafter, we see that the number of visits (of program members) does increase. You're trying to develop loyalty from your customer base, trying to get them to interact more regularly with your company' (Ragone, 2005). LEYE has embraced an element of exclusivity with its frequent diner program by requiring a one-time $25 fee upon signing up. After a diner's first visit to one of the group's restaurants their Rewards Card will be credited $10 and additional $10 on their second and third visits. LEYE offers its members a wide variety of rewards in the form of free meals, spa days and even all expenses paid vacations to Las Vegas.

Instead of discounting, some restaurant loyalty programs are focusing on non-financial incentives for their members as a way to provide differentiated rewards while maintaining their margins. T.G.I. Friday's now offers members of its Earn Your Stripes rewards program a 'Jump the Line' perk upon enrolment. While this approach has been adopted by some restaurants with loyalty programs, the majority still focus predominantly on financial based incentives. As the restaurant industry continues to invest and improve its loyalty marketing programs, a hybrid approach is expected to become the norm, especially in the fine dining segment. Research shows that dining patrons are looking for exciting and entertaining rewards in addition to mere cost savings (Jang and Mattila, 2005).

It has been argued that loyalty must be measured as a combination of attitudinal and behavioural dimensions, and Dick and Basu (1994) have developed a framework for customer loyalty that combines both (see Figure 7.3). Loyal customers have high repeat patronage, but are also less motivated to search for alternatives, are more resistant to counter-persuasion from other brands, and are more likely to pass on positive word-of-mouth. Latent loyalty exists when a consumer has a strong preference for or attitude towards a brand, but does not purchase repeatedly because of situational or environmental constraints. Spurious loyalty occurs when a consumer frequently purchases a brand, but sees no differentiation between brands. Repeat purchase may just be a habit. Finally, no loyalty exists when consumers see few differences between brands and exhibit low repeat purchase patterns. This classification system can be useful to marketers as they try to build or retain loyalty (Javalgi and Moberg, 1997).

Repeat Patronage

High   **Low**

	Loyalty	**Latent Loyalty**
Relative Attitude	■ high repeat patronage ■ less motivated for alternatives ■ more resistant to other brands ■ more likely to pass on positive word-of-mouth	■ strong preference for/ attitude towards a brand ■ do not purchase repeatedly ■ due to situational or environmental constraints
	Spurious Loyalty	**No Loyalty**
	■ frequently purchases a brand ■ sees no differentiation between brands ■ Repeat purchase as a habit	■ see few differences between brands ■ low repeat purchase

Figure 7.3: Service loyalty classification scheme (Source: Adapted from Dick and Basu, 1994).

Finally, one often overlooked benefit of a loyalty marketing program is the wealth of information that it provides businesses about their customers. The quantity and quality of data collected is usually superior to any other source as it represents actual customer behaviour over time. Every tourism and hospitality business can benefit from data-based customer insights. Programs that collect data on customer demographics, behaviour, trends, and marketing performance, all enable companies to target, reach and motivate current and prospective diners better.

Snapshot: Legend Golf & Safari Resort, South Africa

Legend Golf & Safari Resort Signature Course

Legend Lodges Hotels & Resorts is a five-star operation encompassing two safari lodges, two coastal hotels, a country lodge and a state-of-the-art golf and safari resort in South Africa. The Legend Golf & Safari Resort, set in the 22,000 hectare Entabeni Safari Conservancy, features an 18-hole golf course which was built not by just one pro golfer, but by eighteen of the world's top golfers, each responsible for a signature hole. A unique 19th hole is only accessible via helicopter ride to the tee and players drive over an escarpment to a green formed in the shape of the map of Africa.

The Legend Golf & Safari Resort – in the Waterberg Region of the Limpopo Province – includes a hotel, privately-owned homes, the championship golf course, a golf academy, a driving range, recreational facilities, a wellness center, a 'Field of Legends' sports complex as well as a multi-functional conference center.

With facilities promising such lofty standards, service is of necessity a top priority at Legends. 'It is the most important thing we do!' says Michelle Bouic, Senior Marketing Assistant for Legend Lodges, Hotels & Resorts. Wooing guests and keeping them is also top of their priority list. 'We have several different types of customers – independent travelers, tour operators, corporate clients and professional conference organizers, golf event companies and a range of golf event organizers,' Bouic says. In order to service such a broad range of clientele, Legends dedicates specific departments to each segment. Corporate relationship management strategies then feed down to event management departments at each of the properties. Finally there is a dedicated guest relations manager and team of game rangers as frontline service providers. Frontline employees give feedback on all customer service issues to managers via email and during regular meetings.

The company has compiled a list of core values as the foundation of its Customer Relationship Management (CRM) strategy, which are used during new employee induction and posted on notice boards in the Legends properties. These include:

- Create sustainable workforce
- Change industry/customer perception
- B-BBEE (Broad-Based Black Economic Empowerment – a form of Economic Empowerment initiated by the South African government)
- Sales & Marketing
- Profitability
- Workable incentives/benefits schemes
- Innovation development
- Protect what we have
- Fun

A new strategy known as 'Operation Boat Float' is getting right to the heart of the customer by identifying their preferences. 'We have invested in a special Business to Customer (B2C) strategy known as 'Operation Boat Float' (OBF). This defines what floats all our clients' boats – be it their favorite drink, magazine, food, etc. which we then aim to deliver in room, in the restaurants during their stay. OBF information is stored on our CRM system and referred to each time they visit and updated regularly,' Bouic explains. All data is analyzed weekly and fed back to all Legend properties.

In order to further relationships with existing customers, Legend Lodges, Hotels & Resorts hosts its most valued corporate visitors, tour operators and even VIP individuals at special events. 'As an example we are hosting a 'Most Valued Client' day free of charge at one of our properties where we will thank them for their continued support and hand out special awards,' says Bouic. 'We also try and innovate at meetings with them with little treats like zebra-patterned cakes, special torches, etc.' To help management understand the customer, Legends collects rated response forms with sections on all aspects of service delivery. But it is not just statistics which drive customer service and research at Legend. In addition – and more importantly, says Bouic – staff engage with the clients: 'We talk to them and try to understand their unique and specific requirements.'

Another aspect of their service ethos is to train and employ local people. In keeping with the B-BBEE mandate, Legend Resorts established The Legend Sport and Educational Foundation, a non-profit entity, promising culturally and environmentally-friendly development. Its objectives include creating a sustainable financial model focusing on the development of the disadvantaged communities in the area through sport and skill development as well as assisting with the social uplifting of neighboring populations. The Entabeni Nature Guide Training School, Legend Hospitality School and Legend Wildlife Centre have already been established, with sports academies, arts and crafts centers, nurseries and clinics planned for the future. The Foundation is at the heart of the Legend Golf & Safari project which aspires to employ up to 3000 local people in construction and service at the resort. Through scholarships to the Legend Hospitality School and a unique caddy ranger program, the Foundation has already provided new careers for 40 local people.

Sources

Interview with Senior Marketing Assistant, Michelle Bouic, 6 Feb 2011; Interview with Legend's Marketing Director, Pete Richardson, 20 Jan 2008; Anon (2008); Anon (2010); www.legend-resort.com; www.legendlodges.co.za; www.ifahotelsresorts.com

Benefits of relationship marketing

Both parties in the customer–company relationship can benefit from customer retention. It is not only in the best interest of the organization to build and maintain a loyal customer base; customers themselves also benefit from long-term associations. Table 7.2 summarizes the various benefits of relationship marketing for both the company and the customer. Assuming that they have a choice, customers will remain loyal to a company when they receive greater value relative to what they expect from competing organizations. Value represents a trade-off for the consumer between what they give and what they get. Consumers are more likely to stay in a relationship when the 'gets' (quality, satisfaction, specific benefits) exceed the 'gives' (monetary and non-monetary costs). When companies can consistently deliver what the customer considers to be value, the customer clearly benefits and has an incentive to stay in the relationship. Customers may also be rewarded for their loyalty. The snapshot above showed how regular customers at Legend Lodges, Hotels & Resorts are invited to special VIP events such as the 'Most Valued Client' day at one of the properties as a thank you for their continued support. The benefits to an organization of maintaining and developing a loyal customer base are numerous, but they are linked directly to the bottom line. Among service organizations, reducing customer defections by just 5% can boost profits by 25% to 85% (Reichheld and Sasser (1990). Retained customers are much more profitable than new ones because they purchase more and they purchase more frequently, often at a price premium, while at the same time requiring lower operating costs. They also make referrals that cost the business nothing. As Wine for Dudes owner, John O'Connor pointed out in the opening case, word of mouth is the most cost-effective form of marketing so he encourages customers to talk about positive experiences to friends and other travelers. And, of course, the acquisition cost of loyal customers is nothing, which is significant because it costs a company five to seven times more to prospect for new customers than it does to maintain the current ones (Zeithaml and Bitner, 2000).

Chapter 2 introduced the concept of *lifetime value of a customer* to understand the financial value of building long-term relationships with customers. This is a calculation that considers customers from the point of view of their potential lifetime revenue and profitability contributions to a company. This value is influenced by the length of an average lifetime, the average revenues generated in that time period, sales of additional products and services over time, and referrals generated by the customer. The Walt Disney Co., for example, has calculated that a typical household of 3.6 people have a lifetime value of more than $50,000 to the company (Schlaifer, 2006).

Table 7.2: Benefits of relationship marketing to the company and the customer

Benefits to the Company	Benefits to the Customer
Increased purchases	Social benefits
Lower costs	Confidence and trust
Employee retention	Special treatment
Increased profits	Reduced risk
Less customer defection	Increased value
Free advertising through word of mouth	Customized services

One establishment that has seen the benefits of developing a loyal customer base is Port D'Hiver, an opulent, five-star B & B at Melbourne Beach, Florida. The inn was already attracting 25% repeaters while only in its fourth year of business – and that's despite commanding high prices during a recession. The accommodation is topnotch, a rambling, balconied Victorian property restored and re-appointed with plunge pool, fountains, courtyards and lavish rooms, but it is the personal touch that appeals to guests. 'We love to surprise people with treats like finding a couple in the pool and offering to bring them a glass of wine,' says owner, Mike Rydson. He is also savvy with his staff selection, trying to represent the needs of his 25 to 65-year-old clientele: 'There is someone everyone can relate to demographically speaking.' Rydson surveys his clients, brainstorms improvements with his staff and is quick to react to suggestions. 'One of our guests who stayed in the Sunrise room said that they wanted to be able to see the TV from bed and also while sitting on the ocean view porch,' he recounts. 'We thought that was a great idea, so we mounted the TV on a pivoting arm so that guests can turn the TV and watch it from anywhere they like.' In response to early rising business travellers, they developed personalized 'to go' breakfast bags ready to pick up in a handy snack fridge near the parking lot.

Rydson encourages customer loyalty through a frequent stay program, as well as customized birthday and anniversary offers. 'For instance, this month the birthday people got the Carriage House which is usually $525 a night for $195 plus a bottle of wine and free T-shirt,' he says. He sustains a high level of communication with past guests after they leave via social media and direct email. 'We encourage guests to share their experiences on Tripadvisor and other online travel forums. We also have a very active Facebook fan page where guests can interact with us and each other,' he says. He also sends out special offers and events calendars by email and posts offers, giveaways and contests on Facebook.

Targeting profitable customers

A key role of marketing is to identify the customers or segments with the greatest value-creating potential, and target them successfully with retention strategies to reduce the risk of these high lifetime value customers defecting to competitors (Ryals, 2003). In 2004, Lufthansa, one of Europe's largest airlines, invited its 6000 best customers to join the newly created HON Circle program. Clients who collected 600,000 frequent flyer points (equalling approximately 25 first class return flights from Frankfurt to New York) in two calendar years could enjoy 24-hour booking guarantee, limousine pick-up, and check-in at dedicated first class terminals in Frankfurt and Munich (Haenlein and Kaplan, 2008).

The idea of targeting the 'right customers' for relationship marketing has emerged in the literature and in practice over the last few decades. Reichheld and Sasser (1990) for example, stress that companies aspiring to relationship marketing should make formal efforts to identify those customers who are most likely to remain loyal, and should develop their overall strategy around delivering superior value to these customers. Targeting profitable customers for relationship marketing involves studying and analyzing loyalty- and defection-prone customers, searching for distinguishing patterns in why they stay or leave, what creates value for them, and who they are.

Innovative service companies today are beginning to recognize that not all customers are worth attracting and keeping. Many customers are too costly to do business with and have little potential to become profitable, even in the long term. To build and improve upon traditional segmentation, companies are now trying to identify segments that differ in current and/or future profitability to the organization. After identifying profitability bands, these companies offer services and service levels in line with the identified segments. A good example is Federal Express, which has categorized business customers as the good, the bad, and the ugly – based on their profitability. Rather than marketing to all customers in a similar manner, the company now puts its efforts into the good, tries to move the bad to the good, and discourages the ugly (Zeithaml, Rust and Lemon, 2001).

Virtually all companies are aware at some level that their customers differ in profitability—in particular that a minority of their customers account for the highest proportion of sales or profits. This has often been called the 80/20 rule: 20% of customers produce 80% of sales or profits. This 80/20 customer pyramid is shown in Figure 7.4. Of course, this principle does not always hold up. One study of casino patrons, found that a mere 3% of table games customers can generate approximately 90% of all table revenues (Watson and Kale, 2003).

Thomas Cook Travel was one of the first tourism organizations to calculate the profitability of its customers. The company divided its customers into As (those who bring in $750 or more in annual revenues), Bs (those who bring in $250–$749), and Cs (those who bring in less than $250). The company found that 80% of its customers were C's. By focusing in on the more profitable customers

(As and Bs), and by charging Cs for their time-consuming demands (a $25 deposit was taken for researching any trip), the company increased its profits considerably. The growth of the company's A- and B-level clients also increased by 20% (Rasmusson, 1999).

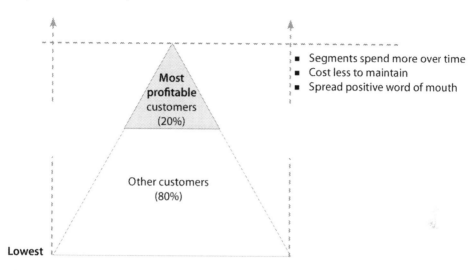

Figure 7.4: The 80/20 customer pyramid. Source: Adapted from Zeithaml and Bitnen (2000).

Kumar and Rajan (2009) suggest customer lifetime value as a basis for segmenting customers. Figure 7.5 illustrates the process of segmenting customers based on loyalty and profitability. From this figure, it is apparent that *True Friends* are the most valuable customers. They buy regularly over time and offer the highest profit potential for the firm. In managing True Friends, firms should indulge in consistent, yet intermittently spaced, communication. *Butterflies* also offer high profits for the firm but they are transient because they look for the best deals and avoid building a stable relationship with any one provider. According to Kumar and Rajan, firms should enjoy their profits while they can, but find the right moment to cease investing in those customers. *Barnacles* are long-term customers but have a low return on investment, so firms should look to ways of decreasing costs of dealing with these customers, or consider up-selling and cross-selling strategies to increase profitability. Finally, *Strangers* are the firm's least profitable customers as they have little fit with the products and services provided. The key strategy in managing these customers is to identify them early and refrain from making any relationship investment as these customers have no loyalty toward the firm and bring in no profits.

Watson and Kale (2003) propose a two-by-two taxonomy of casino customer segments based on customer profitability and level of relationship with a casino (see Figure 7.6). *Prime Customers* represent the casino's most desirable target customers: brand-loyal individuals with a high net worth. *Mobile Customers* comprise less than 1% of a casino's customer base, but are also the highest volume customers. This segment chooses providers on a transaction-by-transaction basis.

They negotiate heavily for high levels of added service before committing their business to any casino. *Valued Customers of Tomorrow* have above average net worth and a serious interest in gambling. Their volume of gambling is high, but individual average bets are far lower than prime customers. But some customers in this segment could become prime customers as their net worth increases over time. Finally *Incidental Customers* are curious and casual gamblers who are not really interested in gaming. *Undesirables* also fall into this segment, those who act inappropriately and disturb more valuable clientele.

High Profitability	**Butterflies** Can contribute high profit potential to the firm. *Managerial implications:* • Ensure satisfaction for each transaction they make. • Do not focus on cultivating long-term customer commitment toward the firm. • Converting them to loyal customers is seldom possible. Ensure profits as long as they are with the firm. • Do not invest in them after they have stopped purchasing from the firm.	**True friends** Have the potential to contribute the most profits. *Managerial implications* • Focus on building long-term relationships. • Send the right number of messages. Flooding them with offers would only chase them away from the firm. Consistent intermittently spaced communication. • Make them buy intensively over time from the firm. • Focus on retaining these customers.
Low Profitability	**Strangers** Exhibit the lowest potential to contribute profits. *Managerial implications* • Do not focus on cultivating relationships with these customers. • Ensure profits from every transaction	**Barnacles** Show little potential to contribute profits. *Managerial implications* • These customers are a drain on company's resources. • Converting these customers into profitable customers involves measuring size and share of wallet. • If share of wallet is low, focus on up-selling and cross-selling. • If size of wallet is small, impose strict cost control
	Low Loyalty	**High Loyalty**

Figure 7.5: Managing loyalty and profitability (Adapted from Kumar and Rajan, 2009, p. 5)

In fact, leading on from the last point, a customer's unprofitability may not be the only reason a company chooses to refuse or terminate a relationship with him or her. For various reasons, the belief that 'the customer is always right' does not always apply in service industries. It would not be beneficial to either the company or the customer for a company to establish a relationship with a customer whose needs the company cannot meet. Every server in the restaurant business has met the 'customer from hell', a paying guest whose behavior is beyond rude and who seems determined to ruin the evening for everyone concerned. These disruptive customers have even been segmented in some research articles, into classifications like 'Egocentric Edgars', 'Freeloading Fredas', and 'Dictatorial Dicks' (Witham, 1998). Such customers are often impossible to satisfy, and may place too much stress on employees and the organization.

Future relationship value

		High	Low
Customer profitability	High	Prime customers	Mobile customers
	Low	Valued customers of tomorrow	Incidental customers

Figure 7.6: A taxonomy of casino customer segments (Source: Watson and Kale, 2003)

Similarly, it would not be wise to forge relationships simultaneously with incompatible market segments. In many tourism businesses, customers experience the service together and can influence each other's perceptions about the value received. For example, a conference hotel may find that mixing executives in town for a serious training program with students in town for a sporting event may not be wise. If the student group is a key long-term customer, the hotel may choose to pass up the executive group in the interest of retaining the students' business. So in some cases, it is desirable for a firm to alienate or even 'fire' at least some of its customers (Zeithaml, Rust and Lemon, 2001; Ryals, 2003). However, a customer abandonment strategy may not be possible in all situations, and requires a careful consideration of benefits and costs. An unprofitable customer who is 'fired' is likely to feel dissatisfied and may spread negative word of mouth (Haenlein and Kaplan, 2008).

Case Study: Service excellence at the Sheraton Suites Calgary Eau Claire

The Sheraton Suites Calgary Eau Claire has a reputation for service excellence. The hotel was awarded the Sheraton Brand Highest Guest Satisfaction from 2001 until 2009 and then placed second 2010 and 2011. This award recognizes exceptional levels of hospitality, service and attention to detail, as well as upscale facilities and variety of amenities. The Sheraton Suites was also the winner of the Alberta Tourism Award (ALTO) for Service Excellence in 2002 and 2005. This particular award honors an organization in the tourism industry that demonstrates a commitment to service excellence, delivering outstanding customer service to visitors, employees, suppliers and other stakeholders.

Gord Minor, Sheraton Suites Calgary Eau Claire

After moving from Fairmont in Toronto, Gord Minor was appointed general manager at the Sheraton Suites in 2008. 'We had a run of eight years in a row of being number one Sheraton in North America up to 2009. We got second in 2010 and last year, which was great, but we've been pushing the envelope to strive to be the best again,' Minor says. He attributes their high ranking largely to the perpetuation of a strong service culture which was launched in 1998. 'There's only so much you can do with the amenities in a hotel room – some are bigger, some are smaller, but what people really remember is the guest experience,' Minor believes.

Driven by desire to be the best – and rival not only other Sheratons but highly-ranked competitors such as the St Regis chain – Minor's first priority is to hire the best people. This is particularly vital, he says, during a recession where there is a 'labor crunch'. Having carefully selected their staff and then trained them thoroughly, Sheraton Suites relies on peer pressure to keep the 260-strong team motivated. 'It's the sixth hotel I've worked at in my career,' says Minor. 'And I've never seen anywhere else where my colleagues put so much pressure on themselves to do this.' He believes that, although having a high quality product and great location helps, service interaction is key to retaining customer loyalty.

The focus on customer loyalty is driven by the 'It's Our Pleasure' program—a recognition and reward program for guests. On every fifth stay, a guest receives a gift, one that is meaningful to the guest, and the value of the gift increases the longer a customer remains loyal. For example, on the fifth stay a guest may receive a bottle of wine in the room, and by the fiftieth stay, a personalized bathrobe could be given as a loyalty gift. 'It's always customized to the particular person, we work out what means something to them,' says Minor. 'At the end of the day it is about acknowledgement.'

The Starwood Preferred Guest program – of which over 70% of guests are members – is also used to reward loyalty via a points system. Through this program, the hotel collects valuable data on the personal preferences of customers and stores it all in a database. For example, if a guest likes extra towels and feather pillows, then these will be waiting in the room when they arrive, with a note saying 'It's our pleasure to provide you with these items…' This anticipation of a guest's needs is no mean feat. Staff members have to look into reservations, research through the database and dig around to find out exactly who the guests are and what their needs are. As Minor says, it is a case of putting in customer service effort both before guests arrive and during their stay. And he doesn't leave it at that. There is work to be done on the customer service level after the guest has left. Social media has been instrumental in making all businesses accountable for their performance. 'It's by no means equal though,' says Minor. 'If something goes wrong it goes a lot further by word of mouth than things that go right but we're always in the top ten on Tripadvisor for Calgary.' His staff monitors everything through Facebook and Twitter and Minor himself responds to almost every comment – negative and positive – on Tripadvisor. 'The good ones are great but the bad ones are also valuable feedback which is a gift to me,' he explains.

Thorough customer service training is also intrinsic to Sheraton Suites' success. Programs include a two-day hotel orientation, a full day spent on the 'It's Our Pleasure' program, and brand-specific programs such as Starwood's 'Building World Class Brands'. Depending on which modules are relevant for a particular job, training can range over 45 days. 'We have added three different modules recently for high guest contact positions,' says Minor. 'We're actually very unique in that we are franchised to Starwood and managed by Fairmont. So we have the best of both worlds and put it altogether to make something that really works.' Part of the training procedure is a coaching program which involves role playing. It's intended to demonstrate how to get the necessary answers from guests and to offer alternative methods.

Empowerment of staff is also vital to on-the-spot customer service and successful service recovery at Sheraton Suites. Energy is put into key contact areas, such as the front door, valet, bellman, reception staff, so that guests are greeted, welcomed by name and made to feel important from the get-go. Communication is also key with front of house and housekeeping staff sharing information via radio throughout the day. Housekeeping are informed of every little foible of the guest – such as how many bottles of water they need – and supervisors double check everything. 'We're a team and everyone looks after one another,' says Minor.

And it's not just about having solid customer service training. 'We've not stood on a pedestal and said you have to do this and you have to do that,' says Minor. 'We supply the ability to let them make decisions on their own. We recognize that every guest is different, and if the staff want to do something for them, if something is not right, they can do it and tell us later why it was not right and then we can correct it for the future.'

Relationship marketing, according to Minor, is not cut and dried but offers a different opportunity with each different guest. Milestone awards for repeat guests vary according to their hobbies and habits. 'When it gets to the real big ones, say 100 stays, we dig deep to find out what their hot buttons are,' says Minor. He recently honored a hiking couple who had notched up 100 stays with gifts of customized hiking sticks. 'We contacted a local artisan who makes walking sticks and had them personalized to mark their anniversary, too, and when we gave them to them, they were nearly in tears. They couldn't believe a hotel could do this,' says Minor. He says it is not just a case of recognizing their loyalty but recognizing them as people, too. It is this high level of engagement with customers that has earned Sheraton Suites recognition by Gallup as a world-class organization.

Another important aspect in relationship marketing is subtlety. Although doormen welcome guests and ask them basic questions such as if they are a new or a returning customer, they don't delay them unnecessarily. 'They have to talk to people in a timely way; we can't have a line going out of the door,' says Minor. Engagement therefore starts off small and develops through various layers of contact during their stay. 'We're family, we treat our team like a family and we treat guests that way, too. It's personable but not intrusive and the guests become very relaxed,' says Minor. Business travel is the primary market and the aim is to make business visitors feel at home even when they are away.

Another important strand of Sheraton Suites' service culture is pride. Housekeepers consider the rooms they clean as '*their* rooms' on '*their* floor'. They are held accountable for 'their rooms' and are also acknowledged for their achievements. This results in a very low turnover of staff and lots of long service awards. 'Last week 51 colleagues were recognized and the year before it was 67,' says Minor. 'And a lot of our employees have been with us or with Fairmont since day one.'

Source

Interview with Gord Minor, 14 February 2012.

References

Anon (2008) 'Legend Golf Resort', *Golf Course Architecture*, p. 63.

Anon (2010) 'Golf Digest Magazine rates new Signature Course at Legend Golf & Safari Resort the Best New Course in South Africa'. Accessed 02/06/2011 from http://www.golfblogger.co.uk/post/golf-digest-magazine-rates-new-signature-course-at-legend-golf--safari-resort-the-best-new-course-in-south-africa

Berry, L. L. (1983) 'Relationship marketing, in L. L. Berry, G.L. Shostack and G. Upah (eds)', *Emerging Perspectives on Services Marketing* (pp. 25-28). Chicago: American Marketing Association.

Berzon, A. (2012) 'Starwood perks up loyalty program', *Wall Street Journal*, 1 February, B7.

Colloquy (2011) The billion member march: The 2011 COLLOQUY loyalty census. Accessed 10/10/12 from http://www.colloquy.com/files/2011-COLLOQUY-Census-Talk-White-Paper.pdf

Dick, A.S. and Basu, K. (1994) 'Customer loyalty: Toward an integrated conceptual framework', *Journal of the Academy of Marketing Science*, **22**, 99-113.

Haenlein, M. and Kaplan, A.M. (2008) 'Unprofitable customers and their management', *Business Horizons*, **52**, 89-97.

Higgins, M. (2011) 'Expanding hotel loyalty rewards', *New York Times*, 1 June. Accessed 22 October 2011 from http://travel.nytimes.com/2011/06/05/travel/small-hotels-offer-new-loyalty-programs-practical-traveler.html

Hlavinka, K. and Sullivan, J. (2011) 'The 2011 COLLOQUY Loyalty Census'. Accessed from http://www.colloquy.com/files/2011-COLLOQUY-Census-Talk-White-Paper.pdf

Jang, D. and Mattila, A.S. (2005) 'An examination of restaurant loyalty programs: What kind of rewards to customers prefer?', *International Journal of Contemporary Hospitality Management*, **17**(5), 402-408.

Javalgi, R. and Moberg, C.R. (1997) 'Service loyalty: Implications for service providers', *The Journal of Services Marketing*, **11**(3), 165-179.

Kumar, V. and Rajan, B. (2009). 'Profitable customer management: Measuring and maximizing customer lifetime value', *Management Accounting Quarterly*, **10**(3), 1-18.

Levere, J.L. (2011) 'A salute to the spenders', *The New York Times*, 18 October, B9.

Ragone, L, G. (2005) 'Loyalty programs drive profits', *Restaurant Hospitality*, Feb, 53-56.

Rasmusson, E. (1999) 'Wanted: Profitable customers', *Sales and Marketing Management*, **151**(5), 28–34.

Reichheld, F. F. and Sasser, W. S., Jr. (1990) 'Zero defections: Quality comes to services', *Harvard Business Review*, **68**, 105–111.

Ryals, L. (2003) 'Creating profitable customers through the magic of data mining', *Journal of Targeting, Measurement and Analysis for Marketing*, **11**(4), 343-349.

Scanlon, L. and McPhail, J. (2000) 'Forming service relationships with hotel business travelers: The critical attributes to improve retention', *Journal of Hospitality & Tourism Research*, **24**(4), 491-513.

Schlaifer, A.N. (2006) 'Build customer and employee loyalty you can be proud of', *The Resort Trades*, July. Accessed 09/15/2011 from http://www.resorttrades.com/articles.php?showMag=Resort&act=view&id=190

Tullo, P. (2008) 'The true value of customers', *Brand Strategy*, May, 30-31.

Watson, L. and Kale, S.H. (2003) 'Know when to hold them: Applying the customer lifetime value concept to casino table gambling', *International Gambling Studies*, **3**(1), 89-101.

Winer, R.S. (2001) 'A framework for customer relationship management', *California Management Review*, **43**(4), 89-105.

Witham, G. (1998) 'Customers from hell', *Cornell Hotel and Restaurant Administration Quarterly*, **39**(5), 11

Yoo, M. and Bai, B. (2007) 'Value creation: The impact of strategic alliance on customer loyalty', *Journal of Quality Assurance in Hospitality & Tourism*, **8**(2), 45-65.

Zeithaml, V. A. and Bitner, M. J. (2000) *Services Marketing: Integrating Customer Focus Across the Firm*, New York: McGraw-Hill.

Zeithaml, V.A., Rust. and Lemon, K.N. (2001) 'The customer pyramid: Creating and serving profitable customers', *California Management Review*, **43**(4), 118-142.

Zemke, R., and Anderson, K. (1990). Customers from hell. *Training*, **27**(2), 25–33.

7

Scan here to get the hyperlinks in this chapter

8 Providing Customer Service through the Servicescape

Everything about Starbucks is staged: the cozy sofa and coffee table arrangements often around a charismatic fireplace, the cheery staff with the 'Can Do' attitude, the pungent aromas of coffee beans, the stories around the walls and on the cups and coffee products, the Italian-sounding names of the drinks. It is a highly recognizable theme which has transcended cultures and borders, persuading even the tea-drinking nations of the world such as China and Japan to switch to coffee.

But none of it came about by accident: it was the brainchild of Howard Schultz who visited Italy in the early 1980s while working for the original Starbucks Coffee Company, a roasting and coffee bean distributor in Seattle, Washington. Having

Howard Schultz, at the company's 40th anniversary celebration at Starbucks Headquarters in Seattle on March 8, 2011. Photo courtesy of Starbucks.

been inspired by the atmosphere and bonhomie of Italian espresso bars, Schultz gave in his notice and set up two coffee shops called Il Giornale – one in Seattle and another in Vancouver – to play out his innovative theme.

He wanted his coffee shops to be everyone's 'third place', a home-from-home for work, play and community interaction. 'If home is the primary or "first" place where a person connects with others, and if work is a person's "second place" then a public space such as

a coffeehouse – such as Starbucks – is what I have always referred to as the "third place",
he says in his book *Onward*. 'A social, yet personal environment between one's house
and job, where people can connect with others and reconnect with themselves.' By 1987
Schultz was able to buy Starbucks Coffee Company from his former employers and use it
as the basis for his global chain of coffee shops.

What Schultz did from the outset was create an inviting, comfortable and compelling
servicescape full of sensory pleasures designed to make his customers relax and linger.
Determined to bring the romance of Italian coffee drinking to the US, he re-created the
ambiance he noticed in Milan and Verona, paying minute attention to layout, furnish-
ing, decor, lighting, temperature, smells and social interaction between employees and
customers.

There were flashbacks to Italy in the decor and in the terminology he developed. Waiters
were called *baristas*, drinks were given names such as *latte* and *frappucino* and sizes such
as *grande* and *vente*. These musical names being shouted out by the *baristas* added to
the geniality which he also encouraged by creating a system of writing the first names of
each customer on the paper coffee cups. This personal touch went a long way towards
making Starbucks seem like a friendly oasis in the midst of the anonymity of a sprawling
city.

A Starbucks cafe looks less like a bar or restaurant and more like a home with its comfy
chairs, fireplaces, coffee smells and camaraderie. Adding free WiFi was an inspirational
touch designed to stop Americans, in the first place, and every nationality eventually,
from grabbing a drink and going. Fighting the whole fast food fad, he encouraged people
to use his coffee shops for computer work, social networking, a meeting place for clients,
a community hub, that 'third place'.

Schultz is famous for his personal visits to stores and it was during one of these in 2006
that he realized that new espresso machines were undermining his carefully crafted servicescape. The machines were too tall, creating a physical barrier between the *barista* and
the customer, precluding conversation and engagement in the coffee making process. He
wrote about this in a memo to his top executives: 'When we went to automatic espresso
machines, we solved a major problem in terms of speed of service and efficiency. At the
same time, we overlooked the fact that we would remove much of the romance and
theater that was in play...' Naturally he put this right, commissioning different machines.

After more than a decade of expansion, Schultz stepped down as ceo (all job titles are
written in lower case at Starbucks) and became chairman to focus more on global strategy than on day-to-day operations. However, he came back to the ceo position in 2008
when he noticed that the leap from 1000 stores in the mid-1990s to 13,000 stores by 2006
had led to a watering down of the Starbucks' Experience. His mandate was to restore
Starbucks to its original goals and refocus on the customer experience.

8

One of the things that had slipped through during his absence from operations was the breakfast sandwich introduced in 2003. Although it was profitable, it became his mission to eradicate it. And his reasoning was totally founded on the servicescape: the smell of melted and burnt cheese was ruining the coffee aromas for which Starbucks was renowned. In his book *Onward*, he wrote 'Where was the magic in burnt cheese? As far as I was concerned, nothing could be further from the romance of the Italian espresso bar.' In fact, he considered the smell of coffee to be 'perhaps the most powerful nonverbal signal' in Starbucks' stores.

He tried everything he could think of in order to eradicate the cheesy odors: he instigated research into different ovens, retrained baristas in cleaning up, replaced the parchment paper which wrapped the sandwiches, narrowed cooking times to prevent cheese dripping, got manufacturers to rework oven vents, improved stores' ventilation, heating, and air conditioning to help extract odors – all to no avail. So, he announced the demise of the breakfast sandwich in January 2008. However, due to divisions among his top executives as well as a public internet campaign, 'Savethebreakfastsandwich.com', they were reinstated with improvements in ingredients, as well as eliminating artificial flavors, dyes, trans fats and high fructose corn syrup. In order to preserve the coffee aroma, Schultz also banned smoking among his employees (dubbed 'partners' internally) and asked them not to wear strong perfumes or colognes.

When he returned as ceo, the huge conglomerate had been threatened by competition and the economic recession. After closing 900 under-performing branches and firing thousands of employees, Schultz started adding new products and slowed down the momentum of expansion. By 2010 Starbucks had increased sales by 10% and doubled its profits, notching up $10 billion per year in revenue, serving nearly 60 million customers per week in 16,000 stores in 54 countries with more than 200,000 employees.

Sources: Schultz, H. (2011); Thompson and Arsel (2004); Venkatraman and Nelson (2008); Strauss, M. (2011)

Elements of the servicescape

An important part of customer service is the physical environment. Because many tourism and hospitality services are intangible, customers often rely on tangible cues, or physical evidence, to evaluate the service before its purchase and to assess their satisfaction with the service during and after consumption. The physical evidence is the environment in which the service is delivered and in which the firm and customer interact, and any tangible components that facilitate performance or communication of the service. The physical facility is often referred to as the 'servicescape', and is very important for tourism and hospitality products such as hotels, restaurants, and theme parks, which are dominated by experience attributes. Disney, for example, effectively uses the servicescape to excite its customers. The brightly colored displays, the music, the rides, and the costumed characters all reinforce the feelings of fun and excitement that Disney seeks to generate in its customers.

General elements of the servicescape are shown in Table 8.1. They include all aspects of the organization's servicescape that affect customers, including both exterior attributes (such as parking and landscape) and interior attributes (such as design, layout, equipment, and décor). Signage is also part of the physical evidence. Beijing attempted to stamp out embarrassingly bad English on bilingual signs in a run-up to the 2008 Olympics. The municipal government issued translation guidelines for signs in hotels, shopping malls, public transport and tourist attractions. At one point before this clean-up, the Park of Ethnic Minorities was identified as 'Racist Park', while the emergency exits at Beijing's international airport read, 'No entry on peacetime'.

Uniforms are also an important part of the servicescape. In 2009, Delta Airlines reintroduced red coats for their customer service agents – intended to be a visible sign of the airline ramping up personal customer service (Jones, 2009). The Red Coats were first introduced in the 1960s but were eliminated in 2005 because of budget cuts. 'We, along with most of the industry, have been driving technology, and we still continue to do that,' said Gil West, Delta's senior vice president, airport customer service. Yet, he said, 'We realize we've got to invest in the human element as well. ... One of our key objectives is to continue to improve our customer service. The bringing back of the Red Coats for Delta is very symbolic of that.' Considered a kind of super-agent who can handle virtually any task, the Red Coats' primary mission is to fix problems. They are equipped with handheld units, similar to those used by rental car representatives, to help them more efficiently assist passengers, directing those who've missed a connection to their new flight, for example, securing boarding passes or even providing food vouchers when needed.

The training of a 'Hooters Girl' for the American restaurant chain is painfully specific, and a key ingredient is achieving and maintaining the Hooters Look. The Hooters Employee Handbook for example, mandates that the white tank tops worn by all the girls may not be midriff-bearing and must always be tucked into the approved Orange Hooters Girl Shorts. Either a white or a nude bra must be worn and no portion of it may be visible. Pantyhose is required at all times and the color is exclusively 'suntan.' But the uniform only scratches the surface in terms of the consistent 'clean, healthy, natural, and vibrant' image Hooters Girls are expected to uphold. For example, drastically different highlighted tones or colors in hair isn't considered attractive or permitted as part of the Hooters Girl Image. The restaurant takes a picture of new staff and it's part of their contract to maintain the precise look for which they are hired. Health and fitness are also emphasized and the restaurant even provides workout tips and a calorie-burning breakdown for various physical activities.

Table 8.1: Elements of the servicescape

Facility Exterior	Facility Interior	Other Tangibles
Parking	Layout	Uniforms
Landscape	Equipment	Business cards
Signage	Signage	Stationary
Exterior design	Air temperature	Invoices
	Interior design	Brochures
	Lighting	Web pages
		Employee dress

The strategic role of the servicescape in delivering service

The servicescape is often one of the most important elements used in positioning a tourism or hospitality organization. According to Zeithaml et al (2007), the servicescape can play four key strategic roles simultaneously.

■ Packaging

The servicescape essentially 'wraps' the service and conveys to the consumer an external image of what is 'inside'. This packaging role is particularly important in creating expectations for new customers and for newly established businesses that are trying to develop a particular image. The opening case showed how Howard Schultz was purposefully trying to position Starbucks to look and feel less like a bar or restaurant and more like a home with its comfy chairs, fireplaces, coffee smells and camaraderie. What Schultz did from the outset was create an inviting, comfortable and compelling servicescape full of sensory pleasures designed to make his customers relax and linger. The Hard Rock Cafes are another good example of servicescape packaging. They use rock-and-roll memorabilia both outside and inside the restaurants to establish an expectation in the mind of visitors. The chain has an unparalleled memorabilia collection, which consists of more than 60,000 pieces that are rotated from restaurant to restaurant, providing the world's most comprehensive 'visual history' of rock 'n' roll. These treasures include a huge collection of classic guitars and other instruments, posters, costumes, music and lyric sheets, album art, platinum and gold LPs, photos and much more. From Jimi Hendrix's Flying V guitar to John Lennon's handwritten lyrics to 'Help' (his favorite Beatles' tune) to one of Madonna's now-classic bustier tops.

The case study in Chapter 1 introduced the Lopesan Group of hotels in the Canary Islands, a company that invests heavily in the servicescape in order to 'package' its offerings. Unlike Las Vegas, where you sometimes feel part of an ineluctable crowd of people from which it's hard to escape, in Lopesan hotels, the atmosphere is serene and there is not so much foot traffic to circumnavigate. Lopesan has also devoted its decorative approach to the village outside the hotels. There is a spacious indoor shopping mall as well as an open air shopping street complete with pavement cafes, restaurants, sports bars, high end boutiques and ice cream parlours. The streets are decorated with water features and statues as well as a bougainvillea-covered walkway as you approach the lighthouse which is perched on the most southerly point of Europe.

Facilitator

The second role the servicescape can play is as a facilitator in aiding the performances of people in the service environment. To encourage the neat appearance of front-line staff, mirrors can be strategically placed so that staff can easily check their appearance before going 'on stage' to meet customers. In fast-food restaurants strategically-located tray-return stands and notices on walls remind customers to return their trays. Grady and Ohlin (2009) have emphasized the importance of physical layout and design for serving guests with disabilities. They suggest that for hotels, both guests and employees should be encouraged to bring forth recommendations for improvement in physical layout and design so that reasonable modifications can be made. They recommend including questions about physical layout or design of the hotel in guest satisfaction surveys specifically designed for guests with mobility impairments. This they say would allow the hospitality operator to gauge whether the physical aspects of the hotel are adequately meeting the guest's needs and would effectively serve as a proxy for whether the property is complying with the Americans with Disabilities Act (ADA).

A well-designed, functional facility can make the service a pleasure to experience from the customer's point of view, and a pleasure to perform for the employee. One thing which can often let down a large five-star, all-inclusive resort is its dining. Buffets are so often unappetizing counters of congealing food, picked through by hundreds of people, with discouraging line-ups for all the best items and waiters more interested in damage limitation, clearing debris rather than serving customers. It can amount to a free-for-all food frenzy rather than a sophisticated, adult night out. On the contrary, at the Baobab, one of the Lopesan hotels in Gran Canaria, there are two huge buffets to choose from, each with indoor and outdoor seating. There is a full wine menu and live entertainment can be heard across the moat encircling the restaurants. Lights are dimmed, waiters are discreet but attentive, and there are two distinct seating times – 6 to 8 pm and 8:30 to 10:30 pm. Fish, seafood and meats are cooked right in front of the customers to order, there is a constant replenishment of fresh items and gluten-free food is available to order. Like many other hotels in the Canary Islands there is complementary Spanish champagne with breakfast daily. And the best part – no plastic wristbands to denote your meal plan, just a room card.

■ Socializer

The design of the servicescape can also aid in the socialization of both employees and customers in the sense that it helps convey expected roles, behaviors and relationships. It was mentioned in Chapter 2 that the lodges owned by Canadian Mountain Holidays (CMH) have been designed specifically to meet the needs of heli-skiers. Each lodge has a dining room and a fully stocked lounge and is equipped with a sauna and hot tub. But the layout of the dining room is the same in each lodge. CMH has discovered over the years, that to encourage socialization at the dinner table, the ideal layout is four tables of 12 people; a total of 44 guests and four staff who sit at the head of each table and interact with customers over dinner. Some all-inclusive resorts like Club Med, and most cruise operators, also design the environment to facilitate customer to customer interactions, as well as guest interactions with staff.

The snapshot in this chapter shows how Incheon Airport in Korea has a very elaborate servicescape that facilitates the socialization of passengers. The free Korean Traditional Cultural Experience Centre, for example, allows passengers to learn about local history, customs, traditional dress, instruments and crafts – all in an interactive manner. The airport also has an on-demand cinema with futuristic egg-shaped booths, another two-screen cinema and a video and media art experience in the Transportation Centre. Forward plans include a 1109 square metre skating rink and performance hall with 11 shops.

■ Differentiator

The design of a physical facility can differentiate a business from its competitors and signal the market segment that the service is intended for. Airlines often employ design consultants to help them differentiate the appearance of their aircraft and employees from those of their competitors. Although some cabin staff look interchangeable, others have really distinctive uniforms that immediately identify them as employees of, for example, Singapore Airlines. In fact, Singapore Airlines has built its reputation on the beauty and hospitality of the sarong-wearing staff known in its global ad campaigns as the 'Singapore Girls'. Chinese airlines are following suit, and tend to employ hostesses who are young, beautiful and practically the same height. They are flaunted as symbols of excellence (Ching-Ching, 2007).

The case study at the end of this chapter shows how the owners of the Cavas Wine Lodge in Mendoza, Argentina have gone to great lengths designing their servicescape in order to differentiate themselves from competitors. They spent around 18 months with architects tweaking the design of the lodge and even hired a theatrical designer in order to achieve the most atmospheric lighting. With great attention to detail, the owners matched staff uniforms to the area and the vineyards and added an 'Argentine touch' with traditional design features for the front desk vests. The theme worked so well that many visitors buy parts of the uniform as souvenirs.

Developing servicescapes

Servicescapes have to be seen holistically, which means no dimension of the design can be optimized in isolation, because everything depends on everything else. Even the arousal elements of scent and music interact and need to be considered in conjunction with each other to elicit the desired consumer experiences. Lin and Matilla (2010) found that in a restaurant setting, consumer satisfaction was highly dependent on the congruency between both the atmosphere and the type of food sold, and the matching of the exterior look of the restaurant and the interior theme or look. A number of restaurants are explicitly designing experiences with themed servicescapes. Examples are the Hard Rock Cafe, Planet Hollywood, or the Rainforest Cafe, where the food is just a prop for what's known as 'eatertainment'. Retailers are also creating themes that tie merchandising presentations together in a staged experience. A popular tourist attraction in Las Vegas is the Forum, a mall that displays its distinctive theme – an ancient Roman marketplace – in every detail. The Simon DeBartolo Group, which developed the mall, disperses this motif through an array of architectural effects. These include marble floors, stark white pillars, 'outdoor' cafes, living trees, flowing fountains – and even a painted blue sky with fluffy white clouds that yield regularly to simulated storms, complete with lighting and thunder. Every mall entrance and every storefront is an elaborate Roman re-creation. Hourly, inside the main entrance, statues of Julius Caesar and other Roman luminaries come to life and speak. 'Hail, Caesar!' is a frequent cry, and Roman centurions periodically march through on their way to the adjacent Caesar's Palace casino.

8

Las Vegas, of course, is home to numerous themed hotels, but perhaps the quirkiest themed hotel chain is the Peabody group found in Memphis, Orlando and Little Rock in the US. In 1932, the general manager of the Peabody returned to the hotel after a weekend hunting trip. Still a bit tipsy on Jack Daniels, he decided to leave a few of his live duck decoys in the travertine marble fountain located in the lobby. The ducks were such a hit with guests that the hotel fountain has not been fowl-free since. In fact, the ducks have become the hotel's biggest attraction, even drawing celebrities like Oprah Winfrey, Michael Jordan and Jimmy Carter (Galloway, 2011). Daily at 11 am, the hotel's 'Duckmaster' leads five Mallard ducks (one male and four females) down a red carpet to the fountain. The ducks march to John Philip Sousa's King Cotton March as onlookers snap photos and applaud. At 5 pm, the ducks march back to the elevator, which returns them to the rooftop Royal Duck Palace, where guests can also catch a glimpse of them through glass windows during off-hours. The ducks only work at the hotel for three months before retiring to a nearby farm, and a new set is brought in to be trained by the resident Duckmaster. Guests interested in being an honorary Duckmaster can book the Ducky Day package, which includes the privilege of helping the Duckmaster lead the daily march and an official brass-headed Duckmaster cane to take home. The twice-daily march of The Peabody Ducks can also be seen at the Peabody hotels in Orlando and Little Rock.

Even golf clubs have introduced theming to differentiate themselves. The Stoke Park Golf Club in Buckinghamshire, England, has a James Bond theme. The club played host to the most memorable game of golf in cinema history – James Bond's victorious round against Auric Goldfinger in the 1964 film. Bond, played by Sean Connery, was driving his souped-up Aston Martin, which was auctioned off in a charity event at Stoke Park a few years ago. In the film, Oddjob, Goldfinger's caddie, threatened Bond by throwing his steel-lined bowler like a discus and knocking the head off a plaster statue. The statue is still there because the film's producers created a duplicate for the beheading in the movie. The club's marketers exploit the links to the movie by showing clips on their golf course website, and the majority of articles that review the course include a mention of James Bond. VisitBritain included a stay at Stoke Park in one if its 'James Bond South of England Itineraries', promoted to film tourists in 2009 after the release of *Quantum of Solace*. For Bond fans, Stoke Park at one time themed its exclusive Colt Bar to reflect the film *Goldfinger*.

Advances in technology are allowing tourism providers to enhance the servicescape in order to create an interactive educational experience for visitors. An example is the Churchill Museum opened in February 2005, which has a unique electronic 'Lifeline' table which allows visitors to journey through Winston Churchill's extraordinary life. The 18-meter-long Lifeline is a computerized filing cabinet, with a virtual file containing items relating to each year, and, in many cases, each month and day of Churchill's career. Touching the strip at the edge of the Lifeline brings up contextual data, documents, films, photographs and even sound tracks that relate to his life whilst providing historical context. The Lifeline includes 4600 pages, 200,000 words, 100 documents, 1150 images, and 206 animations. Exhibit designers, Casson Mann, are proud of their technological and interactive advances, calling it 'a 21st-century museum about a 20st-century giant'. Designers of the British Galleries at the Victoria & Albert Museum in London, Casson Mann are exhibition, museum and interior specialists, who focus on thoughtful and expert communication. They captivate all of the senses by telling interesting stories in intelligent spaces. They aim, through design, to make people feel wanted and comfortable so that they can do what they came to do. This might be to look at art, take in information, to entertain the children, or to have a discussion, to learn, concentrate or relax.

Finally, servicescapes are being developed to attract new segments of tourists. An upcoming case in Chapter 11 discusses the growth of medical tourism in Asia, where Thailand, Singapore, Malaysia, the Philippines and India are all vying for medical tourists. The hospitals they use really emphasize the servicescape in attracting and caring for patients. Thai facilities for example, have created unique atmospheres using art, music, interior design and haute cuisine more at home in a five-star resort. When it comes to hospital food, they try to create multi-cultural food experiences. With calming spa facilities they integrate body, mind and spirit into the healing process. And the facilities – such as Bumrungrad International

Hospital where 60% of patients are internationals – also incorporate bars, restaurants, shops, currency exchange, tour office, transportation office, internet facilities, laundry and postal service. Patients can choose between standard and royal suites with electronically adjusted beds, multi-lingual cable TV, guest sofa-beds, microwave, fridge, in-room safe and Internet.

Snapshot: Incheon Airport: First and last impressions

Photo courtesy of the Korea Tourism Organization

Airports are becoming increasingly representative of the standard of a country's hospitality and tourism offerings. Responsible for the first and last impressions a visitor gets of a destination – and the only impression for transit passengers – they are pivotal in the tourism experience. In response to this, the trend is for better amenities and better standards of service at airports all over the globe. And some airports are becoming attractions in themselves by providing cultural performances and displays, iconic imagery, theaters, knowledgeable personnel, and artwork and decor reflecting the local culture.

Asia and Europe top the charts for great airports these days with Hong Kong and Singapore Changi Airport in particular vying for best ranking. However, they have faced some stiff competition recently in the form of Korea's Incheon Airport in Seoul which has beaten Singapore for six years running in the ACI's ASQ award. Multi-cultural respondents gave Incheon 4.9 out of 5 in every category. In a Skytrax survey over eight million travelers ranked it number one among 190 airports worldwide and it came out third overall.

8

Since opening in 2001, Incheon has refined its customer service strategy to give passengers a seamless, speedy and enjoyable experience, providing both topnotch service and a stimulating servicescape. It aims to exceed expectations at every stage of the journey with high level service, multi-lingual guides, the fastest arrival and departure processing times and advanced IT and customer feedback systems. As well as serving business and tourism visitors via 70 airlines, the airport is a major hub for Asiana Airlines and Korean Air, attracting many transit passengers.

In terms of amenities, Incheon provides 68 shops, an international and Korean food court, lounges and attractions throughout a kilometer-long terminal. Processing around 30 million passengers per year, the spacious facility is still under-utilized, giving visitors a sense of space and peace not typical for busy airports which usually are struggling to provide enough space for customers. Among the free offerings at Incheon are Internet access, public computers, showers and changing rooms. There is a hot buffet lounge – of a standard usually reserved for first class passengers – accessible to anyone. Transit passengers are treated better than most airports and are offered sightseeing tours (between one and six hours) and golf outings to while away their waiting time.

Incheon is able to provide all these facilities by freeing up time in passenger processing through its customer service program. Its Service Improvement Committee (SIC) is a dedicated taskforce with representatives from every department involved with customer contact. The committee monitors and analyzes performance and meets with the heads of departments such as police, customs and immigration. The SIC has outlined four strategies for a customer service blueprint: standardization; creating value; managing the passenger experience; and exporting Incheon Airport's expertise. Through its standardization policy, Incheon Airport has re-structured and streamlined the entire process from check-in to departure and vice versa, in an attempt to cut processing times down. Typically the average is 60 minutes for departures and 45 minutes for arrivals. Incheon has achieved averages of 16 minutes and 12 minutes respectively.

The re-structuring has led to new training programs, a best practice manual, new multi-lingual signage around the terminal and interactive LCD information screens as part of a u-Cyber Terminal program. Closer cooperation and data sharing has been achieved between customs, immigration and quarantine as well as more active liaison between different airport departments, stakeholders, airlines and outsourcing companies. And an incentive program – whereby 5% bonuses as well as 5% penalties can be applied – has been set up to motivate partner companies in service quality. An innovative passenger number forecasting system established in 2004 has resulted in more efficient passenger processing as well as more appropriate staff relocation during busy periods. The immigration sector has been speeded up by 30% by shifting inspectors between arrival and departure sections.

With all the extra spare time passengers now have within the terminal, Incheon has gone on to provide more facilities and entertainments – particularly for transit passengers – to create value. As well as the free restroom and computer facilities, there are ample rest areas and kids' play spaces. The free Korean Traditional Cultural Experience Centre exposes passengers to local history, customs, traditional dress, instruments and crafts – all interactive. There's also an on-demand cinema with futuristic egg-shaped booths, another two-screen cinema and a video and media art experience in the Transportation Centre. Forward plans include a 1109 square metre skating rink and performance hall with 11 shops.

But Incheon hasn't left it there. It has also addressed quality control. In regard to 'managing passenger experience', Incheon espouses the British Airways model which has shown that only 31% of passengers speak up when they have a problem. To counteract this, Incheon has set up a comment program whereby disgruntled passengers can leave feedback via the 'Voice of Customer' complaint system at 23 main touch points (including text messaging, social media, letters, postcards) and 196 computers in the terminal. This valuable feedback is constantly monitored by the customer service team to help identify and rectify weak points. Customer service executives also 'mystery shop' their staff in order to check on standards.

As part of its promise to disperse its innovative customer service strategy, Incheon recently joined with Hainan's HNA Airport Group in China as consultants on international route development and non-aeronautical revenues. Incheon Aviation Academy was Asia's first designated ICAO training center for the TRAINAIR PLUS program. This program is intended to provide enough qualified and competent aviation professionals to operate, manage and maintain the future international air transport system for the area. Hopefully Incheon's example will start to influence busy airports across the world and improve standards for everyone.

Sources

Lee, J.; McCartney, S. (2011); Grossman, D. (2009); http://www.worldairportawards.com/

8

The effect of servicescapes on consumer behaviour

Consumer researchers know that the design of the servicescape can influence customer choices, expectations, satisfaction, and other behaviors. Retailers know that customers are influenced by smell, décor, music, and layout. Arby's, a fast-food chain in North America, uses the servicescape to position its restaurants as a step above other quick-service outlets. With carpeted floors, cushioned seating, and a décor 'superior' to other fast-food chains, the company asserts that the interior

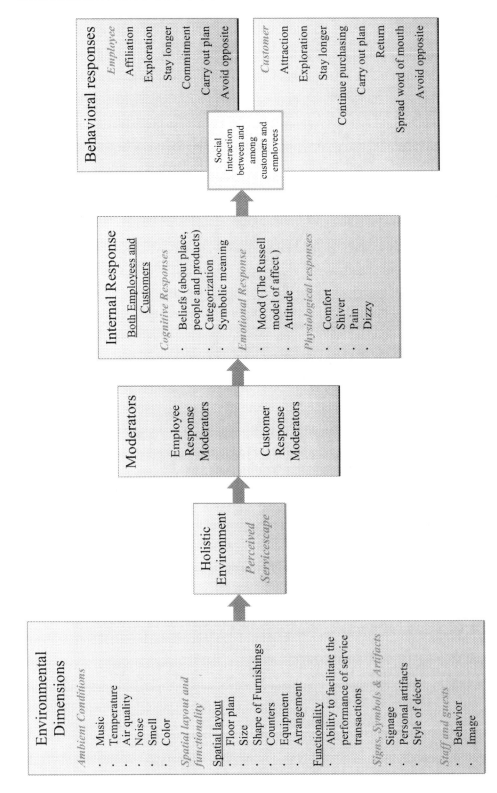

Figure 8.1: How the servicescape impacts consumers and employees (Source: Adapted from Bitner, 2002)

ambience of Arby's outlets contributes to attracting diners. Design of work environments can also affect employees' productivity, motivation, and satisfaction. The challenge in many tourism and hospitality settings is to design the physical space and physical evidence so that it can support the needs and preferences of customers and employees simultaneously.

Bitner (2002) has developed a comprehensive servicescape model which shows the environment and behavior relationships in service settings. This model has been slightly adapted and presented in Figure 8.1. The model has three key elements – environmental dimensions, internal responses, and behavioural responses – all of which will be discussed in turn.

■   Environmental dimensions

Ambient conditions

Ambient conditions refer to the characteristics of the environment that pertain to the five senses. They are composed of numerous design elements that work together to create a desired environment. Even when they are not noted consciously, they may affect emotional well-being, perceptions, and even attitudes and behaviors. The resulting atmosphere creates a mood that is perceived and interpreted by consumers. Ambient conditions include music, temperature, air quality, noise, smell and color. One establishment that understands the importance of ambient conditions in the servicescape is Port D'Hiver, an opulent, five-star bed and breakfast (B & B) at Melbourne Beach, Florida. The accommodation is upscale, a rambling, balconied Victorian property restored and re-appointed with plunge pool, fountains, courtyards and lavish rooms. Breakfast is a bacchanalia of gourmet fare. But they don't just appeal to guests' palates: 'We always try to make sure that all of our guests' senses are engaged from the moment they arrive. From the smell of fresh baked cookies, to music playing and soft lighting when they enter their rooms,' says owner, Mike Rydson. Add to that the aroma of cedar beams, the sounds of the sea and outdoor fountains, crisp high-end sheets, decadent evening hors d'oeuvres and wines and guests really feel like they are being cosseted.

In a service setting music can have a powerful effect on perceptions and behaviors. A number of field experiments have shown the effects music can have on customers. One restaurant study showed that beverage revenue increased substantially when slow-beat rather than fast-beat music was played (Lovelock and Wirtz, 2007). Customers also spent longer in the restaurant if the slower music was playing. Scent is another ambient variable that can permeate a service environment. The opening case showed how Howard Schultz went to great lengths to preserve the smell of coffee in Starbucks stores. At one point he even eradicated the profitable breakfast sandwich because of the smell of melted and burnt cheese that was ruining the coffee aromas for which Starbucks was renowned. He also banned smoking among his employees and asked them not to wear strong perfumes or colognes. Disney is also conscious of the impact of scent. The smell of freshly-baked cookies on Main Street in Disney theme parks is no accident – it is there to relax customers and provide a feeling of warmth as well as igniting their tastebuds. Colors too have a strong effect on people's feelings. Warm colors (red, orange and yellow) are associated with elated mood states, whereas cold colors (blue and green) reduce arousal levels and can elicit emotional responses such as peacefulness, calmness, love and happiness (Lovelock and Wirtz, 2007). Warm colors encourage fast decision making and in service situations are best suited for low-involvement decisions or impulse purchases. Cool colors are favored when consumers need time to make high-involvement purchases. Table 8.2 shows some of the human responses to colors.

Table 8.2: Common associations and human responses to colors (Source: Based on Lovelock and Wirtz, 2007)

Color	Degree of warmth	Common associations and human responses
Red	Warm	High energy and passion; can excite, stimulate, and increase arousal levels and blood pressure
Orange	Warmest	Emotions, expression and warmth; noted for its ability to encourage verbal expressions of emotions
Yellow	Warm	Optimism, clarity, and intellect; bright yellow often noted for its mood-enhancing ability
Green	Cool	Nurturing, healing, and unconditional love
Blue	Coolest	Relaxation, serenity, and loyalty; lowers blood pressure; is a healing color for nervous disorders and for relieving headaches, because of its cooling and calming nature
Indigo	Cool	Meditation and spirituality
Violet	Cool	Spirituality; reduces stress and can create an inner feeling of calm

Spatial layout and functionality

Spatial layout and functionality create the visual and functional servicecape for delivery and consumption to take place. Spatial layout refers to the floor plan, size and shape of furnishings, counters and equipment, and the way in which they are arranged. Functionality is the ability of those items to facilitate the performance of service transactions. Between the two elements, they determined the user-friendliness of the facility to service customers well, and they not only affect the efficiency of the service operation, they also shape the customer experience. Guinness & Co. goes to great lengths to ensure that spatial layout and functionality of pubs deliver the right consumer experience. The company has created a program that supports the launch of authentic Irish pubs by providing advice and resources for entrepreneurs opening and operating pubs, including help with site selection, decor, music and staffing. Because producing the right frothy head for Guinness beer requires care and takes almost two minutes – and is critical to consumers' enjoyment – the company trains the bartenders in pouring techniques. It has even made sure the taps are positioned so that loyal Guinness fans can watch as the beer's foam tops off the glass. And, to guarantee a good product experience for consumers that buy Guinness Draught in cans, the company spent $9 million to engineer and perfect a nitrogen technology that jets a stream of bubbles into the beer when the can is opened, producing the proper thick, creamy head when the can is poured.

Signs, symbols, and artifacts

Signs, symbols, and artifacts are used by service providers to guide customers clearly through the process of service delivery and to teach the service process in as intuitive a manner as possible. Customers become disoriented when they cannot derive clear signals from a servicescape, leading to anxiety and uncertainty about how to proceed and how to obtain the desired service. Examples of explicit signals include signs which can be used to give directions (to the elevators or washrooms, for example), communicate the service script (take a number), and behavioral rules (no smoking, turn off cell phones etc).

Nowhere is signage more important than in an airport. Signs for check-in, security, retail, toilets, gates, transfers, and baggage pick up are important in that they give passengers and visitors guidance. There are a number of companies that specialize in the field of airport signage designs, one of which is GAID from Turkey. When creating signages for an airport, GAID's architects and designers take into consideration and carefully plan the visual surroundings where the signage will be placed. Features such as the background colors on walls, reflection, spacing, windows, lighting and natural daylight, environmental elements and factors are essentially valuable when determining a design for signages in an airport. In a visually crowded environment, it is important that a signage design stands out in its background for maximum effect. Using illumnated signs to enhance readability and vision in airports is very common these days, and more and more airports are experimenting with interactive signs. Dallas and Fort Worth International Airport for example has 11 interactive signs in Terminal D that can be used to find nearby concessions, including shops and restaurants.

Staff and guest behavior and image

Some researchers suggest that the importance of social aspects of the servicescape are often underestimated, and that social variables such as staff behavior and staff image are just as important as tangible elements (Tombs and McColl-Kennedy, 2003; Harris and Ezeh, 2007). These variables have therefore been added to Bitner's original model. Research has shown that the greater the customers' perceptions of staff customer orientation, staff credibility and staff competence, the more likely they are to be loyal to the service provider (Harris and Ezeh, 2007). In addition, Musa and Thirumoorthi (2011) from their study of a popular backpacker hotel in Asia, argue that guest elements such as guest behavior and guest image should be included in any definition of the servicescape.

8

Many customers frequent certain service establishments simply because of the type of people who patronise the place. An example is Abaco, an extraordinarily theatrical and lavish bar in the center of Palma on the Spanish island of Mallorca. Inhabiting the restored patio of an old Mallorcan house, Abaco is filled with ornate candelabra, elaborate floral arrangements, cascading towers of fresh fruit, and bizarre artworks. It hovers between extravagant and kitsch, but the effect is overwhelming and visiting the bar is an experience in itself. Upon opening the door of this bar you are transported to a different world; it feels like you have walked into an ostentatious 17th century Mallorcan house. Atmosphere is low key, with only the sounds of the tinkling courtyard fountain, the songbirds, and classical music in the background. Since opening in 1981, Abaco remains one of Europe's most beautiful and memorable nightspots.

■ Internal responses

Employees and customers in service firms respond to dimensions of their physical surroundings in three ways – cognitively, emotionally, and physiologically – and these responses influence their behaviours in the environment.

Cognitive responses

First, the perceived servicescape may elicit *cognitive* responses, including people's beliefs about a place and their beliefs about the people and products found in that place. 'Handwritten' signs at Starbucks, for example, tend to attract customers by signaling a more authentic experience. One consumer study found that a travel agent's office décor affected customer anticipation of the travel agent's behavior (Bitner, 1990). Research has shown that the servicescape has a direct influence on perceived service quality – particularly for hedonistic services like restaurants (Reimer and Kuehn, 2004).

Emotional responses

In addition to influencing cognitions, the perceived servicescape may elicit *emotional* responses that in turn influence behaviours. The colors, décor, music, and other elements of the atmosphere can have an unexplained and sometimes subconscious effect on the moods of people in the place. Servicescapes that are both pleasant and arousing have been termed 'exciting', while those that are pleasant and non-arousing, or sleepy, are called 'relaxing'. Unpleasant servicescapes that are arousing are 'distressing', while unpleasant, sleepy servicescapes are 'gloomy' (Russell, Ward and Pratt, 1981). Figure 8.2 depicts these feelings experienced in service environments.

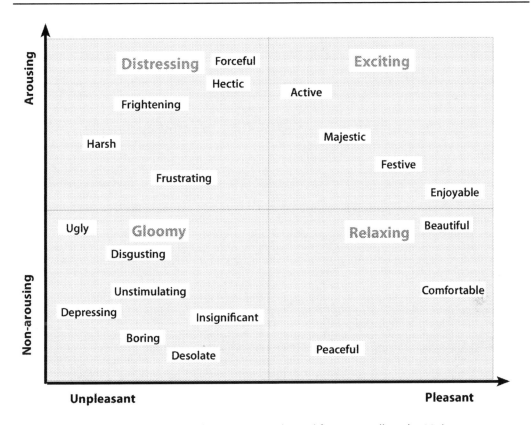

Figure 8.2: The Russell model of affect (Source: Adapted from Russell et al, 1981)

Physiological responses

Finally, the servicescape may affect people in purely *physiological* ways. Noise that is too loud may cause physical discomfort, the temperature of a room may cause people to shiver or perspire, the air quality may make it difficult to breathe, and the glare of lighting may decrease ability to see and may cause physical pain. All of these physical responses will influence whether people remain in and enjoy a particular environment. Music can be particularly important for service providers. A wine store has been found to sell more expensive wine when it is playing classical music than when it plays contemporary music (Areni and Kim, 1993).

In 2004, a Vancouver-based company, Enhanced Air Technologies, developed Commercaire pheromone for the retail sector. The synthetic compound is filtered into a store, and is meant to relax customers so they stay longer and buy more (Brieger, 2004). The company claims retailers can expect revenue growth of between 9% and 20% using the product. While Enhanced Air's sales-stimulating pheromone may be a first, there is a long history of retailers using fake sawdust or fresh bread smells to foster favorable emotions in patrons.

One restaurant in the UK uses sound and smell in a creative fashion to help customers appreciate the food it serves. The Fat Duck in Bray, England, is housed in a 450-year-old pub, and has been awarded three Michelin stars. Owner and Chef, Heston Blumenthal has worked for years with scientists and academics to evolve the restaurant's menu. Increasingly, this means providing nostalgia triggers – using smell to generate emotion, or even headphones to introduce sound – with his tasting menu. Fat Duck's 'Sound of the Sea' signature dish, for example, is made up of seafood (kingfish, kombu-cured halibut, ballotine of mackerel, sea jelly beans, 'edible' sand) served on a box of sand with an iPod in a conch shell playing the sounds of the sea!

Airlines are constantly looking at ways to make long-haul flying more comfortable. Thanks to new technology in Boeing's new 787 Dreamliner, flights are pressured to the equivalent of 6000 feet in elevation, lower than the 8000-foot mark that is typical for commercial passenger aircraft. Boeing says this (coupled with the higher humidity levels possible on the 787) should alleviate headaches, fatigue and reduce the general wear and tear travelers often feel from traveling (Mutzabaugh, 2011). Boeing has also said that the cabin noise on the Dreamliner will be lower than on other jets that typically fly on long-haul routes.

■ Behavioral responses

The internal customer and employee responses discussed above lead to overt behavioral responses such as avoiding a crowded theme park or responding positively to a relaxing environment by remaining there and spending extra money on purchases. At Madame Tussauds waxworks museums, researchers have discovered that customers will stay longer, and have a more satisfactory experience, if they are permitted to touch the exhibits. Most museums have a strict hands-off policy when it comes to their exhibits. At Tussauds, visitors can touch, hug and even kiss the lifelike figures. 'A traditional museum would have ropes up,' said Bret Pidgeon, general manager at Tussauds in Manhattan. 'But this is the closest a lot of people are going to get to an actual celebrity. We allow our guests to get up close and personal' (Klara, 2011). Because of this, the figures – which are made in London and cost up to $200,000 – often get damaged.

As the snapshot in this chapter indicated, airports are going to great lengths in developing elaborate servicescapes in order to change behavioral responses of passengers. Airports today are often noted for their architectural prominence, user features and modern efficiencies. Many are featuring artworks – from Old Masters to contemporary – in order to cast their airport in a positive glow. A Rembrandt hangs in Amsterdam's Schiphol airport, which is home to a branch of the iconic Rijksmuseum. According to spokesperson Kathelijne Vermeulen, the airport museum has seen some very happy travelers. 'Daily we have about 700 visitors', she said. 'And passengers react very positively and enthusiastically' (MacDonald, 2007). Others are putting efforts into the design of commercial areas and stores because the servicescape can have a real impact on passenger spending (Entwistle, 2007).

The importance of aroma was mentioned above, and research suggests that pleasant scents encourage customers to spend more time in the servicescape. This is due to the fact that respiration deepens in the presence of a pleasant aroma whereas unpleasant aroma halts breathing and even causes physical withdrawal (Harris and Ezeh, 2007). Not only do customers stay longer in the presence of pleasant aromas, they also spend more. Studies in the foodservice industry have found that the systematic use of aroma in bakeries increases sales by 300% (Hirsch, 1991).

One recent study of casinos found that customers are more satisfied when they gamble in an attractive physical environment. Their level of satisfaction also affects their intention to revisit the same casinos (Lam et al, 2011). The study found that the dimensions of navigation, ambience and cleanliness are significant predictors of cognitive satisfaction. Navigation also has strong effects on affective satisfaction, but ambience and cleanliness do not. Instead, seating comfort and interior décor are more significant predictors of affective satisfaction. The authors recommend that to create an atmosphere of freedom, comfort and vitality, casino operators should invest more on navigation, ambience and interior décor when building new casinos. Such physical environment relaxes patrons from stress due to gambling, and encourages them to return to the same facilities, which increases gambling revenue.

Waiting line strategies

8

Tourism and hospitality organizations are increasingly aware that today's customers are looking for quick, efficient service with no wait. Organizations that make customers wait take the chance that they will lose their business or, at the very least, make them dissatisfied. It is important therefore to manage the servicescape in order to ensure that waits are kept to a minimum. To deal effectively with the inevitability of waits, Zeithaml et al (2007) suggest that organizations can implement four strategies:

■ Employ operational logic

If customer waits are common, a first step is to try and change the operational process to remove any inefficiencies, as airlines have attempted to do over recent years with self-check-ins. Hotels, too, are streamlining their check-in process; Marriott, for example, allows guests to avoid waiting at the hotel check-in desk altogether. Guests who use a credit card and pre-register can make it from the curb outside the hotel to rooms in three minutes when escorted by a 'guest service associate' who checks the guest into the hotel, picks up keys and paperwork from a rack in the lobby, and then escorts the guest directly to the room. If waits are inevitable, the organization must decide how to configure the queue. Queue configuration refers to the number of queues, their locations, their spatial requirement, and their effect on consumer behavior. Several possibilities exist as shown in Figure 8.3.

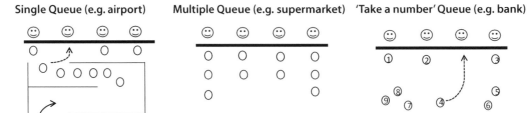

Figure 8.3: Three possible queue configurations (Source: Adapted from Zeithaml et al, 2007)

■ Establish a reservation system

Restaurants, transportation systems and many other service providers use a reservation system to alleviate long waits. Beyond simply reducing waiting times, a reservation system has the added benefit of potentially shifting demand to less desirable time periods. The problem with having such a system is what to do with the 'no-shows'. Some service companies, like hotels and airlines will charge customers who fail to turn up within a given time frame. Others will overbook their service capacity on the basis of past records or no-show percentages.

■ Differentiate waiting customers

On the basis of need or customer priority, some organizations differentiate among customers, allowing some to experience shorter waits than others. Chapter 5 discussed the *Fast Travel* initiative introduced by the International Air Transport Association (IATA) that offers a range of self-service options for passengers in order to speed up the air travel experience. Disney has introduced a virtual queue concept, FASTPASS, developed in 1998, whereby guests could register by computer, go off to enjoy other facilities and then return when their spot was ready. Introduced at five of the top attractions at Walt Disney World in summer 1999, it proved successful enough to expand it worldwide, enhancing the enjoyment for over 50 million visitors per year. Guests are actually given the choice of waiting in the standby line or registering with FASTPASS, giving them an hour's window to wander off. The spin-off has been greater customer satisfaction, more use of less popular rides during the window hour and increased spending per capita in shops and dining facilities. It also takes away the anxiety about how much can be fitted in during the day.

■ Make waiting more fun, or at least tolerable

The type of wait can also influence how customers will react to queuing. In a classic 1985 article entitled *The Psychology of Waiting Lines*, David Maister proposed several principles about waiting, each of which has implications for how organizations can make waiting more pleasurable or at least tolerable. These principles can be seen in Table 8.3.

Table 8.3: The psychology of waiting lines (Source: Maister, 1985)

Occupied time feels shorter than unoccupied time.	In various restaurants, it is common practice to hand out menus for customers to peruse while waiting in line. Apart from shortening the perception of time, this practice has the added benefit of shortening the service time, since customers will be ready to order once they are seated, and will not tie up table space making up their minds.
People want to get started.	One of the other virtues of handing out menus, providing a drinks bar and other methods of service-related time-fillers is that they convey the sense the 'service has started: we know that you are here'. People waiting to make their first human contact with the service organization are much more impatient than those who have 'begun': in other words, pre-process waits are perceived as longer than in-process waits.
Anxiety makes waits seem longer.	Nearly everyone has had the experience of choosing a line at the supermarket or airport, and stood there worrying that he had, indeed, chosen the wrong line. As one stands there trying to decide whether to move, the anxiety level increases and the wait becomes intolerable.
Uncertain waits are longer than known, finite waits	The most profound source of anxiety in waiting is how long the wait will be.
Unexplained waits are longer than explained waits	Most serving personnel are repeatedly asked about the circumstances in waiting situations. The lack of an explanation is one of the prime factors adding to a customer's uncertainty about the length of the wait. Waiting in ignorance also creates a feeling of powerlessness, which frequently results in visible irritation.
Unfair waits are longer than equitable waits	One of the most frequent irritants mentioned by customers at restaurants is the prior seating of those who have arrived later. In many waiting situations, there is no visible order to the waiting line. In situations such as waiting for a subway train, the level of anxiety demonstrated is high, and the group waiting is less a queue than a mob. Instead of being able to relax, each individual remains in a state of nervousness about whether their priority in the line is being preserved.
The more valuable the service, the longer the customer will wait	Our tolerance for waiting depends upon the perceived value of that for which we wait. Airlines have discovered this principle and provided separate lines for those with simple transactions (such as seat selection), medium-difficulty transactions (baggage check-in), and complex transactions (ticket purchase or modification).
Solo waits feel longer than group waits	There is some form of comfort in group waiting rather than waiting alone. This syndrome is evidently in effect in amusement parks such as Disneyland, or in some waiting lines to buy concert tickets when a sense of group community develops and the line turns into almost a service encounter in its own right; the waiting is part of the fun and part of the service. Whatever service organizations can do to promote the sense of group waiting rather than isolating each individual, will tend to increase the tolerance for waiting time

8

Disney has designed a number of different strategies for reducing the perception of waiting. The *Streetmosphere* for example, is a portable entertainment unit which can be moved around different queues. It creates the illusion that the fun has already started, making the line part of the enjoyment and is therefore perceived as a shorter wait time. Providing facilities that enhance waiting conditions also helps counteract dissatisfaction – for example, providing shelter from adverse weather conditions, fitting fans, misters, drinking fountains, toilets, and developing ambient interior design with lighting, palette, temperature, aroma, music, furnishings and layout. During pre-opening tests, Disney found that waiting conditions were compromising customers' enjoyment of the Superstar Theatre at Disney/MGM Studios. They altered the waiting area's temperature and creature comforts to offset this before launching the attraction.

Case Study: Attention to detail at Cavas Wine Lodge, Argentina

Cavas Wine Lodge: Photo courtesy of Cecilia DíazChuit.

Cavas Wine Lodge in Mendoza, Argentina is an idyllic vineyard with an opulent hotel built in the Mediterranean villa style. In the foothills of the Andes, the area is home to around 900 wineries blessed by over 320 days of sun per year. Just 90 minutes flight from Buenos Aires, it attracts wine and culinary tourists as well as those interested in hiking, biking, rafting, horseback riding, year-round golf as well as skiing from June to October.

Cecilia DíazChuit set up Cavas Wine Lodge with her husband, Martín Rigal in 2006. Rigal has academic background in agro-business and marketing and DíazChuit graduated from the Buenos Aires Hotel School. They spent around 18 months with architects Pondal

Malenchini tweaking the design of the lodge. From the outset they were very focused on customer service and getting the servicescape right for maximum impact. 'It was thorough planning as we were building from scratch in a vineyard where there was nothing but vines – enough beauty but no facilities,' says DíazChuit. 'Every aspect of the architecture had to blend in the landscape and have a wow factor. The position of the rooms facing the Andes mountain range, the amount of sun coming into the rooms, the space (the real luxury nowadays), the privacy, the upstairs terrace with a 360-degree view of the endless vineyards. All was important to impress our guests.'

The exterior of building recalls the Spanish and Italian heritage of Mendoza, with a proliferation of patios and rooms which feel totally immersed in the encroaching vineyards. 'We are absolutely surrounded by them, giving each of the 14 rooms, a privileged view and privacy,' says DíazChuit. Designed for comfort and visual impact, the guest rooms are minimalistically furnished with built-in aspects such as concrete bedside tables. The floors, too, are made of concrete with areas separated by arches, exuding an uncluttered, fluid spaciousness. 'We used stone from Mendoza in the bathrooms, many guest have mentioned they would like to change their home bathrooms to look like Cavas's bathrooms – the best compliment,' DíazChuit says. Amid the modernism, history and tradition is maintained with refurbished details such as the 70-year-old bath pipes.

The couple chose bold colors including magenta, bright green and fuchsia as a startling foil to the white linens. They meticulously sourced all fabrics and furniture to complete their vision rather than out-sourcing to interior designers. The impact of this has registered with the guests: 'Our guest comments point out the décor as being unique,' says DíazChuit.

They found music to be one of the more problematic aspects of the servicescape but they learnt a lot through trial and error over the first year. 'We now have a huge music library from soft bossa nova, to sexy modern tango, classical, jazz and international bands. The key here is to find the hotel´s mood,' DíazChuit explains. 'At breakfast time, some classical or soft music, later in the day it can go to crescendo, and playing jazz in the evening matches a chilled glass of Torrontés.'

With great attention to detail, the couple also addressed uniforms for their staff. Bearing in mind the need for durability and practicality, they also had to consider the weather: hot summers, cold winters, and cool mornings in spring and fall. They came up with a color palette to match the area and the vineyards and added an 'Argentine touch' with traditional design features for the front desk vests. The theme worked so well that many visitors buy parts of the uniform as souvenirs.

Objects and works of art have been thoughtfully positioned throughout the elegant lodge accommodation, collected over the 18-month building phase. Based in Buenos Aires at the time, the couple rented a warehouse there as well as a second one in Mendoza, gradually filling them with artwork until construction was finished. 'Having the time allowed us to think of each and every object,' says DíazChuit. Tables for the restaurant were made by local Argentine craftsman, Fernando Moy, who also designed the trendy lobby couch. Salvador Malenchini created the vine chandelier at the entrance to the lodge and they also commissioned him to design the cellar tables.

In order to achieve the most atmospheric lighting in the lodge, the couple hired a theatrical designer, Ruben Amsel. 'He thought out all the indirect lighting in the main building, the rooms and the paths in between the vines – you need to walk under a canopy of 50-year-old vines to get to your room,' says DíazChuit. This is key to the nighttime ambiance of the lodge and was, she says, an important chapter in the planning process.

With any hospitality business, smells are an important aspect of the servicescape. DíazChuit selected a cleaning product with a Kenzo fragrance. 'It smells clean but also fresh. It was presented to us by a local supplier and we have kept it since the opening six years ago. We believe this is Cavas's smell,' she says. To attract locavores and enhance the taste of their food, the couple selects organic fruit and vegetables and local olive oil from the Mendoza region, complemented by their own local wine.

Having established the ideal servicescape, the couple also addresses frontline customer service. They take the time to meet every guest and ascertain their expectations, tailoring each visit to specific needs. 'We like to surprise our guests with a tango evening at sunset or a cooking lesson outdoors,' explains DíazChuit. They encourage guests to take advantage of sunset over the Andes from their terrace with a bottle of their wine. They also take the trouble to select English-speaking drivers for tours around the area's other wineries, making sure they are knowledgeable, friendly and educated. The tours themselves are geared towards small wineries with great attention to detail. 'We combine this with an amazing hike in the Andes and a wine bath in the spa,' says DíazChuit. 'We seek the best experience, effortless for our guests.'

Sources: Personal interview with Cecilia DíazChuit, 2012; www.cavaswinelodge.com

References

Areni, C.S. and Kim, D. (1993) 'The influence of background music on shopping behavior: Classical versus top-forty music in a wine store', *Advances in Consumer Research*, **20**(1), 336-340.

Bitner, M. J. (1990) 'Evaluating service encounters', *Journal of Marketing*, **54**(April), 69-82.

Bitner, M.J. (2002) 'Servicescapes: The impact of physical surroundings on customers and employees', *Journal of Marketing*, **56**(April), 57-71.

Brieger, P. (2004) 'The whiff of a shopping spree', *Financial Post*, 1 & 10.

Ching-Ching, N. (2007) 'Flying the beautiful skies', *The Calgary Herald*, 9 December, E2.

Entwistle, M. (2007) 'Customer service and airport retail: Stimulate passenger spending', *Airport Management*, **1**(2), 151-157.

Galloway, L. (2011) 'Worldwide weird: Make way for marching ducks in Memphis', *BBC Travel*, 27 September. Accessed 03/14/2012 from http://www.bbc.com/travel/blog/20110927-worldwide-weird-make-way-for-marching-ducks-in-memphis

Grady, J. and Ohlin, J.B. (2009) 'Equal access to hospitality services for guests with mobility impairments under the Americans with Disabilities Act: Implications for the hospitality industry', *International Journal of Hospitality Management*, **28**, 161–169.

Grossman, D. (2009) 'Why can't all airports be like Incheon?', *USA Today*. Accessed 03/07/2012 from http://www.usatoday.com/travel/columnist/grossman/2009-06-16-incheon-best-airport_N.htm

Harris, L.C. and Ezeh, C. (2007) 'Servicescape and loyalty intentions: An empirical investigation', *European Journal of Marketing*, **42**(3/4), 390-422.

Hirsch, A.R. (1991) 'Nostalgia: A neuropsychiatric understanding', Paper presented at the Annual Meeting of the Association for Consumer Research, Chicago, IL, October.

Jones, C. (2009) 'Delta brings back Red Coats to help with customer service', *USA Today*. Accessed 11/14/2011 from usatoday.com

Klara, R. (2011) 'Waxing eloquent. Behind the scenes at Madame Tussauds', *USAir Magazine*, December, 42-46.

Lam, L.W., Chan, K.W., Fong, D. and Lo, F. (2011) 'Does the look matter? The impact of casino servicescape on gaming customer satisfaction, intention to revisit, and desire to stay', *International Journal of Hospitality Management*, **30**, 558-567.

Lee, J. (2011) 'Nothing Compares to You: Incheon Airport sets the global standards for customer service excellence', Incheon Airport 10th Anniversary Special Report. Accessed 03/02/2012 from http://content.yudu.com/A1rks6/Incheon/resources/index.htm?referrerUrl-

Lin, IY. and Matilla, A. S. (2010) 'Restaurant servicescape, service encounter and perceived congruency on customers' emotions and satisfaction', *Journal of Hospitality Marketing & Management*, **19**(8), 819-841.

Lovelock, C. and Wirtz, J. (2007) *Services Marketing: People, Technology, Strategy*, 6th edition, New Jersey, USA; Prentice Hall International.

MacDonald, D. (2007) 'The fine art of flying', *The Globe and Mail*, 24 October, R13, R15.

McCartney, S. (2011) 'The World's Best Airport', *The Wall Street Journal*, Personal Journal, D1 and D3

Maister, D. (1985) 'The psychology of waiting lines', in J.A. Czepiel, M.R. Solomon, and C.F. Surprenant (Eds.), *The Service Encounter*, Lexington, MA: Lexington Books, pp. 113-123.

Musa, G. and Thirumoorthi, T. (2011) 'Red Palm: Exploring service quality and servicescape of the best backpacker hotel in Asia', *Current Issues in Tourism*, **14**(2), 103-120.

Mutzabaugh, B. (2011) 'First Dreamliner fliers sing its praises', *USA Today*, 28 October, 1B-2B.

Reimer, A. and Kuehn, R. (2004) 'The impact of servicescape on quality perception', *European Journal of Marketing*, **39**(7/8), 785-808.

Russell, J. A., Ward, L. M. and Pratt, G. (1981) 'An affective quality attributed to environments', *Environment and Behaviour*, **13**(3), 259–288.

Strauss, M. (2011) 'Less Tolstoy, more toys', *The Globe and Mail*, 9 April 2011, B6.

Schultz, H. (2011) *Onward*, Rodale Inc. New York, NY 10017

Thompson, C.J. and Arsel, Z. (2004) 'The Starbucks Brandscape and Consumers' (Anticorporate) Experiences of Glocalization', *Journal of Consumer Research*, **31**, 631-641

Tombs, A. and McColl-Kennedy, J. R. (2003) 'Social-servicescape conceptual model', *Marketing Theory*, **3**(4), 447-475.

Venkatraman, M. and Nelson, T. (2008) 'From servicescape to consumptionscape: A photo-elicitation study of Starbucks in the New China', *Journal of International Business Studies*, **39**, 1010-1026

Zeithaml, V. A., Bitner, M. J., Gremler, D., Mahaffey, T. and Hiltz, B. (2007) *Services marketing: Integrating customer focus across the firm*, Canadian Edition. New York: McGraw-Hill.

 Scan here to get the hyperlinks in this chapter

9 The Impact of Technology on Customer Service

as well as their customers: 'Virgin Atlantic is about fun, energy, pioneering, and a love of flying. We try to live our brand when communicating with customers.' He believes that social media can enhance engagement with consumers if planned and executed in the correct way. 'Engagement must add value or else the customer will lose interest,' he says.

Bradley has been a pioneer of online marketing for over fifteen years. He is an innovator and risk-taker, intent on keeping the company up to speed with – and even ahead of – new developments in tourism marketing. First for Britain's South West Tourism, next for VisitBritain and now for VAA, he is a trailblazer for social media marketing and service. He showed his perspicacity when he espoused 'film tourism' marketing for VisitBritain, leveraging films such as *The Da Vinci Code*, *Casino Royale* and *Elizabeth* for their positive brand reinforcement. Recruited in 2010 by VAA to lead its North America marketing team, Bradley continues to explore new marketing opportunities across a range of online, social and mobile channels.

However, it is not all about advertising. 'Social media has been a game-changer not just for marketing strategies but for the way consumer brands operate,' says Bradley. 'We have certainly stepped up our advertising activity on social channels but only where it is appropriate and relevant to customers. But this really isn't about how budget is divided. It is more about how a brand thinks and the extent to which it moves from being campaign-centric to conversation-centric.'

With its commitment to honesty, value and caring, VAA is using social media to resolve issues, help customers and provide meaningful communication. Virgin's Facebook page includes travel tips from its 'vtravelled' blog – insider information which adds value for the consumer as well as appearing to be honest, informal and caring. The vtravelled site is dedicated to inspirational journeys with customers leading the conversation, exchanging information, stories and advice. Virgin launched it in order to address the extensive planning that consumers are faced with when going on a big trip. Although it does lead to some sales, this site is mainly intended as a brand reinforcement tool which also provides new customer insights.

But social media marketing and customer service cannot just be left to chance; it needs customer relationship management with an emphasis on keeping in character. Virgin Atlantic has a three-member team which monitors and responds to customer feedback from social media channels. 'These comments are captured by social media monitoring software which we also use to share real time customer response and sentiment with the business,' Bradley explains. 'For instance during the introduction of our new economy meal service in November, we encouraged customers on the first flights to share their feedback with us on Twitter which could be captured and reported back to the team managing our product enhancement.'

As keynote speaker at the B2C (Business-to-Consumer) conference, Bradley explained the importance of being genuine and credible on social media in order to create a trusting relationship with the customer. Trust is mainly based on dependable service delivery but when things go wrong, communicating with customers can prevent trust from eroding. During the volcanic-ash crisis in 2010 when hundreds of flights were grounded all over Europe, Virgin had difficulty keeping pace with the rapidly-changing situation on its website, so it turned to Facebook and Twitter to communicate instant updates to its customers.

Bradley realizes that marketers have less control over consumers' brand perceptions on sites such as Twitter and Facebook but he maintains that the consumer is no longer content with traditional advertising messages. Using these more informal means of communication is both more immediate and friendly. 'Our social media strategy was born out of the opportunity social networks gave us in terms of customer service,' he says. 'We knew customers wanted to make contact with us and we see social media as another means to have a conversation with them. Social media is one area where we are able to assist people with questions in real time and that really empowers customers to engage fully with the brand.'

With consumers driving trends in communication, Bradley has noticed a fragmentation of media. 'Consumers are now in the driving seat. They choose where they want to get information from and which brands they want to engage with,' he says. 'This is particularly apparent online where a fundamental change in the engagement dynamic is taking place as customers move from visiting many brand-owned sites to engaging with a small number of platforms and receiving feeds from their favorite sources.'

In order to service this more fragmented arena he suggests a shift towards a conversational approach and away from campaign-driven, traditional advertising. He advocates keeping up with the constantly evolving social media landscape in order to stay relevant to customers and retain avenues for 'meaningful conversation' with them. Social media is giving VAA an opportunity to gather insights into changing consumer needs, allowing them to make timely service improvements. For example, in response to online-community suggestions, it launched a system to arrange taxi sharing for airport transfers with other passengers from the same flight. Fresh insights from social media also reinforce the innovation aspect of the brand as well as improving brand strength and durability.

Ultimately, Virgin Atlantic's social media strategy is not revenue-driven: 'For us, long haul air travel is a carefully considered purchase and the key strengths of social media are driving engagement, continued loyalty and brand preference,' says Bradley. 'We do know through surveying our frequent travelers that those who follow us on Facebook or Twitter are more likely to recommend us to a friend or colleague than those that don't. Alongside this we also have hard metrics such as traffic, revenue and conversion on virgin-atlantic.com.'

Sources: Personal Interview with Simon Bradley, April 2012; Barwise and Meehan (2010); Bradley (2011)

The impact of technological developments on communication

In 1999, Steven Spielberg convened a three-day think tank to gather insights from 23 top futurists for the making of his sci-fi thriller *Minority Report* which depicted the world of 2054. The goal was to create a realistic view of a plausible future. Projecting out from the present day's marketing and media technologies – Web cookies, GPS devices, Bluetooth-enabled cell phones, TiVo personal video recorders, and barcode scanners – the filmmakers gave shape to an advertising-saturated society where billboards call out to you on a first-name basis, cereal boxes broadcast animated commercials, newspapers deliver news instantly over a broadband wireless network, holographic hosts greet you at retail stores, and biometric retina scans deduct the cost of goods from your bank account.

The technologies portrayed in the film were far from science fiction (Mathieson, 2002), and today many are in use or are in development – an indication of the rapid pace of technological progress. Wireless newspapers and magazines that stream news updates – like the *USA Today* seen in the film – are extensions of 'digital paper' technologies currently being developed. Meanwhile, today's GPS and wireless network technologies are close to the place-based, personalized advertising that provides a backdrop for the film's city scenes. GPS-based technologies are used by wireless carriers to target ads to users in specific locations; and new Wi-Fi based Location Enabled Networks (LENs) carve up a wireless network into discrete segments that target users passing through a specified location. As users pass access points, content can be served up based on their position. Of course, for all their commercial potential, these technologies are not free of ethical considerations – a point the movie drives home with a heavy hand. However, what we are witnessing is a rapidly changing communications environment dominated by digital technology – and Spielberg's futuristic world is already upon us.

The marketing communications environment has changed enormously in the last decade. Technology and the Internet have fundamentally altered the way the world interacts and communicates. Traditional approaches to branding that put emphasis on mass media techniques are less and less effective in a marketplace where customers have access to massive amounts of information about brands, product and companies and in which social networks have, in some cases, supplanted brand networks (Keller, 2009).

In the new media environment, consumers are increasingly in control. Not only do they have more choices of media to use, they also have a choice about whether and how they want to receive commercial content. In response, marketers are employing more varied marketing communications techniques than ever before. To communicate effectively and efficiently, tourism marketers have to go where the consumers are – and this is increasingly online. There were over two billion Internet users in 2011, up from one billion in 2005, 420 million in 2000, and

45 million in 1995. Two-thirds of the population in North America and Europe regularly go online. Much of current and future Internet user growth is coming from populous countries such as China, India, Brazil, Russia and Indonesia. The travel sector itself boasted annual online sales of almost $100 billion in 2012, around a third of all global e-commerce activity (Carey, Kang and Zea, 2012).

The Internet has upended how consumers engage with brands to the extent that consumers are promiscuous in their brand relationships (Edelman, 2010). They connect with myriad brands through new media channels often beyond the marketer's familiarity or control. In the past, marketing strategies emphasized brand awareness and ultimate purchase. However, after purchase, consumers may remain aggressively engaged, actively promoting or assailing the products they have bought, and collaborating in the brand's development. The touch points when consumers are most open to influence have changed, requiring a major adjustment to realign marketers' strategy and budgets with where consumers are actually spending their time.

Using technology to improve service during the consumer decision journey

The Internet has fundamentally changed the consumer decision process. In the past, marketers assumed that consumers started with a large number of potential brands in mind and methodically narrowed their choices until they had decided which one to buy. After purchase, consumer relationships with the brand typically focused on the use of the product or service only. This traditional purchase funnel is depicted in Figure 9.1.

Court et al (2009) have introduced a more nuanced view of how consumers engage with brands (see Figure 9.2). They developed their model from a study of the purchase decisions of nearly 20,000 consumers across five industries and three continents. Their research revealed that rather than systematically narrowing their choices until they had decided what to buy, consumers add and subtract brands from a group under consideration during an extended evaluation stage.

9

Figure 9.1: The traditional purchase funnel

After purchase, they often enter into an open-ended relationship with the brand, sharing their experience with it online through social media. The four stages of the consumer decision journey are: 1) consider; 2) evaluate; 3) buy; and 4) enjoy, advocate and bond. As consumers progress through the four stage decision journey, consumer-driven marketing – word of mouth, online research, offline and/or print review – has increasing impact (Court et al, 2009). Social media make the 'evaluate' and 'advocate' stages increasingly relevant. The following section shows how tourism marketers are using technology to engage with consumers at every step of this journey.

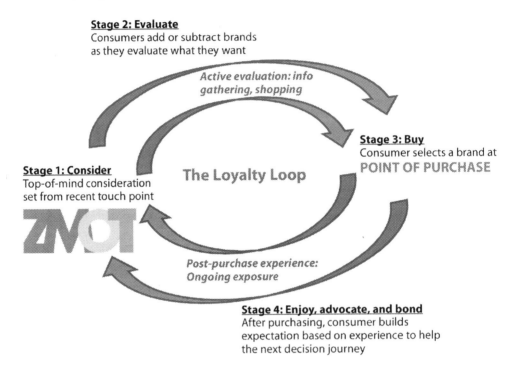

Figure 9.2: The consumer decision journey today (Source: Adapted from Court et al 2009)

■   Stage 1: Consider

The journey begins with the consumer's top-of-mind consideration set: product, services or brands assembled from exposure to ads, a store display, an encounter at a friend's house, or other stimuli. In the funnel model, the consider stage contains the largest number of brands; but today's consumers, assaulted by media and awash in choices, often reduce the number of products they consider at the outset (Edelman, 2010). Off-line channels such as television advertising, in-store browsing and direct word of mouth are at their most influential at this stage, but as the consumer moves from consider to evaluate, the Internet plays an increasingly important role. The model proposed by Court et al has been modified slightly to include the 'Zero Moment of Truth' (ZMOT) a term coined to describe the new reality where marketers have to compete for shoppers' attention online long before a purchase decision is made (Lecinski, 2011).

According to marketing experts, the success factors for marketing tourism on the web include the following: attracting users, engaging users' interest and participation, retaining users and ensuring that they return, learning about user preferences, and relating back to users to provide customized interactions. Research that has looked at content of web pages suggests that it is crucial that content is accurate, attractive, and easily searchable. Interactivity is also an imperative, as the very behavior of consumers changes when they log onto the Internet. They not only search for information but also expect interaction and entertainment. A positive experience on the website increases the time spent at the site and therefore increases the dollar amount spent. According to research, when the first few pages of a website elicit greater pleasure, consumer approach behavior and exploration improves (Menon and Kahn, 2002). One study of customer satisfaction with e-service quality found that online businesses should focus on website design, reliability and security, and customer service (Chang, Wang and Yang, 2009). The website's search function, download speed and organization all need to be considered. Offering diversified contact channels is important so that customers can easily and efficiently communicate with the vendor.

Harris and Goode (2010) have developed a model that links the online service-scape (or the e-servicescape as they call it) with website trust and purchase intentions (see Figure 9.3). They suggest that online physical environments comprise three multi-faceted dimensions – aesthetic appeal, layout and functionality, and financial security. A test of the model found that consumer perceptions of these online dimensions (measured through nine factors) exert a powerful, direct influence over trust that, in turn, is associated with consumers' purchase intentions.

Social media campaigns are increasingly being used at this early consideration stage to drive traffic to websites. For example, in 2011, VisitBritain targeted the Gen Y audience in the US, Canada and Australia on Facebook through its 'Unite the Invite' campaign. Followers of VisitBritain's Facebook and Twitter pages, called Love UK, were invited to register for a Unite the Invite app. Each applicant was asked to upload a picture of himself and was sent the photo of another random registrant, which he was asked to upload to his Facebook wall and encourage his Facebook friends to share so that he could locate his match on the social network. The fastest pair to 'unite their invite' each won a trip for two to the UK. The campaign's goal was to drive traffic to the Love UK Facebook page, where visitors would see digestible chunks of interesting and quirky news about British culture. Twelve thousand people entered Unite the Invite and the Love UK Facebook page gained 25,000 fans during the campaign, according to VisitBritain (Birkner, 2012).

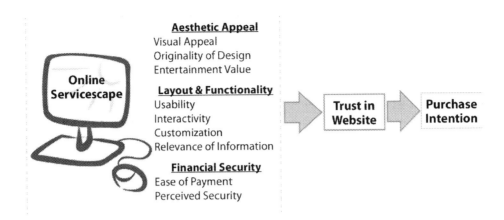

Figure 9.3: A model linking e-servicescape, website trust, and purchase intentions (Source: Adapted from Harris and Goode, 2010, p. 232)

Inviting consumers to upload photographs and videos is a popular social media tactic to generate awareness. In Cape Town, South Africa, destination marketers used social media to engage with potential visitors in a campaign associated with a music video. At the end of 2011, English rock stars Coldplay filmed their music video for the hit single *Paradise* in Cape Town, where the filming was encouraged and supported by the Ministry of Economic Development and Tourism. Understanding the importance of the video in attracting future visitors to Cape Town and the global coverage it would receive, the City and Provincial authorities prioritized the relevant permissions for filming, and ensured the production ran as smoothly as possible. South African Tourism (SAT) then launched a tactical campaign – *My SA Paradise* – to leverage the popularity of the hit single. It took out advertising space on the YouTube video page of 'Paradise', and created a My SA Paradise page on Facebook, through which it ran an online competition. SAT invited people to upload photographs and videos of their South Africa paradise and enter to win a trip around South Africa hosted by SAT.

Twitter is increasingly being used as a stand-alone marketing tool to generate awareness for a tourism product or service. The Virginia Tourism Corporation (VTC) won a marketing award in 2009 for a wine tourism promotion called 'Vintage Tweets' – a cutting-edge public relations effort that utilized social media to promote wine tourism in Virginia. VTC organized Vintage Tweets in September of 2009 in Arlington to kick off October Virginia Wine Month. The state tourism agency used Twitter to target media, bloggers and consumers – all of whom were passionate about wine travel, lived in and around Washington, DC, and had significant numbers of Twitter followers. VTC used Twitter to invite 40 of those consumers to a wine reception, featuring six different wineries from across the state. The guests tweeted about their wine tastings and also took part in Virginia Wine Travel Twitter trivia. In total, Vintage Tweets was able to reach over 43,000 consumers in just 24 hours, providing key facts and travel ideas to potential visitors from across the country.

■ ## Stage 2: Evaluate

At the evaluation stage, consumer outreach to marketers and other sources of information is much more likely to shape their ensuing choices than marketers' efforts to persuade them. One study of a specific model of a television for example, found that at the evaluation stage, consumers didn't start with search engines; rather, they went directly to Amazon.com and other retail sites that, with their rich array of product-comparison information, were becoming the most important influencers (Edelman, 2010).

Blogging websites can be an effective tool to reach consumers during this evaluation stage. South Africa is not alone in prompting consumers to become digital ambassadors for their brands. A well-known example occurred in 2009 when Tourism Queensland embarked on a global search to find an Island Caretaker to explore the Islands of the Great Barrier Reef in Australia and report back to the world about their experiences via a blogging platform. The campaign was called the 'Best Job in the World.' With a salary of $155,000 on offer, over 34,000 would-be caretakers from Azerbaijan to Zimbabwe and everywhere in between uploaded a 60-second video showing their creativity and skills. The job went to 'ostrich-riding, bungee-jumping' charity worker Ben Southall from Hampshire in England, who was still, two years later, reporting via blogs on his adventures. The campaign generated $80 million of global publicity for an investment of just $1 million (Sweney, 2009).

By giving out an opportunity to win a free vacation, marketers involved with these types of campaigns create excitement, interest and commitment among competitors and hope to raise awareness of their destination by generating free media coverage. In 2009, the Orlando Convention & Visitor's Bureau initiated a 67 Days of Smiles contest, promising two lucky winners the chance to visit Orlando for 67 days. The idea was that it would take a tourist 67 days to experience everything the Orlando area has to offer. Kyle and Stacey were chosen for the job and recorded their trip on a 67 Days of Smiles blog. By the end of their experience, the Days of Smiles website had recorded over 67,000 hits and their Twitter account had almost 1000 followers. The traveling duo was also featured by several media outlets including the New York Times.

Offering virtual tours is one way of allowing customers the ability to evaluate a service before purchasing, and many destinations offer potential visitors the ability to take virtual tours of an extensive selection of places. Golf courses for example, often provide virtual tours of their courses. One such product is the Heli Golf Guide that is based on PGA-style hole-by-hole video. Using low-flying aerial footage combined with ground level footage, professional narration and music, Heli Golf Guide creates videos for each individual course. Heli Golf Guide is a division of Blue Coconut Media Inc based in Ontario, Canada, and also makes videos that showcase entire resort properties – a useful tool for selling events, memberships and real estate.

9

Having a presence in an online virtual world is another opportunity for marketers to showcase services. An example is Second Life, an online world with a million registered users and a thriving virtual economy. Second life allows its users to create a new, and improved, digital version of themselves. 'Residents' can buy land, build structures and start businesses. The service is fast becoming a three-dimensional test bed for corporate marketers, including Sony BMG Music Entertainment, Sun Microsystems, Nissan, Adidas, and Toyota. Retailers have set up shops to sell digital as well as real world versions of their products, and musicians can even promote their albums with virtual appearances. Starwood Hotels and Resorts created an elaborate digital prototype for a new chain of hotels called Aloft before the first real hotel opened in 2008. Projects like Aloft are designed to promote the venture but also to give its designers feedback from prospective guests. Futurists predict that by 2020, people will spend a large amount of time in virtual-reality worlds in which they will compete, socialize, relax, be entertained and do business. This will likely have an impact on business travel. Virtual meetings and events doubled in value from 2008 to 2009 and the industry is expected to grow to $18.6 billion by 2015, a 56% annual growth rate from 2010 (Global Futures and Foresight, 2011).

Online brand communities can be another effective online tool at this evaluation stage. Brand communities are defined as 'specialized, non-geographically bound communities, based on a structured set of social relationships among admirers of a brand' (Bagozzi and Dholakia, 2006: 45). The emergence of brand communities has coincided with the growth in consumer empowerment. They are venues where intense brand loyalty is expressed and fostered, and emotional connection with the brand forged in customers. Research on such communities has found that commitment to a brand can be influenced (positively) by encouraging interactions with groups of like-minded customers and identification with the group in social context offered (and sponsored) by the firm and the brand, but controlled and managed primarily by the consumers themselves. A challenge in building and managing online brand communities is that consumers can easily associate marketers' efforts with extrinsic motives of profit exploitation and thus become less likely to engage with, and contribute to, such a community (Algesheimer, Dholakia and Herrmann, 2005; Lee, Kim and Kim, 2011). One possible solution is to develop a platform of online brand communities encouraging consumers to share and exchange their ideas voluntarily rather than imposing the organization's own ideas, such as sales coupons or sweepstakes. This implies that marketers should employ a passive role when facilitating brand communities.

A good example of this passive engagement in a brand community is the Walt Disney World Moms Panel. This is a forum where online 'Moms' answer questions and offer advice about family vacations to Disney. The 'Moms' are selected to be panelists because they have demonstrated an excellent knowledge of Disney products. Being familiar with the Parks, resort hotels, dining and entertainment, shopping, and recreational activities, they can offer the help and tips consumers need when planning their vacations. As Leanne Jakubowski, who oversees the program, says 'It is important that the Moms Panel is made up of real guests and represents a diverse spectrum of thoughts and perspectives so we can offer honest, heartfelt and useful information' (Walt Disney World, 2011). Panelists receive a trip to the Walt Disney World Resort for their participation and in 2012 the Panel boasted 43 panelists whose expertise spanned Walt Disney World Resort, Disney Cruise Line, Disney Vacation Club, Adventures by Disney and Disneyland Resort offerings. The Moms Panel offers guests vacation insights on a variety of platforms including exclusive 'How-To' videos from panelists and celebrities, dedicated Facebook content, personal Disney Parks Blog posts and in-park meet-ups.

■ Stage 3: Buy

Point of purchase – which exploits placement, packaging, availability, pricing, and sales interaction – is an ever more powerful touch point. For tourism marketers, however, this 'buy' stage is often likely to occur online, given that the travel sector accounts for around a third of all global e-commerce activity (Carey, Kang and Zea, 2012). When customers are buying online, they want to find their desired products easily and complete the order efficiently (Chang, Wang and Yang, 2009). Website owners also need to pay high attention to privacy and security; customers will only shop online when they perceive it is safe to transmit private information.

One recent study found that the leading factor in determining great customer service is speed of delivery (STELLAService, 2010). This may not often apply to tourism and hospitality websites, as they are not delivering physical products, but the helpfulness of customer service representatives and the ease of access to information on a website are also at the top of the list for important elements of service for online transactions (see Figure 9.4).

For many tourism marketers, social media platforms are fast becoming more than a customer relationship tool. Many hotels, for example, now offer room-booking technology on their Facebook pages, which is leading to incremental sales (Blank, 2011). Westin Hotels & Resorts for example, introduced in 2011 a 'Shop' tab on its properties' Facebook pages. The shopping widget serves as a fully contained shopping transaction, instead of working as a link from Westin's website. Bolongo Bay Beach Resort in St. Thomas, US Virgin Islands, also sports a unique, free-standing booking engine on its social-networking site; an engine that has proved to be very successful. Fairmont and Omni Hotels & Resorts are two examples of chains that tweet or Facebook last-minute special offers in hopes of unloading their un-booked inventory.

9

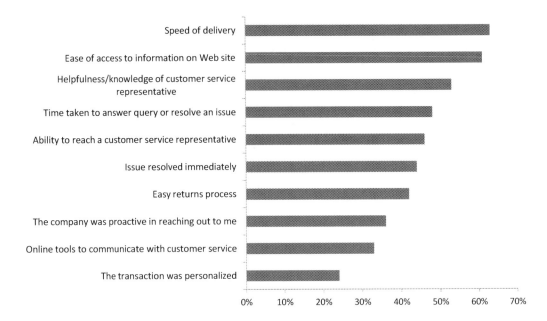

Figure 9.4: Leading factors for great customer service online (STELLA Service, 2010, p. 5)

■ Stage 4: Enjoy, advocate, and bond

Interestingly, after purchase, a deeper brand connection begins as the consumer interacts with the product and with new online touch points. For example, Court et al (2009) found that more than 60% of consumers buying facial skin care products conduct online research about the products *after* purchase – a touch point not entirely captured in traditional purchaser funnel models of communication.

Vail Resorts has capitalized on this 'enjoy, advocate, and bond' stage with its new EpicMix social media campaign profiled in the case study at the end of this chapter. Hotels, too, are leveraging technology to provide additional customer service after the purchase stage. An increasing number of them are employing virtual concierges in addition to the human type. Many upscale brands, for example, offer location-specific information accessible via the Internet, iPhone apps and even live chats. Intercontinental Hotels in 2007 began creating videos starring individual hotel concierges offering destination-specific advice. The majority of the brand's 170 or so hotels have now created videos, which are available on each hotel's website and on YouTube and iTunes. In 2010, Marriott International Renaissance hotels introduced a program called Navigator that offers suggestions for dining, drinks, shopping and sightseeing. This information, generated by Wcities, an online destination content provider, and by hotel employees, can be found on each hotel's web page and on an iPhone app.

Other hotels are distributing iPads and similar devices to customers in an effort to tap the buzz surrounding tablet computers. Using third party software developers, they are introducing apps to order food, browse hotel amenities and local attractions, request wake-up calls, schedule housekeeping, message other guests, and arrange car services. In embracing the digital format, hotels can quickly update menu changes and deliver up-to-the-minute information about facilities and deals. The Phoenician in Scottsdale Arizona, for example, sells a 'Dinner on the 9th green' package through its app.

One relatively new social media platform that is helping tourism and hospitality businesses engage with consumers at this final stage of the consumer decision journey is the emergence of geo-location sites such as Foursquare, Gowalla and Loopt. Foursquare encourages consumers to broadcast their whereabouts (or 'check-in') in exchange for discounts or coupons, etc. Foursquare recently hit one billion check-ins (Mogg, 2011). People use the Foursquare app on their smartphones to check in to places like restaurants, pubs and hotels, and just about any other type of physical and even nonphysical location. Once they check-in, users often share that information with friends, families and followers on Facebook and Twitter. Foursquare users compete for badges, points, and 'mayorships', awarded to those who check in to a place most frequently. Business owners claim their venue on Foursquare (for free) and reward people simply for checking in, for checking in a certain number of times, for checking in with friends, or reward the person who checks in the most (the 'mayor'). For example, Chili's Grill & Bar, a national restaurant chain in the US, rewards its customers with free chips and salsa every time they check in. Chili's makes money on the deal because customers don't walk into Chili's just for free chips and salsa and leave. They order appetizers, entrees and drinks.

Brand communities were mentioned as important influencers in the evaluation stage of the consumer decision journey, but because brand community members have a strong interest in the product and in the brand, they can also be a valuable source of innovation. In a study of brand community members, research found that the stronger the identification with the brand, and the higher the brand trust, the more likely a consumer was willing to contribute to open innovation projects initiated by a brand. This activity has been called 'crowdsourcing', a term coined in 2006 by *Wired* magazine's Contributing Editor, Jeff Howe (Sullivan, 2010). Crowdsourcing-led innovation means opening the door to allow customers, employees, or the general public at large into the innovation process to help improve products, services or marketing efforts. Consumers get a direct line to the company and the opportunity to steer offerings to reflect their needs better, while companies benefit from getting more insights, opinions and wisdom that can be translated into actionable innovation ideas for less money than a typical R&D initiative. Dell, for example, created an online venue called IdeaStorm to give customers a central location where they could share ideas with the company. In the first three years, IdeaStorm crossed the 10,000 idea mark and implemented nearly 400 ideas.

As mentioned in Chapter 6 Virgin Atlantic Airways uses social media opportunity to gather insights to drive continual incremental improvements (Barwise and Meehan, 2010). The opening spotlight explained how, in response to online-community suggestions, VAA launched a system to arrange taxi sharing on arrival with passengers from the same flight. Fresh insights from social media also reinforce the innovation aspect of the brand. Facebook interactions helped the company appreciate the extensive planning that goes into a big trip, so they launched vtravelled, a site dedicated to inspirational journeys. Customers moderate the conversation and exchange information, stories, and advice. The site leads to some sales, but, as Simon Bradley asserts in the opening spotlight, its main benefit to VAA comes from brand reinforcement and new customer insights.

Another airline in Europe, Estonia Air, recently launched an online crowd-sourcing campaign 'My Estonian Air' to solicit ideas on airline innovations and improvements. The project proved an immediate success with more than 300 responses received the day the website was launched. While initial feedback covered aspects of company style or culture as well as overall direction, Estonia Air began issuing weekly themes to gain more focused as well as in-depth feedback from travelers. Although the website's primary goals were to solicit ideas and establish expectations, secondary functions proved just as important, namely the ability to interact and explain company rationale for specific decisions as well as sell the company and services to customers.

In an interesting spin-off from crowdsourcing, an Australian startup has developed a human-powered budget website called FlightFox. Amateur travel agents called 'flight hackers' compete for a nominal (starting at $29) finder's fee to identify the lowest available online airfares. While the traveler must pay the finder's fee when booking the 'winning' or lowest priced flight, the website claims average savings of around $350 per flight, although the savings and websites itself are apparently geared more toward long-haul and international flights.

Other tourism organizations are using social media at this final stage to respond to consumer complaints. Southwest Airlines for example, which has 1.2 million Twitter followers, has a team of ten staff from communications and customer relations which monitors the account from 5am to 11pm, hours in which the airline operates (Holmes, 2011). At least one person from each unit monitors the account, fielding questions about lost baggage, delayed flights and misplaced drink coupons. If someone tweets a complaint to @SouthwestAir, the reply may come from the team: 'So sorry to hear about your lost luggage. Have you filed a claim? Any progress yet?'

Service Snapshot: Barbados leveraging social media to attract medical tourists

Barbados Fertility Clinic. Photo Courtesy of Veronica Montgomery

A great example of the adoption of new technology for interacting and engaging with perspective tourists comes from Barbados, one of many countries seeking to attract the growing and lucrative medical tourism segment. The Barbados Fertility Clinic (BFC) uses augmented reality and interactive TV to demonstrate to prospective medical tourists that BFC is a cutting-edge center of excellence for fertility treatment – treatment that costs the medical tourist an average of $5,750. An active social media strategy compliments these activities to drive business to the clinic. For example, in a three-month period of 2011 the company reached 93,789,951 people through Facebook and Google paid searches in the UK and the US – one million people a day – resulting in 12,613 new patient enquiries in the same time period. The clinic has found that fertility patients are very keen to get more information and interact online, so in 2011 they launched a Fertility application for iPhone and iPad for couples who have decided to start a family.

Despite the small size and population of Barbados, the BFC was established in April 2002, combining traditional medicine with holistic therapy for locals and, more importantly, medical tourists. This combination, says Marketing Manager, Veronica Montgomery, helps facilitate the relaxation of patients. The tropical location is another stress-reliever: 'Given the negative impact of stress on fertility treatment and our tropical location, it seemed a perfect fit for patients to come to Barbados, unwind in the natural beauty of the island, then undergo IVF,' Montgomery explains.

Patients are greeted at the airport and taken by luxury vehicle to their choice of accommodation before being presented with a full itinerary of clinical appointments and holistic therapies, such as acupuncture, reflexology, massage and a session with a counselor

9

trained in dealing with the negative emotions associated with IVF. 'We have always tried to be at the top of our game and pride ourselves on finding new techniques to improve every couple's chance of success,' says Montgomery. 'We believe the combination of de-stressing, leaving their everyday lives and the pressures of work, and undergoing holistic treatments means that our patients are at their optimum to receive fertility treatment.' Patients are also treated individually and offered tests and medications not necessarily available in their home countries.

To disseminate information about this cutting-edge treatment, the BFC also has to be forward-thinking in its marketing. The message it wants to convey, says Montgomery, is 'that there is an easier way to go through IVF treatment and that it can even be an enjoyable experience.' To facilitate this, it launched The Fertility App for iPhone and iPad in October 2011. This includes an ovulation calendar and advice on pre-conception sup-plements and recommends that if a couple has failed to conceive after 12 months they should seek medical advice. 'The calendar also alerts the patient of which medication to take when, with push notifications – again reducing stress,' says Montgomery. It features healthy lifestyle tips, a full medical glossary of medical terms, treatments and medication. Couples can confer directly with the medical team, speak to other patients in the support forum and connect with the clinic via social media channels.

The app was officially launched at the Fertility Show in London in November 2011 with an iPad giveaway each day as well as iPad demonstrations of the interactive TV and augmented reality messages. 'Augmented reality is similar to QR codes: you hold the device (in our case an iPad) over a trigger image – the same as you would with a QR code – except the trigger was a palm tree,' Montgomery explains. Virtual images are then launched including an animation of a beach to emphasize the relaxing environment, an animation of the cutting edge technology used to achieve a pregnancy at the clinic and also an animation of someone doing yoga, highlighting the clinic's 'Healthy Mind Body Program'. 'These were the three key messages that we wanted patients to leave our stand with,' Montgomery says. 'We also had a flat graph of success rates, which was the trigger to launch animated graphs and figures to come to life.'

Another attraction on the BFC stand was an information video (for use on an iPad) layered with interactive buttons. Montgomery says that IVF patients are 'very information hungry' so the clinic tries to give them as much information as possible including specifics about the treatment, explanations about IVF, success rates, etc. 'All these interactive buttons take them out of the video to a website and when they are done, they resume the video where they left it,' she explains. The high-tech approach has really helped demonstrate to prospective patients how the Barbados Fertility Clinic differs from other facilities.

As part of its digital advertising strategy, the clinic utilizes 'pay per click' sponsored words on Google. It also targets patients in the UK, Canada and the US by city: 'We target patients who have direct flights to Barbados and, more specifically in the UK. We target patients who are looking for donor eggs as there is such a shortage since new laws mean that UK donors are no longer anonymous,' says Montgomery.

The BFC Facebook page has now been 'liked' by thousands of readers: 'This is very much our patient community of prospective patients with current and past patients talking to one another with us leading the conversation,' Montgomery explains. She says that the digital campaign has been really effective, resulting in around 4000 new patient enquiries per month. 'This has been the most transparent form of advertising for us and is where the majority of our marketing budget is now spent,' she adds.

Statistics show that on average 36 % of Americans talk about health care per day. A growing number are doing this online, particularly teens and the 20-30 age-group. Interest in social media in the health care sector has been increasing, along with expectations and budgets for leveraging the advertising and marketing potential.

Sources: Interview with Veronica Montgomery May 2012; Pirovano (2011)

Delivering service through electronic channels

As more aspects of everyday life converge toward digital, opportunities for tourism organizations to interact with consumers expand dramatically. Social media and new mobile phone technologies give companies unprecedented access to data on customer interaction, while the technologies are changing the nature of the interactions themselves. Given the speed of technological development, it is likely that self-service facilities will continue to evolve and will play an even more important role in service delivery than they do currently (Beatson, Lee and Coote, 2007). Table 9.1 summarizes some of the advantages and disadvantages of electronic distribution of services.

Table 9.1: Advantages and disadvantages of electronic distribution of services.

Advantages	Disadvantages
Consistent delivery for standardized services	Privacy and ethical issues
Low cost	Inability to customize with highly standardized services
Customer convenience	Security concerns
Wide distribution	Competition from widening geographies
Customer choice and ability to customize	Price competition
Quick customer feedback	Loss of control over the consumer evaluation process
Potential for building customer relationships	Keeping abreast of changes in technology
Vast amounts of consumer data	Ability to data mine

On the positive side, using electronic channels overcomes some of the problems associated with service inseparability and allows a form of standardization not previously possible in most services (Zeithaml et al, 2007). This method of delivery can also be more cost-effective for organizations, and they can reach a wide distribution much more efficiently. Investment in self-service technology can result in increased speed of delivery and customization of the service delivery process; reduced labor costs through less staff contact; increased productivity through fewer staff and opening hour restrictions; improved competitiveness; and differentiation through a technological reputation (Beatson, Lee and Coote, 2007). Jetstar, for example, was promoting its Automatic Check-in service in 2011 as the first Australian complete and consistent self-service check-in. Jetstar CEO Bruce Buchanan said, 'removing the check-in process altogether is another example of a Jetstar innovation improving the air travel experience for its customers' (FlightCentric, 2011).

Technology also allows organizations to provide 24-hour, 7-day service response to customers. In fact, the main reason consumers have adopted the Internet is that it enables them to shop 24/7 in the comfort of their home with no time zone worries. Many consumers, too, are looking to build relationships on the web. Godin introduced the concept of permission marketing (Godin, 1999), in which consumers volunteer to be marketed to on the Internet in return for some kind of reward. This type of marketing uses the interactivity offered by the web to engage customers in a dialogue and, as a consequence, in a long-term interactive relationship. Permission marketing is based on the premise that the attention of the consumer is a scarce commodity that needs to be managed carefully. Its emphasis is on building relationships with consumers instead of interrupting their lives with mass marketing messages.

Computer software and Internet reservations systems like OpenTable and Rezbook have pushed restaurant service to another level, allowing them to amass a trove of data with ease. Because of advances in technology, many restaurants are tracking their customers' individual tastes, tics, habits and even foibles (Craig, 2012). Increasingly they are recording whether you are a regular, a first-timer, someone who lives close by, or a friend of the owner or manager. Even a single visit to somewhere like the RedFarm in New York can prompt the creation of a computer file that includes diners' allergies, favorite foods and whether they are wine 'whales', likely to spend hundred of dollars on a bottle of wine. That is valuable information, considering that upward of 30% of a restaurant's revenue comes from alcohol.

Customers – whether they be restaurant patrons or airline passengers – are willing to adopt technology because it gives them a wider choice, allows them to customize and makes the buying process more convenient. Research has shown, for example, that business travelers have a positive perception towards hotel e-commerce and IT applications (Yeh et al, 2005). They are willing to pay for the convenience of using a hotel's e-commerce facilities, and they prefer to shop the Internet for a better deal in terms of price. In fact, business travelers will be more satisfied and tend to be more loyal with a hotel if e-commerce and IT applications are implemented. However, self-service technology makes it difficult for organizations to establish suitable service recovery strategies in the event of service failure (Beatson, Lee and Coote, 2007). The potential loss of interpersonal contact may also lead to a loss of social bonds and a lack of up-selling opportunities.

There are other challenges associated with service delivery and technology. One such challenge facing online marketers is the concern over security and privacy. Social media websites, for example, remain one of lowest-scoring categories of websites when it comes to customer satisfaction. User concerns about privacy, including being targeted for advertising, continue to be problematic for these websites (ACSI, 2011). In 2011, the social media category earned a score of 70 on the American Consumer Satisfaction Index's (ASCI) 0 to 100 scale. Wikipedia topped the social media category with 78, benefiting from its non-profit position that allows users to surf, create, and edit content without intrusion from commercial messages. Google-owned YouTube came in second place with 74, while Facebook scored a low 66. Facebook is facing intense scrutiny from consumers, courts and regulators worldwide about how it handles the data it collects from its 845 million users (Sengupta, 2012). The scrutiny is at its most intense in Europe: a proposed Europe-wide law requires Facebook, along with every online business, to expunge every bit of personal data at a consumer's request.

Another disadvantage of electronic distribution for tourism marketers is the fact that the Internet has made it easy for customers to compare prices for a wide variety of services. One customer-driven pricing strategy that has increased in popularity due to the Internet is the reverse auction. Travel e-tailers, such as Priceline.com, Hotwire.com, and Lowestfare.com, act as intermediaries between prospective buyers, who request quotations for a product or service, and multiple suppliers who quote the best price they are willing to offer. Buyers can then review the offers and select the supplier that best meets their needs.

A further downside to the proliferation of online social networking for tourism and hospitality companies is the loss of control over the consumer evaluation process (Kim and Hardin, 2010). While reasonable criticisms taken from social networking sites could lead to further improvements in services, consumers can easily distribute damaging information using social media, without the opportunity for companies to resolve consumer complaints. Tourism and hospitality companies can counteract this by implementing their own social networking sites where customer reviews can be more closely monitored. Marriott Hotels has assigned full-time personnel to monitor customers' reviews and to generate daily reports. A recent study found that few hotels are actively managing their reputation on sites such as TripAdvisor. Despite a facility to respond to criticism, few hotels use this option on the TripAdvisor site, calling into question how seriously hotels are managing user-generated content (O'Connor, 2010).

Staying abreast of rapid changes in technology can also present its problems. Marcos Van Aken conference manager for Ten Travel (see spotlight in Chapter 5) has the challenge of keeping up with changes in technology on a small island. Due to its remote location, Tenerife is not as advanced as mainland Europe or the US when it comes to IT. When Ten Travel was planning conferences and incentives for Microsoft in 2010, Van Aken had to work swiftly with the local telephone company to get WiFi into all the delegates' rooms and the common areas. 'When 250 delegates all came out of their conference and switched on their computers, of course the WiFi went down. But over the next few hours we got it sorted out,' says Van Aken. 'These are the kind of challenges we get here when the client comes from overseas and the island isn't necessarily culturally up to date.' Having diverse contacts with local services and businesses is vital in coping with these types of problems quickly.

Finally, the data analysis (or data mining) is both a challenge and an opportunity for tourism marketers in the digital era. Travel companies have access to mind-boggling data: everything from basic personal information to preferred airline seats, in-flight entertainment preferences, favored television channels in hotels, meals in restaurants, and credit card usage. They have the means to paint detailed pictures of consumers that will drive marketing initiatives to engage them deeply. Yet few of them truly maximize the potential of the data at their disposal (Carey et al, 2012). Those in the travel sector could follow the example of Amazon, who became the thorn in the side of every bookseller by mining data to craft individualized customer experiences full of conversion-ready streams of recommendations. Disney Destinations has turned to Merkle, an independent customer relationship marketing agency, to help leverage the information it knows about the millions of Facebook users who are fans of Walt Disney World and Disneyland theme parks based on other interactions with them, such as visits and digital trip planning applications. On Facebook, Walt Disney World has more than 7.3 million fans, and Disneyland has more than 10.6 million fans (Steel, 2011).

Case study: Vail Resorts using apps to enhance the customer experience

In the old days of providing customer service, something as insignificant as a ski lift pass would not really have provided managers with much opportunity. It used to be a scrap of paper, attached to a jacket with a metal or plastic clip, flapping in the wind and getting caught on tree branches and other obstacles, but needing to be visible to lift attendants. However, with modern 'smart card' technology, ski resorts all over the world are using lift passes for all manner of conveniences including easy access to ski lifts without having to take it out of a pocket and doubling it up as a resort credit card.

Photo courtesy of Vail Resorts

Vail Resorts in the US has gone even further with its EpicMix technology. Each season pass or multi-day lift ticket has a built-in radio frequency ID chip, and can be used at all seven Vail Resorts ski hills and kept year after year for re-use. The lift pass, in the form of a hard plastic card, can remain in a pocket all day. It can be loaded with money or linked to credit card details for resort spending. Furthermore, it can be hooked up to an EpicMix ski app, enabling the user to log runs, lifts taken, and vertical mileage. There are also challenges to take part in around the resorts with 'pins' awarded for various achievements. The EpicMix account can be loaded with personal photos and also used to load free professional photos taken by EpicMix photographers stationed around the resorts. It acts as a trail map and a GPS to hook up with friends and family around the mountain, too. Guests can also use and access the technology without smart phones, by visiting the online site www.epicmix.com

EpicMixers can collate all this information with the Mountain Remix feature into a computerized collage of their day and transmit it instantly by Facebook, Twitter and email to all their contacts. The strategy behind all this is two-fold: 1) to provide the consumer with as much added value as possible for their ski pass and 2) get priceless engagement and advertising via an enhanced social media presence for Vail Resorts. Not only has the social media presence increased dramatically, it has been achieved by candid and credible consumers promoting the product themselves and not directly by Vail Resorts marketers.

The innovative idea has also captured the attention of prominent travel and ski journalists resulting in many articles in magazines and newspapers including the prestigious travel section of the Los Angeles Times, Skiing magazine and Denver's Huffington Post. Furthermore, the app has secured Vail Resorts coverage in more unusual outlets for a ski company such as Mashable, CNET, Wired, Popular Mechanics, FastCompany, and other tech focused publications. Launching the service, Vail Resorts CEO Rob Katz said 'We want to make a change in how people experience the mountains. Our mission is to give people the experience of a lifetime.'

According to Vail Resorts the idea behind their high-tech trendsetting is to encourage story sharing about skiing and snowboarding experiences. Robert Urwiler, CIO Vail Resorts, was a co-creator of EpicMix. 'Capturing memories on mountain is a big part of the experience and being able to share with friends and family is particularly important on a ski vacation,' Urwiler explained. In the past those amateur pictures were often compromised by adverse factors such as weather conditions, lighting, lack of skill and inability to ski with the requisite equipment.

Around 15% of Vail Resort guests used EpicMix during its first season (2010/11), creating 275,000 social posts and 35 million social impressions from 55 billion vertical feet of skiing and snowboarding – all in real time. 'We've been very surprised who it attracts – it's been all ages,' said Urwiler. The most vertical feet last season was clocked up by 'Charles A', who is in his sixties. 'This kind of brand exposure is hard to match right now,' Urwiler said. 'We are essentially creating brand advocates.' He considered it a great return on investment, calling it a strategic investment and discretionary marketing spend. The Word of Mouth Marketing Association agreed – they awarded Vail Resorts a gold 2011 Wommy award for the most effective mobile campaign.

Vail Resorts are real pioneers in this field, combining indirect marketing with customer service and added value. Ski resorts have traditionally charged for photographic services on the hill and usually don't provide any action shots. Vail Resorts saw the value in advertising spin-offs of providing photos for free in order to encourage skiers and snowboarders to send out more professional-looking tweets and Facebook photos of themselves. Vail Resorts was also the first ski hill to use its lift pass system as an app. They have created their own resort blogs about EpicMix with information as well as testimonials from consumers.

As Urwiler says, it is not just youthful skiers and riders who are taking advantage of such techie toys in Vail, Beaver Creek, Keystone, Breckenridge, Heavenly, Northstar and Kirkwood. All age groups are enthralled with tracking stats, outdoing previous performances and crowing to their office-bound buddies back home about their skiing experiences. And it is attracting locals as well as tourists. Beaver Creek tour guide, John Merritt loves his EpicMix app, using it to track mileage during his complimentary resort tours as well as during free skiing with the Vail Club 50. 'I spent a whole day trying to do all the lifts at Vail to get the pin but didn't quite make it as I missed the lower half of one of the village gondolas,' he said. 'It's fun to have the challenge and I see people of all ages using it.'

Once skiers and riders start using the app, it seems they become hooked. Ski Independence rep, Victoria Thurlby (33) says she's addicted to it and so are her British guests. 'We all check our mileage even before we take off our ski boots,' she said. Thurlby, a former freestyle competitor, skis with all the local Vail hotshots, the token girlie among the macho group. Her best vertical so far is 40,288 feet in one day. Jason Plante, a 22-year Vail veteran, is one of her ski buddies, also obsessed with the app. A regular heli-skier, Plante (44) is not above tracking his on-piste progress, aiming for that 50,000 feet pinnacle.

Sources: Interviews with Robert Urwiler, John Merritt and Victoria Thurlby February 2012; Hudson (2011); Lewis (2010)

References

ACSI (2011) 'Social media websites struggle with customer satisfaction', *ACSI Commentary* July 2011. Accessed 03/06/2012 from http://www.theasci.org.

Algesheimer, R., Dholakia, U.M. and Herrmann, A. (2005) 'The social influence of brand community', *Journal of Marketing*, **69**, 19-34.

Bagozzi, R. and Dholakia, U. M. (2006) 'Antecedents and purchase consequences of customer participation in small group brand communities', *International Journal of Research in Marketing*, **23**(1), 45-61.

Barwise, P. and Meehan, S. (2010) 'The one thing you must get right when building a brand', *Harvard Business Review*, **88**(12), 80-84.

Beatson, A., Lee, N. and Coote, L.V. (2007) 'Self-service technology and the service encounter', *The Services Industries Journal*, **27**(1), 75-89.

Birkner, C. (2011) 'Sharing the LOVE', *Marketing News*, **45**(3), 20-21.

Blank, C. (2011, March 28) 'Facebook leads to hotel revenue', *HotelNewsNow.com*. Accessed 04/13/2012 from http://www.hotelnewsnow.com

Bradley, S. (2011) 'Virgin Atlantic: Long-Haul Social Media Strategies', presented at Marcus Evans B2C Marketing Summit, 7-8 Nov 2011, Colorado Springs, CO.

Carey, R., Kang, D. and Zea, M. (2012) 'The trouble with travel distribution', *McKinsey Quarterly*, February.

Chang, H.H., Wang, Y-H. and Yang, W-Y. (2009) 'The impact of e-service quality, customer satisfaction and loyalty on e-marketing: Moderating effect of perceived value', *Total Quality Management*, **20**(4), 423-443.

Court D., Elzinga, D. Mulder, S. and Vetvik, O.J. (2009) 'The Consumer Decision Journey', *McKinsey Quarterly*, June. Accessed 11/17/2011 from https://www.mckinseyquarterly.com/The_consumer_decision_journey_2373.

Craig, S. (2012, September 5) 'Getting to know you', *New York Times*, D1, D5.

Edelman, D. (2010) 'Branding in the digital age', *Harvard Business Review*, **88**(12), 62-69.

FlightCentric (2011) 'Jetstar goes fully self-service', *FlightCentric*. Accessed 04/25/2011 from http://www.aviationrecord.com.

Global Futures and Foresight (2011) 'The Futures Report 2011,' report prepared by Global Futures and Foresight, Kingston upon Thames, UK.

Godin, S. (1999) *Permission marketing*, New York: Simon & Schuster.

Harris, L.C. and Goode, M.M.H. (2010) 'Online servicescapes, trust, and purchase intentions', *Journal of Services Marketing*, **24**(3), 230-243.

Holmes, E. (2011, December 9) 'Tweeting without fear', *Wall Street Journal* (New York, NY), p. B1.

Hudson, L (2011). 'Technology at ski resorts offers skiers info, images of day on slopes', Los Angeles Times. Accessed 12/11/2011 from http://www.latimes.com/travel/la-tr-tech-20111211,0,7911087.story

Keller, K. (2009) 'Building strong brands in a modern marketing communications environment', *Journal of Marketing Communications*, **15**(2/3), 139-155.

Kim, J. and Hardin, A. (2010) 'The impact of virtual worlds on word-of-mouth: Improving social networking and servicescape in the hospitality industry', *Journal of Hospitality Marketing & Management*, **19**(7), 735-753.

Lecinski, L. (2011) *Winning the Zero Moment of Truth*, Published 5 August 2011 in Knowledge@Wharton

Lee, D., Kim, H. and Kim, J. (2011) 'The impact of online brand community type on consumer's community engagement behaviors: Consumer-created vs. marketer-created online brand community in online social-networking web sites', *CyberPsychology, Behavior & Social Networking*, **14**(1/2), 59-63.

Lewis, M. (2010) 'Vail Resorts' CEO on new Epicmix application', Transworld Business. Accessed 03/30/2012 from http://business.transworld.net/46344/features/vail-resorts-ceo-on-new-epicmix-application/

9

Mathieson, R. (2002) 'The future according to Spielberg: *Minority Report* and the world of ubiquitous computing', *Mpulse Magazine,* August. Accessed 10/05/2011 from http://www.rickmathieson.com/articles/0802-minorityreport.html

Menon, S. and Kahn, B. (2002) 'Cross-category effects of induced arousal and pleasure on the internet shopping experience', *Journal of Retailing,* **78**(1), 31-40.

Mogg, T. (2011) 'Foursquare hits a billion check-ins, looking forward to the next quadrillion', *Digital Trends,* 20 September. Accessed 03/05/2012 from http://www.digitaltrends.com/mobile/foursquare-hits-a-billion-check-ins-looking-forward-to-the-next-quadrillion/

O'Connor, P. (2010) 'Managing a hotel's image on TripAdvisor', *Journal of Hospitality Marketing & Management,* **19**, 754-772.

Pirovano, D. (2011) 'Interest and Activity in Social Media Intensifying Across All Health Care Sectors'. Accessed 07/12/2011 from http://www.holmesreport.com/opinion-info/9923/Interest-and-Activity-in-Social-Media-Intensifying-Across-All-Health-Care-Sectors.aspx

Sengupta, S. (2012) 'Risk and riches in user data. Scrutiny of Facebook threatens its top asset', New York Times, 27 February, B1.

Steel, E. (2011) 'Facebook's brand of loyalty', *Wall Street Journal,* 3 October, B9.

STELLA Service (2010) *The Value of Great Customer Service: The Economic Impact for Online Retail and Other Consumer Categories.* Accessed 09/07/2011 from http://media.stellaservice.com/public/pdf/Value_of_Great_Customer_Service.pdf

Sullivan, E. (2010) 'A group effort', *Marketing News,* 28 February, 22-28.

Sweney, M. (2009) 'Best job in the world' campaign storms Cannes Lions advertising awards', *The Guardian,* 23 June. Accessed 03/25/ 2012 from http://www.guardian.co.uk/media/2009/jun/23/best-job-advertising-awards

Walt Disney World (2011) 'Love sharing your knowledge of Mickey's California crib? Raced around every attraction at Walt Disney World Resort?' *PRNewswire,* 12 September, Lake Bueba Vista Florida. Accessed 02/02/2012 from http://multivu.prnewswire.com/mnr/disneyparks/48532/

Yeh, R.J., Leong, J.K., Blecher, L. and Wei-Tang, H. (2005) 'Analysis of e-commerce and information technology applications in hotels: Business travelers' perceptions', *Asia Pacific Journal of Tourism Research,* **10**(1), 59-83.

Zeithaml, V. A., Bitner, M. J., Gremler, D., Mahaffey, T. and Hiltz, B. (2007) *Services Marketing: Integrating Customer Focus across the Firm,* Canadian Edition. New York: McGraw-Hill.

 Scan here to get the hyperlinks in this chapter

10 The Importance of Service Recovery

'At your service' Spotlight: Paul Hudson - solving problems for travelers

Paul Hudson has a wealth of experience solving problems for travelers. Having worked in the travel industry for more than 30 years, Hudson has held previous roles as Head of Overseas Operations at Neilson Active Holidays, Product Development Manager at Cosmos Holidays, and Regional Manager Spain and Winter-Ski operations at First Choice Holidays. Hudson is currently Operations Director at Luxury Family Hotels, where he is responsible for the operation of eight hotels in the UK recently purchased from the Von Essen Group.

Hudson realized the importance of service recovery very early on in his career. 'When I worked as a travel representative, and my customers had a problem with the hotel or the airline, I got sick of these companies passing

Paul Hudson, Luxury Family Hotels. Photo Courtesy of Paul Hudson

the buck and saying 'it is not my problem'. The problems could easily have been solved but they couldn't be bothered. I decided that as soon as I was in a position to manage the supply chain, I would make sure these things didn't happen.'

Hudson acknowledges that many problems in the travel industry are unforeseen and/or uncontrollable. 'Naturally there are myriad examples in tourism where holidays or flights get overbooked. Most of the time, though, you try to train staff to do things that they don't have to do but that they want to do to keep everyone happy. I encourage staff not to wait until the problem arises, but to anticipate the issue. For example, if you are a waiter you have to look around for people who have not been quickly served and if you see someone who has been waiting for too long, you go and offer them a free drink before they even get the chance to complain.'

One problem Hudson had to deal with a few years ago was a forest fire in Greece that disrupted the holiday of his guests. 'Basically we had a forest fire in Greece behind one of our hotels and had to evacuate everyone, which was quite a scary experience for them. We put them all up in another hotel and when everything was under control some people stayed and went back to the hotel but others were too traumatized and preferred to travel home. So my team went to those who were going to fly back home and invited them to come back a few weeks later for another trip for free. We had no obligation to do this but it was a gesture that they appreciated when they came back for another visit. I feel that the feedback and the word of mouth was more than worth it.'

How does Hudson train his staff in the art of service recovery? 'We use case studies, many of them real-life, role plays, and letters of complaints, and then ask them "what would you have done to solve this?" We also look at previous complaints and learn from them. I try and get my staff to encourage guests to tell us everything about their holiday experience – both good and bad - so that we can learn from it.'

Hudson believes that although empowerment is critical, employees have to work within a framework when making decisions on service recovery: 'It is no good throwing money at a problem without working out what the problem was in the first place and how to prevent it in future. It is also important to find out what the customer values in a service, and exactly what we can do to put a problem right. For example, it would be foolish to give a free night's accommodation for a whole family if just one meal was cold in the restaurant. And there is no point giving the customer a free bottle of wine if he/she doesn't drink. A free swimming lesson for the kids might be the perfect remedy, and it costs us very little.'

Hudson encourages his staff to think outside the box in terms of what value they can add. 'You have to work with each particular guest as they all perceive things differently. At the end of the day, they should always go one step further – solve the problem and go a bit extra. It is not always a question of money – experiences, such as a free ride on a speedboat are sometimes valued more by the customer. Our adage is 'Fix it, plus one' – blow the customer away without costing too much money. Buy them a bottle of champagne after they have already bought the wine so they are still paying their usual amount but you give them something extra. We sometimes ask our suppliers to help. For example, we had a problem in our New Forest hotel, and we knew the family wanted to go to Beaulieu, so we got them tickets. Free for us but huge value for the customer. It is all about knowing your customer – interacting with them so you can surprise them.'

Source: Personal interview with Paul Hudson, July 2012

Service recovery

Service delivery failure is likely to occur at some point in time for organizations in the tourism and hospitality industry. Though it is unlikely that businesses can eliminate all service failures, they can learn to respond effectively to failures once they do occur, as is shown in the opening spotlight. This response is often referred to as service recovery, defined as the process by which a company attempts to rectify a service delivery failure. One study of hotel customers found that their level of satisfaction and lasting impression of a hotel is based first and foremost on what happens when something goes wrong (Johnston, 2004). Mostly, customers accept that mistakes happen; the problem begins when there is no strategy in place to rectify the situation easily.

Despite the significance of the tourism sector both economically and as a source of customer complaints, there has been little research that explicitly addresses complaining behavior and service recovery. Research that does exist is relatively recent and still evolving. In the tour operating sector, Schoefer and Ennew (2004) examined customer evaluations of tour operators' responses to their complaints. They found that even when a firm recovered effectively from a service failure, satisfaction was not guaranteed, which is at variance with results reported by other researchers like Smith and Bolton (1998). In the hospitality industry, Lewis and McCann (2004) focused on service failure and recovery in the UK hotel industry, finding that guests who were satisfied with the hotel's response to their problems, were much more likely to return than those who were not satisfied with recovery efforts. Leong, Kim and Ham (2002) studied the impact of critical incidents of service failures and recovery efforts in a hotel, finding that only complete resolution results in repeat patronage, while partial resolution and unresolved service failures served as a deterrent to the guest's return patronage. O'Neill and Mattila (2004) presented findings from a survey of 613 hotel guests indicating that guests' overall satisfaction and intention to revisit were much higher when they believed that service failure was unstable and recovery was stable. Finally, the influence of service recovery on satisfaction and revisit intention was also stressed by the study of Yavas et al (2004).

In the restaurant sector, Hoffman, Kelley and Rotalsky (1995) examined service failures and recovery strategies commonly occurring in the industry, and Leong and Kim (2002) focused on recovery efforts in fast-food restaurants, finding that reasonable care in providing a service failure resolution that meets the customer's expectation may influence customer loyalty. Lastly, Sundaram, Jurowski and Webster (1997) investigated the impacts of four types of service failure recovery efforts in restaurant service consumption situations that differ in the degree of criticality. They argued that the importance of the situation to the consumer plays a significant role in their responses to service failure recovery efforts.

10

The service recovery paradox

Some researchers have suggested that customers who are dissatisfied, but experience a high level of excellent service recovery, may ultimately be even more satisfied and more likely to repurchase than those who were satisfied in the first place (Hart, Heskett and Sasser, 1990; McCollough and Bharadwaj, 1992). This idea has become known as the service recovery paradox (see Figure 10.1). There are somewhat mixed opinions on whether a recovery paradox exists, but customer complaints about defective services may represent an opportunity for the company to improve its image and perceived quality since it permits the company to make a positive correction or to resolve the complaint (Albrecht and Zemke, 1985; Grönroos, 1990; Heskett, Sasser and Hart, 1990).

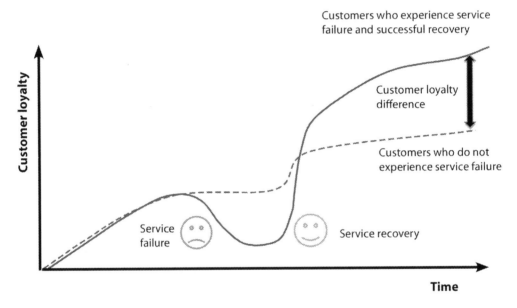

Figure 10. 1: The service recovery paradox (Source: Adapted from Schindlholzer, 2008)

McCollough, Berry and Yadav (2000) tested the service recovery paradox for airline passengers, finding that customer satisfaction was lower after service failure and recovery than in the case of error-free service. Hudson and Moreno-Gil (2006), however, found that hotel customers in Spain who had experienced a recovery encounter, perceived a higher level of service quality for intangible attributes (assurance, trust, reliability, responsiveness, and empathy), than non-complaining customers, supporting, to some extent, the service recovery paradox. The results showed that resolving customer problems related to intangible aspects of the service in a hotel has a strong impact on perceived service quality and thus customer satisfaction. Sousa and Voss (2009) studied service recovery in an e-commerce setting and also found a recovery paradox effect but only for a small proportion of 'delighted' customers: those who perceived an outstanding recovery. They concluded that despite not being a viable strategy in general, delighting customers in the recovery may make sense for profitable customers.

But given the mixed opinions on the extent to which the recovery paradox exists, 'doing it right the first time' is the best and safest strategy in the long run.

The service recovery process

Every tourism and hospitality organization should have a systematic plan for winning back customers who have been disappointed by some facet of service delivery. One such plan is proposed by Zemke and Schaaf (1989) which is a five-step procedure.

1 Apology

The process of service recovery begins with an apology. As Isadore Sharp from the Four Seasons says: 'Whatever the issue, making it right starts with a sincere apology' (Sharp, 2009: 232). Once an organization accepts that failure sometimes occurs, it can instill in its employees the necessity of extending a genuine apology when a customer is disappointed. This simple act can go a long way to framing the customer's perception of his value to the organization and helps pave the path for subsequent steps to regain goodwill (Fisk, Grove and John, 2000). One restaurant study found that recovery strategies that included personal service interaction with customers were more successful than strategies that included monetary compensation (Silber et al, 2009). When contact employees treat customers with respect and courteousness during a service recovery, customers will report significantly higher satisfaction levels (Swanson and Hsu, 2009).

2 Urgent reinstatement

The next step is to do something to remove the source of customer disappointment. Urgent means the action is taken quickly; reinstatement means making an effort to correct the problem. If an organization is slow to address customer dissatisfaction or fails to present evidence that it is taking some action, the customer is likely to perceive that his or her problems are not important, and may well defect at this point. Customers who complain and have their problems resolved quickly are much more likely to repurchase than those whose complaints are not resolved. In fact, research by TARP (1986) showed that if complaints are resolved quickly, 82% of customers will re-purchase. However, if complaints are resolved, but not necessarily quickly, only 52% of customers will return. Urgency is therefore the key, and employees must therefore be empowered to solve problems as they occur. For G Adventures (profiled in Chapter 3) with over 1300 staff, one of the key components to employee satisfaction is empowerment. 'Our whole success ratio comes from empowering our staff to deal with things on the ground,' says founder Bruce Poon Tip. For example, if guests miss arrival transfers for

10

whatever reason and end up getting themselves a taxi to their hotel, his staff is empowered to deal directly with the problem. 'Most tour leaders tell the guests they have to write to the company on their return, but we cut in and refund on the spot – no arguments,' he says.

3 Empathy

Empathy means making the effort to understand why the customer was disappointed with the organization. If service employees can put themselves in the shoes of the customers, they may be able to grasp the disappointment felt by the customer, and successfully display that understanding. An important part of the service recovery process is not economic reimbursement, but empathy and responsiveness of employees (Liden and Skalen, 2003). The payoff of empathy is the customer's realization that the organization is in fact sensitive to the service failure. Tax and Brown (1998) have suggested that customers are looking for three specific types of justice following their complaints: outcome fairness, procedural fairness, and interactional fairness. Outcome fairness concerns the results that customers receive from their complaints; procedural fairness refers to the policies, rules and timeliness of the complaint process; and interactional fairness focuses on the interpersonal treatment received during the complaint process.

4 Symbolic atonement

The next step in the recovery process is to make amends in some tangible way for the organization's failure, and this may take the form of a room upgrade, a free dessert, or a ticket for a future flight. This step is called symbolic atonement because the gesture is designed not to replace the service, but to communicate to the customer that the organization takes responsibility for the disappointment caused and is willing to pay the price for its failure. At this point, it is important for service organizations to determine customers' thresholds of acceptability. In order to calculate how much compensation a firm should offer after service breakdown, Lovelock and Wirtz (2007) suggest that managers need to consider the positioning of the firm, the severity of the service failure, and who the affected customer is. But the overall rule of thumb for compensation for service failures should be 'well-dosed generosity'. In fact, Timm (2008) believes that companies should go beyond symbolic atonement and always go the extra mile in the eyes of the complaining customer.

At Walt Disney World, staff are empowered to use a 'No Strings Attached' (NSA) Card to fix 'accidents' that might occur in the park – even if Disney is not at fault. For example, if a guest spills a drink on a t-shirt and needs to purchase a replacement, the card (worth up to $50) can be used to keep the guest happy. However, Disney is renowned for going above and beyond in the area of service recovery. On one occasion, a young girl left her favorite teddy bear behind at the park, and the parents called up to see if it could be found. The next day, the teddy arrived in the post with a letter to the girl. In the letter, Disney empathized with the girl for missing her favorite teddy, but assured her that the teddy had a terrific time while he was at the park on his own. Attached to the letter were photographs of the teddy on every single ride in the park! Other tourism and hospitality companies that give employees discretion in how to solve guest complaints include YUM! brands and Ritz Carlton. At the Ritz Carlton on Hainan Island (see end of chapter case study), employees have $2,000 at their disposal per service episode to resolve complaints or service failures for guests (Susskind, 2010).

5 Follow-up

By following up to see if the gesture of symbolic atonement was well received, an organization can gauge how well it placated the customer's dissatisfaction. The follow-up can take many forms depending on the service type and recovery situation. Follow-up gives an organization a chance to evaluate the recovery plan and identify where improvements are necessary. A study of service recovery in the hotel sector found that many hotels did not follow-up and are thus missing out on effective way of satisfying guests and informing themselves of the adequacy of their recovery strategies (Lewis and McCann, 2004). The final encounter in a service interaction is critical in determining overall satisfaction, so service providers should ensure that encounters end on a good note.

The consequences of an effective recovery process

Research has shown that resolving customer problems effectively has a strong impact on customer satisfaction, quality and bottom-line performance; (Heskett et al, 1990; Berry and Parasuraman, 1993; Kelley, Hoffman and Davis, 1993; Tax, Brown and Chandrashenkaran, 1998; Tax and Brown, 1998). An effective recovery will retain customer loyalty regardless of the type of failure. In one study, customer retention exceeded 70% for those customers who perceived effective recovery efforts (Kelley, Hoffman and Davis, 1993). Retained customers are much more profitable than new ones because they purchase more and they purchase more frequently, while at the same time requiring lower operating costs. British Airways calculates that service recovery efforts return $2 for every dollar invested. In fact, the company finds that 'recovered' customers give the airline more of their business after they have been won back.

An effective recovery process may also lead to positive word of mouth, or at least diminish the negative word of mouth typically associated with poor recovery efforts. One study reported that customers who experienced a service failure told nine or ten individuals about their poor service experience, whereas satisfied customers told only four or five individuals about their satisfactory experience (Collier, 1995).

In fact, research by US firm TARP back in 1979 shows that for every 26 unhappy business to business customers, only one will lodge a formal complaint

10

with management. Instead, on average, each unhappy customer will tell ten people, who in turn will tell five others. Therefore, an average of 1300 people will hear about at least one of these unhappy customers' experiences. This 'Customer Complaint Iceberg' is illustrated in Figure 10.2. Further, repeated service failures can aggravate employees. The cost in employee morale is an often overlooked cost of not having an effective service recovery program.

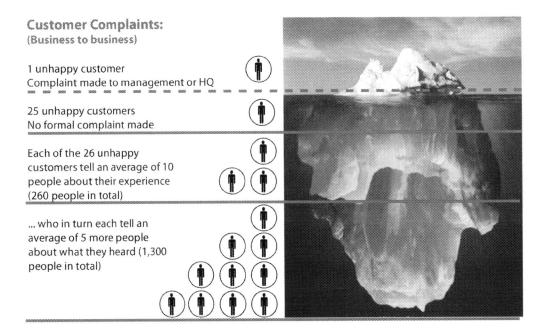

Customer Complaints:
(Business to business)

1 unhappy customer
Complaint made to management or HQ

25 unhappy customers
No formal complaint made

Each of the 26 unhappy
customers tell an average of 10
people about their experience
(260 people in total)

... who in turn each tell an
average of 5 more people
about what they heard (1,300
people in total)

Figure 10.2: The Customer Complaint Iceberg (Source: based on TARP, 1979)

The service recovery process can be used to improve the overall quality of service delivery as the service occurs. This is possible if the customer provides feedback during the service experience, which allows the organization to refine its service process. Keeping track of sources of dissatisfaction that create a need for recovery can also help the organization. Careful collection and storage of information regarding the incidents may produce a rich database of information on service quality. In analyzing this data, patterns may emerge that specify particularly troublesome aspects of its service delivery system. As mentioned in Chapter 1, the Lopesan Group in the Canary Islands uses the results of audits and surveys to enhance customer service and also to evaluate and reward managers and staff. Based on customer feedback, the group creates a top ten problem list across the chain and then provides a fund to help solve these problems. A good solution in one hotel can then be applied across other hotels in the chain, making it more cost-effective if they have had to invest in the solution.

Snapshot: Recovery via social media

Tourism and hospitality organizations are using social media to respond to consumer complaints. It's an efficient way for customers to be heard and an effective means of solving problems and being seen to solve problems. Southwest Airlines, for example, has 1.2 million Twitter followers, with a team of ten staff from communications and customer relations that monitors the account from 5am to 11pm, hours in which the airline operates. They field questions about lost baggage, delayed flights and misplaced drink coupons. If someone tweets a complaint to @SouthwestAir, the reply may come from the team: 'So sorry to hear about your lost luggage. Have you filed a claim? Any progress yet?'

Jason Bangerter, Oliver & Bonacini Restaurants. Courtesy of Stacey Newman Photography

Many companies are responding to this new way of servicing customers' needs. Social media has affected G Adventures – an outdoor adventure travel company – by enhancing transparency of the customer service culture. 'When there were floods in Peru, we had a group stranded,' founder Bruce Poon Tip recounts. 'They needed evacuation but the CEO was having problems getting confirmation for the helicopter because of the sheer expense.' The ensuing tweets revealed all the negotiations to the people involved as well as their Twitter networks. Another example was when a guest's flight delay was preventing her from meeting her ship in time. 'She tweeted that she was going to be late and, although it was after hours, our people jumped on it and got her a direct flight with Air Canada which worked out better for her in the end,' explains Poon Tip.

Interacting with customers using Facebook and Twitter can improve customer service and speed up resolution and service recovery. 'It's enabling us to accelerate that conversation and make those connection points in ways that weren't before possible,' says Andy Kauffman, the vice president of commerce at Marriott Hotels. 'But the principles behind it are all rooted in good service and, if something happens, great service recovery.' Marriott International has two full-time people who work on the Twitter feed. One of them is on the customer service team; John Wolf, the director of public relations, is the other. He says that brand loyalists sometimes point him to people who are tweeting about problems they've had at Marriott hotels. 'We'd rather know that there's an issue than not know it, and we'd rather be given the opportunity to solve the problem,' Wolf says. This strategy has successfully recovered previously dissatisfied customers. It also gives Marriott the ability to solve problems for customers as they arise.

Other major hotel chains also have some version of this personalized customer service. In addition to its Hyatt Concierge Twitter service, Hyatt guarantees answers within 24 hours to questions that are posted on its Gold Passport Loyalty program Facebook page. 'We really don't know whether [responding to customers on Twitter and Facebook] pays off or not,' Carroll says. 'However, at the same time, we do know that the conversations are going on and…that it probably is advisable to be part of the conversation.'

Virgin Atlantic Airways also uses social media to solve problems. During the volcanic-ash crisis in 2010 which grounded hundreds of planes in Europe, VAA's website couldn't keep pace with the rapidly changing situation, so it used Facebook and Twitter to update customers.

Elsewhere in the hospitality industry there is diversity of opinion about the appropriateness of new technology. While many restaurants around the world are banning cellphones while dining, a Toronto executive chef Jason Bangerter – from Oliver & Bonacini Restaurants – uses Twitter to keep up with his customer's needs. He allows phones, picture taking and tweets during meals so that diners feel in touch at all times and feel important.

Listening to social media is one thing; effective responses to the information can be more difficult to design. Interflora was one of the first companies to leverage the information they garnered from Twitter in an innovative way. In response to people moaning about a bad day, they sent bouquets of flowers to cheer them up – in other words, acting like a caring friend rather than a company. Surprising people like this can lead to many favorable tweets among Twitter networks, resulting in brand reinforcement for the company. For Interflora, this was all part of its social media strategy designed by a company called We are Social. The company advised Interflora to monitor Twitter to find people in need of cheering up, contact them via their postal address and then send them flowers. Adam Hart is the online marketing manager for Interflora. 'At Interflora we are focused on exceeding people's expectations and delivering a personal, trusted service that will brighten up their day,' he said in an interview with Marketing magazine.

A Canadian company, FreshBooks has followed suit, sending flowers to console customers, even when the problem is nothing to do with their service. It seems that public relations is turning more personal these days with a nod to the old-fashioned, one-on-one service expected in a small business but not anticipated from larger corporations. Misty Harris, a reporter for the Calgary Herald, calls these new PR managers 'Twitter troubadours'. 'The micro-blogging site is turning public relations into personal relations as more companies hire social media 'firefighters' to snuff out online complaints, foster one-on-one customers relationships and act as Twitter troubadours for their brands – all in 140 characters or less,' she says.

Sources: Kessler (2010); Teotonio (2011); Shearman (2010); Harris (2009)

Guidelines for soliciting, tracking and handling complaints

Complaints are inevitable, but each grievance represents a chance to correct a flawed process, educate a customer and strengthen loyalty. TARP's first study for the White House in the 1970s referred to earlier, revealed that consumers with problems who did not complain were less loyal than those who did and had their issues resolved. Subsequent studies have continued to confirm TARP's initial findings that every problem presents an opportunity to enhance both loyalty and word of mouth (Goodman, 2006). The challenge is soliciting complaints, since over 90% of customers who are dissatisfied with service never bother to complain (Bigger and Bigger, 2010). Harari (1997) offers eight guidelines for handling complaints.

1 Make it easy for customers to complain

Companies should aggressively solicit complaints through multiple channels, such as survey cards that are easy to fill out, suggestion boxes in as many sites as possible, electronic accessibility to central terminals, phone numbers on all business cards, and by calling customers and ex-customers with a list of specific questions. Online customer reviews in particular provide customers with an easy mechanism to spread their voice without fear of identification (Black and Kelley, 2009). Managers can also hold regular small focus groups to solicit feedback from customers. The Sheraton Suites Eau Claire for example, a hotel profiled in Chapter 7, hosts a weekly cocktail party at the hotel, which gives guests the opportunity to offer suggestions as to how service could be improved.

2 Respond quickly to each and every complaint

This is where empowerment comes in. If employees of an organization are not given the information and authority (including spending authority) to resolve problems quickly, then the organization's concern about complaints is not commitment, but rather lip service. Empowerment also implies responsibility. Somebody in the organization has to 'own' each complainer – that is, see that the problem is fixed, follow up to ensure customer satisfaction, and champion appropriate changes in the organization. At Sandals Resorts, when a guest complains to an employee or 'team member', the team member owns the complaint and ensures that the procedure for following guest complaints is carried out.

Andrew Dunn, from Scott Dunn Travel, who was profiled in Chapter 2, works on the philosophy that Scott Dunn will do anything to rectify problems. So the ash cloud which disrupted airports all over Europe in 2010 was an opportunity to show the company's mettle. Dunn had to decide on the Tuesday whether to wait and see if airports would open in time for his guests' Sunday flights or immediately commandeer coaches just in case. 'I had to decide do we send coaches – which will cost us real money – or do we wait. We did in fact send the

10

coaches – and then within 48 hours there were no more coaches to be had for anyone. Other people in the travel business hadn't done that; they hadn't even thought of it,' he says. His clients were among the few people who got home on time and it became more apparent when they returned how well they had been looked after by Scott Dunn when thousands of other travelers were still stranded all over Europe and beyond.

3 Educate employees

Employees should be taught about the strategic and financial value of complaints, about the need for urgency in responding, and perhaps most important, and that everyone owns the problem – not just the 'customer service' people. This can be done in orientation, in management-development sessions, in memos and briefings, and in meetings and speeches. The interactive role of front stage personnel has been found to be decisive for effective complaint management (Skaalsvik, 2011). Managers or executives should also be aware of the benefits of an effective complaint handling process.

Employees also need appropriate coping and problem-solving skills to handle customers as well as their own feelings in difficult situations (Bitner, Booms and Mohr, 1994). Employees can also be taught to recognize characteristics of situations (e.g. unexpected peaks in demand, inordinate delays) and anticipate the moods of their customers so that some potential problem situations can be avoided completely or alleviated before they accelerate. In the opening spotlight, Paul Hudson of Luxury Hotels UK, trains his staff in the art of service recovery using case studies, role-plays, and letters of complaints.

4 Approach complaints as operational problems and strategic opportunities

Approaching complaints as opportunities means putting complaints in the category of 'research and information'. It means replacing blame analysis with problem analysis. It means viewing complaints in the Renaissance tradition, in which the critic was an ally who helped the object of the criticism to focus better on reality. Paul Hudson looks at previous complaints to learn from them. 'I try and get my staff to encourage guests to tell us everything about their holiday experience – both good and bad – so that we can learn from it.'

5 Make complaints and complainers visible

Harari suggests that companies post quantitative complaint data publicly (for employees and for customers). These should be raw, unedited letters or phone call transcripts, and should be posted on bulletin boards, reprinted in newsletters, or posted on the web. The responses to the complaints should also be publicized, with employees who did the responding identified and applauded. Complainers should be invited to address people in the organization and to work with them on improvements. A 'customer panel' in every management retreat would also make sense.

6 Adjust quality measures, performance reviews, and compensation accordingly

Quality measures should always incorporate pervasive customer complaints. Key questions for managers' performance evaluation and pay might include the following: How many complaints have you solicited? How many 'firefighting' teams have you been on? How have you used the input of complainers to improve this organization? Rewarding managers for discovering and acting on complaints should be encouraged. Winners of the Nova Scotia Pineapple Awards for service excellence in Canada, for example, are often employees whose service recovery goes above and beyond what is expected to enrich a visitor's stay in Nova Scotia.

7 Reward complainers

Complainers can help a business prosper, and their advice is often priceless. Visible displays of gratitude not only make good common sense but also send a signal to complainers and to the organization. Companies should consider thank-you notes and phone calls, small cash rewards, plaques and certificates, gifts, 'consultant of the month' awards, feature stories in company newsletters, and periodic celebrations with complainers as guests of honor.

8 Stop calling them 'complainers'!

Hararis' final suggestion is not to call customers who complain 'complainers' or 'difficult customers' or even 'jerks'. They are critics, allies, consultants, or guests of honor. What they are called should reflect their contribution to the success of the organization.

Service guarantees

A growing number of tourism and hospitality organizations are offering customers a service guarantee, promising that if service delivery fails to meet predefined standards, the customer will be entitled to one or more forms of compensation, such as an easy-to-claim replacement, a refund or a credit. They are finding that effective service guarantees can complement the company's service recovery strategy. Table 10.1 highlights some of the reasons why service guarantees are powerful tools for both promoting and achieving service quality, and also lists the criteria for designing effective guarantees. One of the reasons for having a service guarantee is to build marketing muscle, and research has shown that providing a service guarantee in advertising materials significantly enhances consumers' intentions to buy (Boshoff, 2003). Research has also found that a service guarantee has a positive, long-term effect on both employee motivation and customer intention to return, although there are suggestions that organizations need to make better use of the information and knowledge gained from invocations of a service guarantee (Hays and Hill, 2006).

10

Table 10.1: Reasons for having a service guarantee and criteria for designing guarantees (Source: based on Hart, 1988; Zeithaml et al, 2007)

Reasons for having a service guarantee
A good guarantee forces the company to focus on its customers
An effective guarantee sets clear standards for the organization
A good guarantee generates immediate and relevant feedback from customers
Information generated from the guarantee program can be used for continuous improvement
When the guarantee is invoked there is an immediate opportunity to recover
Guarantees build 'marketing muscle' by reducing the risk of purchase decision
Employee morale and loyalty can be enhanced as a result of a good guarantee program

Criteria for designing guarantees
The guarantee should be totally unconditional
It must be easy to understand and communicate to the customer
It must be meaningful to the customer and compensation more than adequate
The guarantee must be easy to invoke
It should be easy to collect
The guarantee should be credible

From the customer's perspective, the primary function of service guarantees is to lower the perceived risks associated with purchase. In response to the threat of hurricanes, hurricane guarantees are now offered by many tour operators and travel agents for travelers going to the Caribbean. Resorts like Beaches, Sandals, SuperClubs and Club Med promote policies that allow travellers to rebook for another time without penalty if a hurricane ruins their vacation.

But companies should think carefully before deciding to introduce an unconditional service guarantee. Service firms whose quality is truly uncontrollable because of external forces would be foolish to consider a guarantee. Also, companies that already have a reputation for excellent service may not need a guarantee – introducing one may confuse the market. It has been argued by Isadore Sharpe, chairman of Four Seasons Hotels, that service guarantees are unnecessary for any organization that has quality at the center of its operating philosophy (Callan and Moore, 1998).

Kandampully and Duddy (2001) suggest that a service guarantee maintains both a marketing and operational function that will simultaneously enhance an organization's internal and external marketing effectiveness and operating competency. They illustrate this impact of service guarantees on marketing and operational functions in Figure 10.3. They also argue that service guarantees facilitate feedback, ensure customers are rewarded for their comments, and effectively compel an organization to respond to customer feedback. Tourism organizations that are willing to offer a service guarantee, and also prove capable of delivering on that promise, will gain a powerful competitive advantage.

Figure 10.3: The impact of service guarantees on marketing and operational functions (Kandampully and Duddy, 2001, pp. 36)

Case study: China's 'Hawaii': Climbing the curve of customer service

China is slated by many tourism agencies to become the world's most popular destination. Inbound tourist arrivals are forecast by the World Tourism Organization to grow to 210 million by 2020, with foreign tourist revenue set to reach US$58 billion. China is widely seen as an exotic new destination, and both domestic and inbound tourism are growing at unprecedented rates. Currently about 75% of all Chinese travelers go to Hong Kong or Macao, the earliest beneficiaries of a still-evolving policy to permit Chinese from certain areas to travel on their own. However, with the rise of low-cost airlines, people with relatively low income levels are able to travel by air for the first time, and they are setting their sights on more exotic locations in China.

Michel Goget, General Manager of the Ritz-Carlton Sanya, Hainan on the hotel's terrace. Photo courtesy of Michel Goget

An example is Hainan Island off the south coast of mainland China. Known as 'China's Hawaii', Hainan is a tropical island. Its capital, Haikou, with streets lined with palm trees, is the main port and business center for the island. Hainan Province has also been a Special Economic Zone since 1988 and has as such become a magnet for investment and tourism

10

development. The total number of domestic visitors increased by 7.4% in 2005 to 14.7 million.

Meanwhile, the island is attracting international tourists, and overseas visitors grew 40% in 2005 to 431,900. In June 2006, Mytravel, the UK-based tour operator, launched its first packaged holiday to China, sending British tourists to Hainan. The southern beaches in the Sanya area and the tropical climate are the main attractors, even though originally Hainan was a remote and exotic place of exile, culturally backward and disease-ridden. It has a rich historical background of piracy, banishment, various indigenous peoples with distinct cultures and customs, plus Japanese occupation and atrocities.

With a current population of around eight million, Hainan is the second largest island off the China coast (Taiwan being the biggest). It is thickly forested and has an agrarian value for China, particularly with its production of rubber in the lush interior as well as rice, coconuts, palm oil, sisal, tropical fruits, coffee, tea and sugarcane. It is also rich in minerals and hardwoods and has a thriving fishing industry both for edible seafood and pearls. A lack of energy resources, however, has held industry back and, with an economic recession in the 1990s, Hainan has refocused its growth on the tourist industry.

The island is linked to the mainland at Guangdong Province by ferry links and there are also two airports, Meilan Airport in Haikou as well as Sanya Phoenix International Airport. A 12-hour railway link between Guangzhou, on the mainland, and Hainan, with a ferry crossing included, is hoped to increase both tourism and economic development on the island. The project cost US$583 million and was planned to compete with the well-established tourist and financial areas of Hong Kong and Macau. Another bonus for foreign tourists is the visa-upon-arrival policy, initiated in 2000 with 21 countries as part of a strategy to attract visitors from abroad. Usually, visitors to China have to fill out lengthy forms and satisfy pernickety requirements in advance of their trip for visas. But, being a Special Economic Zone, Hainan is exempt from the economic policies of the mainland.

Famed for its lush greenery, white sandy beaches and clean air, Hainan island is also home to various traditional temples, the most notable being Five Officials' Temple. Hairu Tomb, built in 1589, is a key national cultural protection site, reinforcing the island's position as an important cultural tourism destination. The island also boasts hot springs, volcanic gardens, rivers and other scenic zones but visitors do experience difficulties in locating these as very little tourist information exists in English. Historically the island did not have a good reputation, with off-putting labels such as 'an antechamber to Hell' coined by an imperial civil servant. However, nowadays its remoteness, its reputation for housing the ethnic minority group with the longest life span in China (the Miao), and its unexplored flora and fauna could all help establish it as an environmental tourism mecca. Naturalist literature about the island is scarce, and access to the innermost areas, which are home to around 4,200 plant species, is limited, but there are several reservations which protect endangered species such as the Hainan gibbon and Eld's deer as well as mangroves.

Sanya is the most hotel-dense area in Hainan Island and, indeed, the whole of China. These are mainly luxury international hotels and resorts. Recent figures released by Hainan Tourist Bureau list 209 starred hotels, including 22 five-star properties, a number that will be doubled by 2014. There are many more hotel projects currently in development, at least half of which are planned for Sanya, which is fast becoming a tropical-style resort often comparable to Hawaii with its luxury accommodation and surfing beaches. This development has all happened over the past 15 years with the past two seeing the most rapid growth along Yalong Bay, Sanya's most popular beach, and Haitang Bay. Along with increasing affluence and tourism opportunities within a nation, comes a more discriminating and demanding customer. With growing expectations, there is more chance of service failure and the need for better recovery strategies in order to retain customer loyalty. This is vital for Hainan Island where competition for high-end tourists is fierce.

The Ritz-Carlton Sanya – arguably Hainan's most luxurious five-star resort – was built in 2008 on Yalong Bay, Hainan Province, overlooking the South China Sea and 40 minutes from the Sanya Phoenix International Airport. The resort is owned by the China Jin Mao Group Company, Ltd and managed by Ritz-Carlton. There are 450 rooms including 33 private villas complete with their own plunge pools, lotus ponds and butlers, part of the exclusive Ritz-Carlton Club which also has a private lounge serving five complimentary food and beverage selections per day. There are four outdoor pools, tennis courts, fitness centre, Ritz Kids Club, spa, conference and wedding chapel and facilities, and eight different eateries. It also houses a designer boutique shopping arcade with five of the world's top brands – Louis Vuitton, Salvatore Feragamo, Tod's, Paul & Shark and Ermenegildo Zegna – the first high-end hotel retail arcade for Hainan Island.

Michel Goget has been General Manager of the Ritz-Carlton Sanya since it opened and also the Chairman of Sanya Tourism Association since 2011. The same year he was named 'Outstanding Entrepreneur' by the Sanya City Government and Tourism Bureau, after leading the Ritz-Carlton to more than 78 tourism industry awards. With experience in seven different countries over two decades, Goget is charged with keeping the Ritz-Carlton Sanya at the number one position in Hainan Island. Managing a team of 1000 staff is no mean feat. The majority are Chinese with college educations in hospitality. 'We have a lot of lovely employees who are very young: the average age is 23 years old,' says Goget. 'They are 98% Chinese with a very limited amount of expatriates. We have an Italian chef and maitre d' and there's me, of course.' Goget is a French-born, US citizen and has a home in Washington DC. He has worked all over the US and Europe. Many of his staff members come to the Ritz-Carlton to gain experience during their college degrees and then return to work there full-time after graduation. 'We put them through a very rigorous training process. There are currently about 200 undergoing training,' Goget says.

Named by Training Magazine as the best company in the US for employee training, Ritz-Carlton is also known worldwide as a leader in customer service. Its quaintly old-fashioned mandate is to provide 'ladies and gentleman to serve ladies and gentlemen'.

10

But how does this translate to a remote island in the South China Sea? 'Our whole philosophy – the three steps of service and our gold standard – is the same here as our other hotels,' says Goget. 'What's really amazing is that I have worked in seven different countries and frankly I see no difference here in the culture.' Firstly, the staff searching process is very thorough, selecting only those individuals with a passion to connect with the guest. 'The real challenge we have culturally is that it is very difficult for a Chinese local to identify themselves as the same rank as the guest so we really have to train them to engage with the guest and have confidence to look them in the eye,' Goget explains. 'We work on making sure they are comfortable using the guest's name, pronouncing the name correctly, and breaking the ice. That would be our toughest challenge – encouraging genuine engagement like you have in America.'

The Ritz-Carlton policy is to do considerable groundwork in advance of guests' arrival to ensure that things do not go wrong at their properties. For example, they have thoughtfully provided a 'romanceologist' to orchestrate romantic evenings, proposals and engagements to create the perfect environment for couples. Goget, who has experienced these services firsthand, says that with considerable differences in his Russian, Chinese and Western clientele, the romanceologist has to be well versed in the intricacies of many cultures. 'We get a lot of couples so we try to anticipate these guests' needs. We have romanceologists in our hotel, who work on ways to do something really cool for couples. If they have booked into one of our 33 villas they will have their own butlers and a beautiful villa. But we ask them if there is anything else we can do for them, any particular requirement. We recommend the spa; if they want a romantic dinner on the beach we can arrange it; and if they want to get engaged, we will come up with something to help that out to make it memorable. We have whole list of items we can provide and romantic spots on the island for couples to go to.'

Ritz-Carlton prides itself on its 'lineup' tradition – borrowed from French chefs – where staff gathers to reinforce procedures and learn from daily incidents. 'Every shift we get together to review various kinds of culture, alignment, what's happening today, what's happening tomorrow, discuss issues and challenges, review VIP arrivals, and so on,' says Goget. With intensive training, regular on-the-job reviewing and research into clients' specific needs, Goget tries to avoid any customer service problems before they happen. But when something does go wrong his team is well equipped to provide speedy remedies. One quite frequent example is forgotten passports. 'In a situation where the guest is on the way to the airport and realizes he has forgotten his passport, he calls back to the hotel,' says Goget. 'If, for example, he was staying in one of our villas, there is a 24-hour butler on hand who will figure out a way to find the passport. If it is still locked in the safe, then we have procedures to open it and he will then jump in a cab and rush to the airport so the guest doesn't miss his plane.' Another recent incident was a lost iPhone which was speedily found on the beach when 15 staff members instigated a search. One more serious problem that occasionally occurs is having a guest get into trouble swimming. 'It is really amazing that lots of Chinese guests spending their vacation with us can't swim; we have even had some drownings on the island. Thank goodness our employees are well trained for this and are able to rescue them, get them back on their feet. I am very proud of our employees taking the initiative in this sort of instance,' says Goget.

One of Ritz-Carlton's most remarkable policies is to permit every employee to spend up to $2,000 if required on making any single guest satisfied. This doesn't get used very often, however, but it does indicate the level of confidence management has in its team of staff. Goget says it would be relevant if they had a situation whereby a guest arrived to find he had no room booked. 'We would have to upgrade them, that has a considerable cost factor. Also, sometimes, being on an island, guests arrive early in the morning and we have no room ready for them, so we have a waiting room available for families, there's complimentary Chinese soup and noodles in the restaurant,' Goget explains. 'It is not their fault that they have to arrive early, so we make sure the experience is not overbearing; we make it as comfortable as we can.'

Sources: Interview with Michel Goget, April 2011; Reiss (2009); Anon (2006); Gubler et al (2008); Staff (2011)

References

Albrecht, K. and Zemke, R. (1985) *Service America*. Homewood: Dow Jones-Irwin.

Anon (2006) 'Market profiles on Chinese cities and provinces: Hainan Province'. Accessed 10/20/2011 from http://www.hktdc.com/sc-supplier/

Berry L.L., Zeithaml, V.A. and Parasuraman, A. (1990) 'Five imperatives for improving service quality', *Sloan Management Review*, **31**(4), 29-38.

Berry, L. and Parasuraman, A. (1993) 'Marketing de los servicios: La calidad como meta', Paramón ediciones, S.A. Madrid.

Bigger, A.S. and Bigger, L.B. (2010) 'Customer service: Serve today as our jobs may depend on it tomorrow', *Executive Housekeeping Today*, August, 6-8.

Bitner, M.J., Booms, B.H. and Mohr, L.A. (1994) 'Critical service encounters: The employee's viewpoint', *Journal of Marketing*, **58**, 95-106.

Black, H.G. and Kelley, S.W. (2009) 'A storytelling perspective on online customer reviews reporting service failure and recovery', *Journal of Travel & Tourism Marketing*, **26**, 169-179.

Boshoff, C. (2003) 'Intentions to buy a service: The influence of service guarantees, general information and price information in advertising', *South African Journal of Business Management*, **34**(1), 39-44.

Callan, R.J. and Moore, J. (1998) 'Service guarantee: A strategy for service recovery', *Journal of Hospitality & Tourism Research*, **22**(1), 56-71.

10

Collier, D. A. (1995) 'Modeling the relationships between process quality errors and overall service process performance', *Journal of Service Industry Management*, **64**(4), 4–19.

Fisk, R.P., Grove, S.J. and John, J. (2000) *Interactive Services Marketing*, Boston: Houghton Mifflin Company.

Grönroos, C. (1990) *Service Management and Marketing*, Lexington, Mass: Lexington Books.

Goodman, J. (2006) 'Manage complaints to enhance loyalty', *Quality Progress*, **39**(2), 28-34.

Gubler, W., McCarter, M., Seawright, K. and Zhang Y. (2012) 'Service recovery in transition economies: Russia and China', *Managing Global Transitions*, **6**(1): 23–51.

Harari, O. (1997) 'Thank heavens for complainers', *Management Review*, **86**(3), 25–29.

Harris, M. (2009) 'Customer service getting shorter and tweeter', *Calgary Herald*, 11 July, A10.

Hart, C.W.L. (1988) 'The power of unconditional service guarantees', *Harvard Business Review*, **64**(4), 54-62.

Hart, C.W.L., Heskett, J.L. and Sasser, Jr., W.E. (1990) 'The profitable art of service recovery', *Harvard Business Review*, **68**(4), 148-156.

Hays, J.M. and Hill, A.V. (2006) 'An extended longitudinal study of the effects of a service guarantee', *Production and Operations Management*, **15**(1), 117-131.

Heskett, J., Sasser, W. and Hart, C. (1990) *Service Breakthroughs: Changing the Rules of the Game*, New York: The Free Press.

Hoffman, K.D., Kelley, S.W. and Rotalsky, H.M. (1995) 'Tracking service failures and employee recovery efforts', *Journal of Services Marketing*, **9**(2), 49-61.

Hudson, S. and Moreno-Gil, S. (2006) 'The influence of service recovery and loyalty on perceived service quality: A study of hotel customers in Spain', *Journal of Hospitality & Leisure Marketing*, **14**(2), 45-66.

Johnston, R. (2004) 'Towards a better understanding of service excellence', *Managing Service Quality*, **14**(2/3), 129-133.

Kandampully, J. and Duddy, R. (2001) 'Service system: A strategic approach to gain a competitive advantage in the hospitality and tourism industry', *International Journal of Hospitality & Tourism Administration*, **2**(1), 27-47.

Kelley, S. W., Hoffman, K. D. and Davis, M. A. (1993) 'A typology of retail failures and recoveries', *Journal of Retailing*, **69**(4), 429–452.

Kessler, S. (2010) 'The future of the hotel industry and social media', *Mashable Business*. Accessed 04/03/2012 from http://mashable.com/2010/10/18/hotel-industry-social-media

Leong, J.K. and Kim, W.G. (2002) 'Service recovery efforts in fast food restaurants to enhance repeat patronage', *Journal of Travel & Tourism Marketing*, **12**(2/3), 65-93.

Leong, J.K., Kim, W.G. and Ham, S. (2002) 'The effects of service recovery on repeat patronage', *Journal of Quality Assurance in Hospitality & Tourism*, **3**(1/2), 69-94.

Lewis, B.R. and McCann, P. (2004) 'Service failure and recovery: Evidence from the hotel industry', *International Journal of Contemporary Hospitality Management*, **16**(1), 6-17.

Liden, S.B. and Skalen, P. (2003) 'The effect of service guarantees on service recovery', *International Journal of Service Industry Management*, **14**(1), 36-58.

Lovelock, C. and Wirtz, J. (2007) *Services Marketing: People, Technology, Strategy*, 6th edition, New Jersey, USA; Prentice Hall International.

McCollough, M.A., Berry, L.L. and Yadav, M.S. (2000) 'An empirical investigation of customer satisfaction after service failure and recovery', *Journal of Service Research*, **3**(2), 121-137.

O'Neill, J.W. and Mattila, A.S. (2004) 'Towards the development of a lodging service recovery strategy', *Journal of Hospitality & Leisure Marketing*, **11**(1), 51-64.

Reiss, R. (2009) 'Leadership: How Ritz-Carlton stays at the top', Forbes.com. Accessed 04/10/2012 from http://www.forbes.com/2009/10/30/simon-cooper-ritz-leadership-ceonetwork-hotels.html

Schindlholzer, B. (2008) 'The service recovery paradox: Increased loyalty through effective service recovery'. Accessed 04/16/2012 from http://www.cxacademy.org/the-service-recovery-paradox-increased-loyalty-through-effective-service-recovery.html

Schoefer, K. and Ennew, C. (2004) 'Customer evaluations of tour operators' responses to their complaints', *Journal of Travel & Tourism Marketing*, **17**(1), 83-92.

Sharp, I. (2009) *Four Seasons. The Story of a Business Philosophy*, New York: The Penguin Group.

Shearman, S. (2010) 'Interflora cheers up glum Twitter users', *Marketing*, Accessed 04/03/2012 from http://www.marketingmagazine.co.uk/news/1033403/Interflora-cheers-glum-Twitter-users/

Silber, I., Israeli, A., Bustin, A. and Zvi, O.B. (2009) 'Recovery strategies for service failures: The case of restaurants', *Journal of Hospitality Marketing & Management*, **18**, 730-740.

Skaalsvik, H. (2011) 'Service failures in a cruise line context: Suggesting categorical schemes of service failures', *European Journal of Tourism Research*, **4**(1), 25-43.

Smith, A.K. and Bolton, R.N. (1998) 'An experimental investigation of customer reactions to service failure and recovery encounter: Paradox or peril?' *Journal of Service Research*, **1**(1), 65-81.

Sousa, R. and Voss, C.A. (2009) 'The effects of service failures and recovery on customer loyalty in e-services', *International Journals of Operations & Product Management*, **29**(8), 834-864.

10

Staff (2011) 'Hainan island: Heaven or hell for luxury hotels? Experts express concerns over the fast-expanding hotel scene in "China's Hawaii"', CNN GO. Accessed 04/03/2012 from http://www.cnngo.com/shanghai/visit/hainan-island-heaven-or-hell-luxury-hotels-855468

Sundaram, D.S., Jurowski, C. and Webster, C. (1997) 'Service failure recovery efforts in restaurant dining: The role of criticality of service consumption', *Hospitality Research Journal*, **20**(3), 137-149.

Susskind, A.M. (2010) 'Guest service management and processes in restaurants: What we have learned in fifty years', *Cornell Hospitality Quarterly*, **51**(4), 479-482.

Swanson, S.R. and Hsu, M.K. (2009) 'Critical incidents in tourism: Failure, recovery, customer switching, and word-of-mouth behaviors', *Journal of Travel & Tourism Marketing*, **26**, 180-194.

Tax, S.S. and Brown, S.W. (1998) 'Recovering and learning from service failure', *Sloan Management Review*, **40**(1), 75-80.

Tax, S.S., Brown, S.W. and Chandrashenkaran, M. (1998) 'Consumer evaluation of service complaint experiences: Implications for relationship marketing', *Journal of Marketing*, **62**(2), 60-76.

Technical Assistance Research Program (TARP) (1979) *Consumer Complaint Handling in America: A Final Report*. Washington, DC: White House Office of Consumer Affairs.

Technical Assistance Research Program (TARP) (1986) *Consumer Complaint Handling in America: An Update Study*. Washington, DC: White House Office of Consumer Affairs.

Teotonio, I. (2011) 'DC eatery bans mobile devices while Toronto chefs welcome them', thestar.com. Accessed 04/03/2012 from http://www.thestar.com/printarticle/1049300

Timm, P.R. (2008) *Customer service. Career success through customer loyalty*, Upper Saddle River, N.J: Pearson Prentice Hall.

Yavas, U., Karatepe, O., Babakus, E. and Avci, T. (2004) Customer complaints and organizational responses: A study of hotel guests in Northern Cyprus. *Journal of Hospitality & Leisure Marketing*,**11**(2/3), 31-46.

Zeithaml, V. A., Bitner, M. J., Gremler, D., Mahaffey, T. and Hiltz, B. (2007) *Services marketing: Integrating customer focus across the firm*, Canadian Edition. New York: McGraw-Hill.

Zemke, R. and Schaaf, D. (1989) *The Service Edge*, New York: Plume.

Scan here to get the hyperlinks in this chapter

Promoting Customer Service Internally and Externally

Elena Ulko, CEO, UlkoTours. Photo Courtesy of Elena Ulko

Russia is not renowned for its exemplary customer service, but one Russian tour company is going against the grain and specializing in personalized customer attention. UlkoTours is a verified member of the American Society for Travel Agents (ASTA), running private shore tours for cruise passengers in the Baltics. The company, based in St Petersburg, also sets up tailor-made tours for air and train passengers, concentrating on city itineraries in Moscow, Tallin, St Petersburg, Stockholm, Helsinki and Berlin.

How it differs from other – bigger – operators is in its personalized service message and delivery. The website reads like an invitation to come on a family vacation with founder and CEO, Elena Ulko, whose smiling photograph dominates the center of the home page. She is also pictured with her family at the top of a column advocating family travel to Russia. The text reads: 'Being a Happy Mom of two kids I know what it feels like to travel with these little noisy bundles and I'm happy to assure you that no matter how old your children are, we will create a unique program concentrating on making everyone happy and excited about Saint-Petersburg.' Ulko says her intention is to create a strong personal connection with customers: 'I have included personal information for the clients to know that I am a real person standing behind UlkoTours and from personal experience I know that it creates an emotional attachment when you visualize the person you're communicating with and when you are able to obtain some personal information about the person you are dealing with.'

On the website, Ulko goes on to outline all the free extras she offers to families, such as an upgrade to mini-van, water bottles and baby equipment – all available on request at no charge. She adroitly uses the emotional appeal of a picture of her happy family, perfectly posed in summer attire much like a US family portrait. She emphasizes the value of exploring the Baltics on a private tour with an educated local and introduces her web audience to everyone involved: her office team, her guides and her drivers. Her tagline is 'Superior Customer Service & Real People behind the website'. Again her objective is to connect with website readers and create a real-life story about the company for them. 'Other companies include information on their staff and even write descriptions about those people,' she says. 'But having a vague description just makes you feel one of the many, whereas having a personal story, something that comes directly from your heart, connects instantly to your potential clients.'

And this emotional connection pays off in bookings for the boutique tour operator. 'I can say with 100% confidence that every "possible" client who actually has read that section about my family has booked tours with us,' says Ulko. She believes her methods inspire trust among potential clients. 'Every client who has read the description does want to meet with me,' she says. 'They always ask if I would like them to bring something for myself or for my family from the US and they get upset if we cannot meet.' The same applies when her managers take charge of tour arrangements, with clients hoping to meet and get to know them.

Another unique aspect of the company is the dinner party option. Visitors can meet with Ulko and her family for a private dinner and tour of her home. Tapping into this kind of fly-on-the-wall, reality show trend, Ulko offers the intimate family dinners as the perfect ending to a tour day: a way to unwind with authentic local foods and beverages as well as learning about everyday life in Russia. 'It's not something that people book very often,' she says. 'But those who have done it have become my close friends and my family visits them now and then when we are in the US.'

Her mandate is to provide high quality service at every touch point for what she thinks of as a 'once-in-a-lifetime' trip for her customers. Phone lines are advertised as open from 1 am until 9 pm EST. Elsewhere on the website, Ulko offers free visa support for her customers if required. The motivation behind all these customer service extras is to encourage more US visitors to the region now it has opened up to tourism, dispelling all the 'cold war' myths and prejudices. She uses photos and testimonials from happy US clients to try and reinforce the message both on her website and on Tripadvisor.

The Russian government is keen to increase international visitation numbers but there still remain some barriers to easy travel in the region. Independent travelers have to register with government officials in each city visited and the transit system can be rudimentary. Along with a $12 billion blueprint in place to improve facilities and encourage tourism to Russia, the government also recently launched its cruise ship terminal in St Petersburg. It is all part of a plan to attract around 40 million tourists per year by 2016. Ulko considers the communication of customer service improvements to be paramount for the area in reaching out to target markets. 'Because many US travelers visiting Russia and the Baltics have hardly any knowledge of the language and the countries, they feel better when there's somebody that can guide them through the process, answer their questions not with standard answers, but with a highly personalized approach,' she explains. Although many clients take the opportunity to call the company and discuss the finer details over the phone, she says 90% of her customers leave all the arrangements for the entire tour program to her and her staff.

As a member of ASTA, UlkoTours is able to reach out to a network of over 22,000 US travel agents, cruise line and tourist board personnel. Ulko also offers a price match with any competitors' tours. These include large bus tour companies which deal with thousands of customers per season. 'For them, clients come and go,' says Ulko. 'For us, smaller folks, it's not the volume that matters, but the quality. Yes, our tours are sometimes more expensive but people get more in terms of personal approach and overall experience.' Another advantage of using a more personalized company is the quick response time when something goes wrong. 'We have never had any out of order situations, to be honest,' says Ulko. 'The only "disaster" happened last season when by mistake we assigned an English-speaking guide to a French-speaking group from Canada.' All correspondence for the tour had been conducted in English but the group had requested a French-speaking guide. Realizing the mistake, Ulko managed to find a substitute guide just two hours into the tour.

Communicating with potential customers always reaps rewards. Having noticed the provision of bottled water and welcome gifts during tours, one jocular client sent a message, saying 'Did that say a free bottle of water or a free bottle of Russian vodka?' Ulko went along with the joke with the response, 'Mmm...I think I can persuade my manager to leave our last bottle of vodka for you: As a ransom for the guide. A driver is part of the welcome gift!' The tour was booked immediately, she says, after this personalized banter.

11

Whenever prospective customers call, she is happy to divulge personal information and experiences, creating a relationship over the phone: 'They start asking more questions, more personal, and minute by minute they realize they already know you and can't wait to go on tour with you.'

In a savvy cross-marketing project, UlkoTours now has an office based in St Petersburg, Florida. Clients making telephone inquiries are always curious as to whether they are talking to someone in the US or the Russian office. 'When I was taking client calls while in the US, all of the clients asked if they were talking to the US office or Russian office,' says Ulko. When she told them she was in the US with her family but was usually based in Russia, the conversation would invariably lead to the clever connection between the Florida St Petersburg and the Russian one. 'We would then talk about the weather and kids going to school...and voila, next day comes their tour booking,' says Ulko.

It is all very well connecting emotionally with customers when trying to close the sale, but there is still the task of continuing that connection both during their visit and afterwards. Ulko works hard to perpetuate this personal connection by meeting with clients during their tours, giving them welcome gifts and posing for photos with them. After their holiday, communication continues with picture sharing, feedback and client referrals. 'Not everybody is like that, there are people who do not like to communicate and don't like to be bothered, it's just the way it is,' she notes. 'In those cases, we give detailed and precise answers to their questions so that they would get exactly what they need.'

Sources: Interview with Elena Ulko, April 2012; Matthews, L (2011); http://ulkotours.com/

Developing an integrated communications strategy for customer service

The 'gaps model' of service quality, introduced in Chapter 6, showed the importance of external communications in setting customer expectations given that a major cause of poorly perceived service is the difference between what a firm promises about a service, and what it actually delivers. The opening spotlight is a good example of a tour operator going out of its way to close that gap. To avoid broken promises, companies must manage all communications to customers, just as Elena Ulko does with UlkoTours, so that inflated promises do not lead to overly high expectations. This difference between what is promised and what is delivered can cause customer frustration, perhaps driving the customer to the competition. As Jim Knight, Senior Director of Training for Hard Rock International says: 'the worst mistake a business can make is to over-promise and under-deliver' (Knight, 2009, pp. 12).

Perhaps one of the most important advances in marketing in recent decades has been the rise of integrated marketing communications (IMC) – the unification of all marketing communications tools, as well as corporate and brand messages, so they send a consistent, persuasive message to target audiences. This approach recognizes that advertising can no longer be crafted and executed in isolation from other promotional mix elements. As tourism markets and the media have grown more complex and fragmented, consumers find themselves in an ever more confusing marketing environment. Tourism marketers must address this situation by conveying a consistent, unified message in all their promotional activities. IMC programs coordinate all communication messages and sources of an organization. An IMC campaign includes traditional marketing communication tools, such as advertising or sales promotion, but recognizes that other areas of the marketing mix – such as social media – are also used in communications. Tourism and hospitality consumers also receive communications from servicescapes and everyday interactions with employees. Planning and managing these elements so they work together helps to build a consistent brand or company image.

■ Branding and service providers

Before discussing in detail different approaches to managing service promises, it is important to consider the concept of branding and how it applies to service providers. The subject of branding has received increased attention over the last few decades. In an increasingly competitive global marketplace, the need for tourism and hospitality organizations to create a unique identity—to differentiate themselves from competitors—has become more critical than ever. A brand in the modern marketing sense offers the consumer relevant added value, a superior proposition that is distinctive from competitors', and imparts meaning above and beyond the functional aspects.

The process of building a brand should begin with an analysis of the current situation. This stage should consider how contemporary or relevant the brand is to today's consumer and how it compares with key competitors. Once this market investigation is complete, the next stage is to develop the brand identity. Critical to the success of any brand is the extent to which the brand personality interacts with the target market. A brand's personality has both a head and a heart: its 'head' is its logical features, while its 'heart' is its emotional benefits and associations. Brand propositions and communications can be based around either.

The third stage in brand building is to communicate the vision and launch the brand. This may be done through a single announcement or as a part of huge international advertising campaign. This stage involves translating the brand personality and proposition into deliverable messages. A logotype or brand signature and a design style guide, which ensures consistency of message and approach, should also reinforce the brand values. The vision should be expressed in the brand's core values that are consistently reinforced through the product or serviceand in all marketing communications. Every execution in all media contributes to maintaining brand presence. The final stage is to evaluate the

11

brand's performance in the marketplace. Continuous monitoring and evaluation of the communications is the key here, in conjunction with open-mindedness and a willingness to embrace change on the part of the brand managers. Any change must be managed with the overall consistency of the brand. The secret is to evolve continually and enrich the original brand personality, building on the initial strengths to increase their appeal and broaden the market.

Chapter 9 discussed the importance of social media in today's communications mix, and Table 11.1 below shows how Virgin Atlantic Airways (VAA) employs social media to deliver on the four qualities that make it such a successful brand (Barwise & Meehan, 2010).

Table 11.1: How Virgin Atlantic Airways (VAA) employs social media to strengthen its brand (Source: Based on Barwise & Meehan, 2010)

Qualities that make successful brands	How VAA uses social media to deliver each quality
1. Offer and communicate a clear, relevant customer promise	The VAA customer promise is innovation, fun, informality, honesty, value, and a caring attitude. This customer promise is reinforced at every touch point, and VAA uses social media to support these brand values. For example, the most-read section of its Facebook page includes travel tips from crew members – communication that comes across as honest, informal, and caring.
2. Build trust by delivering on that promise	Trust is mainly about service delivery, but when things go wrong, keeping customers informed can prevent that trust from eroding. During the volcanic ash crisis in 2010, VAA's website couldn't keep pace with the rapidly changing situation, so it used Facebook and Twitter to communicate with customers.
3. Drive the market by continually improving the promise	For VAA, like many companies, the greatest social media opportunity lies in gathering insights to drive continual incremental improvements. For example, in response to online community suggestions, it launched a system to arrange taxi sharing on arrival with passengers from the same flight.
4. Seek further advantage by innovating beyond the familiar	Fresh insights from social media reinforce the innovation aspect of the brand. For example, Facebook interactions helped the company appreciate the extensive planning that goes into a big trip, so they launched vtravelled, a site dedicated to inspirational journeys. Customers moderate the conversation and exchange information, stories, and advice. The site leads to some sales, but its main benefit to VAA comes from brand reinforcement and new customer insights.

Managing service promises

Zeithaml et al (2007) suggest that there are four strategies that are effective in managing service promises. These are shown in Figure 11.1. Service guarantees are discussed in Chapter 10 but the following section looks at the three other strategies.

Figure 11.1: Approaches for managing service promises (Source: Based on Zeithaml et al,2007)

■ Create effective services advertising

One of the key ways that services promises are communicated is through advertising, but the intangibility of services makes advertising difficult for marketers. Before buying services, consumers have problems understanding them, and after purchase, they have trouble evaluating their service experiences. Various strategies have been proposed to overcome these problems. One is to present vivid information and evoke strong emotions. Advertisers of destinations, for example, often try to build a mood or image around the destination, such as beauty, love, or serenity, creating an emotional relationship between the destination and potential visitors. This was the case with the print advertisement shown which uses the promise of top-notch customer service to target golf tourists. It is a full-page print ad promoting golf in Bermuda that was placed in *Travel + Leisure Golf* magazine in 2008. The print ad was part of an integrated 'Bermuda. Feel The Love' campaign, which also used television and radio. The campaign was designed to position the island as an exceptionally convenient, relaxing and friendly getaway that pampers and caters to every wish with a smile. The two heads – a male and a female – sculptured from the landscape of the golf course grab the reader's attention, and this visual image works with the print copy to gain the reader's interest and to provoke the desire in him or her to travel to Bermuda. The website is included at the bottom of the ad to inspire action.

11

Love is par for the course.

Less than 2 hours from the East Coast, Bermuda is the ideal spot to relax, release and indulge in your passions. Eight world-class golf courses to perfect your swing. Over seventy tennis courts to fine-tune your serve. Dozens of luxurious spas to refresh your inner being. Bermuda. Do it all or nothing at all.

For affordable packages and to book reservations, please visit bermudatourism.com. Bermuda. Home of the 2008 PGA Grand Slam of Golf.

BERMUDA
feel the love

Bermuda promoting golf that was part of the 'Bermuda. Feel The Love' campaign. Courtesy of Bermuda Department of Tourism

Research has showed that appealing to a consumer's emotional responses can be very effective in terms of creating a favorable attitude towards a service brand (Matilla, 1999). Tourism advertisers are realizing the importance of touching emotions and getting into the consumer psyche, and destinations like Las Vegas, Australia and Canada have begun to focus on promoting experiences as opposed to products and service (Hudson and Ritchie, 2009). Hotels, too, are promoting the experience of staying in their properties as opposed to physical attributes. Hilton Hotels, for example, in its 'Travel Should Take You Places' ad campaign, attempts to engage guests at an emotional level, instead of trying to entice guests through rational product attributes, winning their hearts rather than their heads.

In order to promote the promise of good customer service, employees are often featured in advertising, as in the two ads below. In the Delta Airlines ad, the company is promoting customer service in two ways. First, by showing an employee in a red coat, and by saying *'the red coats are back'*. It was mentioned in Chapter 8 that, in 2009, the company reintroduced red coats for their customer service agents – intended to be a visible sign of the airline ramping up personal customer service. Considered a kind of super-agent who can handle virtually any task, the Red Coats' primary mission is to fix problems. They are equipped with handheld units (shown in the ad) to help them more efficiently assist passengers, directing those who've missed a connection to their new flight, for example, securing boarding passes or even providing food vouchers when needed. The second way customer service is promoted by Delta is in the headline copy *'Customer service shouldn't fluctuate with the price of oil'*. This suggests that despite rising costs, the customer service is reliable. Reliability has been consistently shown to be the most important determinant of perceptions of service quality (Parasuraman, Zeithaml and Berry, 1985).

A Delta print ad promotes customer service. Courtesy Delta Airlines.

In the Seabourn ad, several cruise employees are show in uniform, and the tagline *'Clairvoyance is a job requirement'* advances the idea that employees at Seabourn will anticipate your every want and need. Seabourn has a fleet of six ships carrying between 208 and 450 guests each, exclusively in ocean-view suites. They are served by nearly the same number of hand-picked crew, who are consistently ranked as the finest at sea, earning Seabourn honors as the *World's Best Small Ship Cruise Line* (and this accolade is used in the copy) in surveys of readers by *Condé Nast Traveler* and *Travel + Leisure*.

A Seabourn print ad advances the idea that employees will anticipate your every want and need.
Courtesy of Seabourn

Another successful campaign that used real employees in advertising copy was a hotel campaign called 'Portraits', which consisted of beautiful black and white portraits of Four Seasons employees, such as Liloo, the concierge at the Four Seasons Toronto. The headline was *'Liloo is warm, knowledgeable, gracious, absolutely ruthless in the fulfillment of your every wish'*. The copy continued *'not only can our incandescent concierge find you a secretary fluent in Japanese, but also deftly corner the first-class seat on the evening flight. Moreover, she possesses the worldliness that opens doors to the newest bistros and makes sold-out tickets appear before your eyes. For Liloo, like all our employees, believes accommodating you must not merely be a livelihood but a life passion'*.

■ Coordinate external communication

As mentioned above, one of the most important yet challenging aspects of managing brand image is the unification of all marketing communications tools, as well as corporate and brand messages, so they send a consistent, persuasive message to target audiences. These marketing communications tools include advertising, websites, sales promotions, public relations, direct marketing and personal selling. Chapter 9 stressed how technology and the Internet have fundamentally altered the way the world interacts and communicates. One luxury golf resort in South Carolina, Kiawah Island Golf Resort, uses a number of communication tools to promote the customer experience including an interactive website. KiawahMoments.com invites resort guests, property owners and residents to share their Kiawah Island experiences online. The resort uses a 'Capture Your Kiawah Moment' advertising theme to portray memorable experiences, tell a story and prompt readers to visit KiawahMoments.com for the rest of the story. The engaging, interactive site invites users to upload and share their experiences via videos, photos and blogs. The campaign won a 2008 Magellan Award from *Travel Weekly*, which honors best practices in travel. Kiawah Island Resort is also very active in public relations, and management is extremely hospitable to media, recognizing the importance of favorable stories about the resort.

Public relations can be used in other ways to build a positive image and a reputation for service excellence. The case study at the end of the chapter shows how Thailand Medical Travel & Tourism (TMTT) promotes medical tourism in the country by attending international conferences. At the Medical Tourism Congress in Chicago in 2011, TMTT's PowerPoint presentation showed images of beautiful Thai nurses in couture uniforms, serving banquet standard food, while, in the lobby, glamorous entertainers play chamber music in lacy white dresses. Attending this type of conference is part of TMTT's strategy to spread the word about their business and set up connections.

Winning awards can also provide excellent publicity. As in the Seabourn ad, third-party endorsements can be used in advertising to build credibility and attract customers. It is advisable therefore, to apply for industry awards on a regular basis. An example is the International Association of Golf Tour Operators (IAGTO) Awards, the official annual awards for the golf tourism industry. One winner in 2007 was Vietnam, which won the Undiscovered Golf Destination of the Year. Dr Nguyen Ngoc Chu, general secretary of the Vietnam Golf Association, said 'we used to think of ourselves as the world's best-kept secret, but with the announcement of this award, the secret is out. Vietnam is ready for the big time' (IAGTO, 2007). Another winner that year was Ginn Reunion Resort in Orlando, Florida, which won the North American Golf Resort of the Year Award. Peter Bonnell, VP of Sales and Marketing said 'this award is going to brand us. It puts us in an elite status now that we have to protect and maintain.'

Publicity stunts can also generate much-needed publicity and Virgin's CEO Richard Branson's trademark is outlandish publicity stunts. His innovative flair has trickled down to Virgin's marketing department, displayed in a subtle marketing initiative at Heathrow Airport in 2004. Passengers, who had just disembarked from Virgin's trans-Atlantic flight from Los Angeles, witnessed a bright-red Virgin-branded carton of eggs making its way around the luggage carousel. On the carton it said 'Please excuse the short wait, this is how much we take care of your bags'.

Virgin-branded carton of eggs make its way around the luggage carousel at Heathrow Airport

One relatively new communication tool that blurs the line between advertising and public relations is branded entertainment (Hudson and Hudson, 2006). BMW expanded the boundaries of advertising formats on the web where its short films featuring BMW automobiles were the attraction, not an advertising distraction. The company launched its first round of films online in the summer of 2001 and the short-film *The Hire*, featuring the Z4 and X5 models, also spawned its own comic book collection. A 2008 marketing campaign from Ritz-Carlton and American Express featured three short original online films to promote the brands to younger guests. The films were all expertly done. They were sleek and provocative, luxuriously set at Ritz-Carlton properties and subtly incorporated the Amex card in each.

A still from the Ritz-Carlton's film ad, 'The Delay'

One film focused on customer service and service recovery in particular. Called *The Delay*, the film features a young woman on a weekend getaway (after a boyfriend has broken-up with her) to see a Duncan Sheik concert. She suffers a flight delay that causes her to miss the event and the airline loses her luggage. The story is about how everything begins to get better after she arrives at the Ritz-Carlton. In the final scene, the hotel concierge really goes above and beyond by arranging for Duncan Sheik to come to hotel to play for the woman.

In a related but different method of communicating customer service, the Restaurant Association of Singapore and the Singapore Hotel Association in 2010 supported a reality show called 'Can You Serve?' The television series was the first to put contestants' customer service skills to the test. Nine contestants competed against each other over eight episodes in various challenging roles for the top prize of S$70,000 in cash and S$30,000 in training opportunities. The winner was Jacquelyn Yvonne Chan, who owns a backpacker hostel called Rucksack Inn. Interviewed after the show, she said 'In my opinion, delivering good service is about going the extra mile and exceeding customer's expectations because that is what sets you apart from the rest' (Ong, 2011). The service snapshot below describes how the Burj Al Arab hotel in Dubai promoted its premier customer service via a 'behind the scenes' television show produced by The Discovery Channel.

Service Snapshot: Behind the scenes at the Burj Al Arab courtesy of The Discovery Channel

Back in 2003, Burj Al Arab, in collaboration with the Dubai Department of Tourism and Commerce Marketing (DTCM), revealed in a unique 'behind the scenes' documentary on Discovery Channel, the secrets of what it takes to provide guests with the luxurious level of service and experience at the Burj Al Arab Hotel in Dubai. Ten journalists from ten different countries around the globe were invited by Discovery Channel to view the documentary at Burj Al Arab, when the show premiered on Discovery Channel.

The Burj Al Arab in Dubai. Courtesy of Dubai Department of Tourism and Commerce Marketing

11

The show was called The *World's Most Luxurious Hotel* and included footage of the incredible architecture, advanced technology and sterling service personnel which includes a team of butlers. There is also a team of marine biologists who take care of the aquariums – complete with coral reef and 40 species of fish.

The sail-shaped Burj Al Arab is owned by Jumeirah Group, a Dubai-based luxury hospitality company and a member of Dubai Holding. Construction started in 1993 and took over five years to complete. The hotel offers luxurious and spectacular facilities and it provides exclusivity, security and privacy. It was built on a man-made island 280 meters offshore, reached by a causeway. Each of the 202 duplex rooms is set on two floors connected by a spiral staircase. Every floor has its own check-in desk. There are private elevators in two Royal Suites, ensuring both privacy and security. Butlers are available for guests' every need and they enter suites via separate entrances to guarantee the least disruption to the visitor. The Royal Suites are decorated in marble and gold, have revolving four-poster canopy beds, private cinema, and dressing rooms larger than average hotel rooms. No expense was spared on the hotel's design or its rococo furnishings, fit for a sheik's palace. The whole building is shaped like a ship's sail soaring over 321 meters high.

The hotel boasts the world's tallest atrium in the world. Gold pilasters and enormous aquariums are situated alongside the escalators. Restaurant facilities are equally luxurious, in particular the sealife-encircled Al Mahara Seafood Restaurant. The Skyview Bar, 200 meters above the Arabian Gulf, is reached by an express panoramic lift, traveling at six meters per second.

Sources: Dalrymple (2002); Fannin (2005); http://www.ameinfo.com/29264.html; Correspondence with Izabela Hamilton, PR Manager, Burj Al Arab 6 September 2012

■ Make realistic promises

To be appropriate and effective, marketing communications about customer service must accurately reflect what customers will actually receive in service encounters. Chapter 3 explained how customer expectations can be influenced by explicit and implicit promises from the service provider, and if expectations are not met then customers will become frustrated and are likely to complain. Therefore it is important for marketers to understand the actual levels of service delivery in an organization before making any promises. For example, in the Delta advertisement critiqued above, the company is making the promise of a high (because of the Red Coats) and reliable (the copy text makes the promise) customer service. But some industry observers have commented that although this is bold campaign for an airline with one of the worst records of customer service, these promises may be challenging to live up to, especially in an industry that is so volatile (Johansmeyer, 2010).

Making realistic promises means there needs to be effective internal communication in an organization. As the material in Chapter 4 already suggested, managers need to pay significant attention to the communication of marketing strategies and objectives to employees, so that they understand their own role and importance in the implementation of the strategies and in the achievement of the objectives. Because service advertising promises what people *do*, frequent and effective communication across functions – *horizontal communication* – is critical. If internal communication is poor, perceived service quality is at risk. If company advertising and other promises are developed without input from operations, contact personnel may not be able to deliver service that matches the image portrayed in marketing efforts. Communication mechanisms may come in the form of company meetings, training sessions, newsletters, emails, annual reports, or videotapes. Fairmont distributes a bi-monthly newsletter in each hotel as well as a company-wide newsletter to keep staff up to date on new company procedures. Southwest Airlines created a 'Culture Committee' whose responsibility is to perpetuate the Southwest spirit. Members promote the company's unique, caring culture to fellow employees, appearing anywhere, at any time, to lend a helping hand. Southwest also has a blog called 'Nuts about Southwest' which addresses employees concerns, relays information about changes in the company, and tries to boost employee morale.

In 2006, Four Seasons published a white paper to communicate the importance of customer service called *The Power of Personal Service* (Talbott, 2006). Originally intended for internal use only, the paper was published by Cornell University, and discusses the power of personal service, why it matters, what makes it possible, and how it creates a competitive advantage. The paper suggests that Four Season's success depends on choosing employees who provide service that is genuine and innovative, on developing standards that are both meaningful and flexible, and on maintaining a unique cultures that makes delivery of both possible. The case demonstrates that personal service can be a source of superior profitability, reputation, and growth.

Ethical issues in communication

Lovelock and Wirtz (2007) suggest that few aspects of marketing lend themselves so easily to misuse (and abuse) as advertising and selling, so service providers must be conscious of acting ethically when promoting customer service in order to attract business. As we have seen, communication messages often include promises about the benefits that customers will receive and the quality of service delivery. Although some unrealistic promises are the results of poor internal communication between operations and marketing, unethical advertising and sales practices can also play a role. For example, with the rapid growth of the Internet, many travelers rely on hotel photos and marketing descriptions, but frequently they say that these photos and marketing information do not accurately portray the hotels and lead to disappointing stays (Stoller, 2011).

11

Ethical behavior is also important in service recoveries. Alexander (2002) exposed consumers to two different types of service failures with different levels of service recovery in vignettes. One of the scenarios, for example, had a very important customer arrive at a hotel to find his reservation had been lost. In one version, the hotel manager gave this customer a room at the expense of another customer who was arriving later (but who was not such an important customer). In another version, the managers suggested to the loyal customer that he stay in the sister hotel next door in the same type of room at the same rate. Respondents were asked to evaluate each scenario on an ethical basis. The results showed higher satisfaction and quality ratings for the ethical recovery attempt and higher intentions to complain in unethical recovery attempts.

Finally, product placement was mentioned above, and there are some ethical concerns over its use as a marketing tool, the main concern centering on the issue of deception. Product placements are not labeled as advertisements and therefore may be viewed as hidden but paid messages (Balasubramanian, 1994). Research has confirmed that consumers are concerned about the 'subliminal' effect of product placement (Tiwsakul, Hackley, and Szmigin, 2005). The issue of subliminal marketing is an extremely controversial topic. The idea of advertising which affects people below their level of conscious awareness, so that they are not able to exercise conscious control over their acceptance or rejection of the message, creates ethical issues for both marketers and consumers.

Case Study: Thailand promoting medical tourism with a personal touch

Out of the 16 million annual tourists to Thailand, around two million are medical travelers, including over 180,000 Americans. There are 15 JCI (Joint Commission International) accredited hospitals and since 1997 the number of private medical facilities in Thailand has risen from 2% to almost 50%. Some of these clinics are almost exclusively for international patients. The boom period during the 1990s resulted in considerable investment in Thailand's medical facilities, particularly in first-rate private hospitals and clinics.

Kiana Bright – TMTT. Courtesy of Kiana Bright

Thailand is really taking advantage of the new wave of medical tourism. A report, *Research and Markets*, undertaken by an Irish company in 2008, revealed that Thailand's international patient numbers were the highest in Asia. With a large ex-patriot population in the region, there has long been a demand for Western medicine in Thailand. However, now it seems the West is not just coming there as professionals but as patients.

Thailand Medical Travel & Tourism (TMTT) has recognized the potential for medical tourism, providing a travel service to help patients from Hawaii, mainland USA, Canada and beyond choose their destinations, smooth their travel and assist throughout their medical procedures and tourist activities while in Thailand. VP and Partner of TMTT, Kiana Bright says they attract medical tourists from as far away as Australia, the Maldives, and the Emirates. 'They come from all over the world. Mainly through word of mouth and also through the affiliate companies in and outside the US that we work with,' Bright explains.

Naturally, many of the medical tourists are attracted to foreign facilities such as the Thai hospitals because of affordability: savings can be up to 50% compared to home hospitals. However, the hospitality side is far superior to typical Western standards. Just looking at the hospital advertising literature puts one in mind of a hotel or resort rather than a medical facility. At the 2011 Medical Tourism Congress in Chicago, TMTT's PowerPoint presentation showed images of beautiful Thai nurses in couture uniforms, serving banquet standard food, while, in the lobby, glamorous entertainers play chamber music in lacy white dresses. A far cry from a sneak-peek at the British National Health Service or a drop-in clinic in the US. Attending this type of conference is part of TMTT's strategy to spread the word about their business and set up connections. 'At big conferences, what we gain from that is not only work with consumers, but networking with affiliate companies,' says Bright. She works with around 30 travel agents in the US and Canada who include Thailand on their itinerary but need TMTT for their medical know-how.

Bright set up the full-service medical travel agency with her mother-in-law, Cherie Bright in 2008 as a subsidiary of their company International Travel Services, Inc. She had been working in Thailand in tourism since 2000 and saw the need for a highly personalized medical tourism service with an emphasis on affordability, enjoyment and carefree travel. 'I started in Thailand with a travel agency and saw tourists coming there, receiving health care but there was no service in place, no company to assist them going through the whole process,' says Kiana.

Now, from offices in Hawaii, San Diego and Thailand, TMTT networks with hotels, resorts, transportation companies, hospitals and clinics in order to coordinate all aspects of diagnosis, treatment and convalescence, building in sightseeing tours to complete the experience. During their stay, patients benefit from a complete concierge service.

11

TMTT handles everything, starting with airport to hotel transfers as well as an in-country personal assistant to help with taxis, appointments and medical communication. In between appointments, patients can take tours in the region and later recuperate on Thailand's beautiful beaches. TMTT is able to fast track medical services and ensures one-on-one nursing during hospital visits, private rooms, and an extra night's stay. The Brights' modus operandi is a customer-focused attitude including respect of patients' needs and beliefs and the reduction of language and cultural barriers. Prices are not outlined on the website, but are quoted for individual needs.

The quality of the Thai health system and the level of customer service are communicated in a very personal way by TMTT via intimate social gatherings in Hawaii and California where prospective patients listen to presentations and can speak with experienced medical tourists. 'These are casual social functions where potential clients who are thinking about going to Thailand, and other clients who have been, can talk to each other,' says Kiana. 'These presentations really work well for us.'

Thai medical practitioners are renowned for their compassionate customer care which is facilitated by a nurse to patient ratio of 1:1. All nurses have had four years of training and a third have a masters or doctorate degree. The doctor to patient ratio is 1:4 and 500 Thai doctors are US board certified. Treatments include heart, vascular, musculoskeletal, spinal, cancer, brain and spinal cord, orthopedic, stem cell and regenerative medicine, ophthalmology, plastic surgery. Despite all these qualifications, any kind of surgical procedure is a frightening experience for most people and the trials of foreign travel could compound the anxiety. TMTT addresses this on its website with a reassuring testimonial from a US veterinarian, Joanne Woltmon, with photos and snippets from her travel diary. The testimonial page goes on to outline the experiences of 10 more US and Canadian citizens who used TMTT to facilitate their Thai medical and travel experiences. Bright says this is an important emotional connection for prospective clients: 'What we work on is trust, it is all about trust, it doesn't matter what your website looks like or what your presentation is like, if they don't trust your company.'

Personal referrals are the mainstay of TMTT's business. 'We don't really go for online marketing; instead we spend our time and energy on existing clients. When we get a client who goes to Thailand, we ensure that everything is taken care of and cover every single aspect of their trip so that they have peace of mind,' she says. This level of service extends to family and friends back home who TMTT communicate with regularly to keep them apprised of the outcome of medical procedures. 'Then – one of our main strategies when we have a client who comes back happy to the US – we still continue communication with the person and make sure that, if there is something that they need to follow up on or any questions they have for the doctors, we help with that, too,' says Bright. 'A lot of companies once they send a client to a destination, their job is done but we don't stop at that; we go to the next level to get a relationship with the client and then that person will refer us.'

The TMTT website outlines the specialties of a variety of Thai medical facilities. Since 2002, the JCI has been accrediting Thai hospitals following strict international guidelines. Bangkok Hospital Medical Centre is the flagship of the largest private hospital chain in Thailand, hosting over 150,000 international patients per year. Other JCI accredited facilities include Bangkok Hospital Phuket, Bangkok Hospital Pattaya, Bangkok Nursing Home (BNH), Bumrungrad International and the three Samitivej facilities.

Bumrungrad was founded in 1980 and is the largest multi-specialty hospital in Bangkok with over 550 beds and 30 plus specialty centers. Encompassing diagnostic, therapeutic and intensive care facilities, it is a one-stop medical facility serving over a million patients annually, including 400,000 internationals. Many of these are ex-patriots from the region as well as visitors from 190 different countries. English is widely spoken and the medical coordination office provides interpreters for all nationalities.

Thai medicine is also more focused than Western counterparts on preventative care. Reflecting this, there are Health and Holiday Packages available such as a three-day stay at the Peninsula, Bangkok and BNH Hospital or Bumrungrad Hospital. The package includes a grand deluxe suite or room with 'Gold' medical check up at the hospital, same day results, medical report sent to overseas address if required, round trip hospital transfers by limo and round trip airport transfers.

Thai medical treatments are under-cutting North American prices in all areas including dentistry. For example, a basic dental package cost around US $125 and includes a check-up, radiograph of teeth and jaw bone, full mouth de-scaling and oral hygiene instructions and a permanent filling for one tooth at RSU Dental Centre, Rangsit University, Pathum Thani. Many of the top dental practitioners in Thailand were trained either in the US or Australia. Prices are cheaper still at Pattaya on the coast where there are fabulous beach benefits to make a dental visit more palatable.

But it is not just about the bottom line with TMTT clients. Cherie Bright says that many of the alternative medical procedures they are seeking are not available in the West. 'Some people go to Thailand even for procedures which are covered by insurance at home. So that means they end up costing more in Thailand but their physician told them that the quality of care is better. And others go because they want the best care possible,' she explains. A personal proponent for Thai medicine, she has had several procedures herself starting with a barbed wire accident when she experienced the emergency facilities: 'Four doctors took care of me and I couldn't believe the system.' Since then she has experienced both alternative medicine and dentistry in Thailand.

Although TMTT anticipates every eventuality during a patient's stay with its large network of in-country support staff, there are occasions when things go awry. 'We had one seriously ill patient who ended up in the emergency room before the scheduled surgery date. We were concerned beforehand that something may go wrong, so Kiana flew over there to handle it personally,' Cherie recounts. 'Other times, you have doctors who change the schedule so you have to be in complete communication and in control. Most companies don't have the means to make changes like that. Also, you have to be able to change depending on how the patient's feeling – they may think that they will want to go on tours and then won't be up to it or they may think they won't want to do any touring and then it turns out they feel well enough to. You need that flexibility to be able to cater to them and allow them to be completely relaxed.'

11

Running the finance and business side of TMTT from the Hawaii office, Cherie is fulfilling a childhood dream to be involved in the medical industry. 'I've always been fascinated by the world of medicine and medical tourism is a growing thing. It was only just beginning when Kiana started her initial company in Thailand and now it has two million tourists a year, one of the fastest growing businesses in the world. Price Waterhouse says it is the second largest business after apps for iPhones.'

Sources:

Interview with Kiana and Cheri Bright, 2012; Lunt, N. and Carrera, P. (2010); Verrastro, N. (2011); Woodman, J. (2009); France, T. (2011);

http://www.medical-tourism-in-thailand.com/;

http://www.health-tourism.com/thailand-medical-tourism/;

http://medicaltourismtothailand.com/;http://www.thaimedtraveltourism.com/;

http://www.patientsbeyondborders.com/_;

www.tourismthailand.org/us

References

Balasubramanian, S.K. (1994) 'Beyond advertising and publicity: Hybrid messages and public policy issues', *Journal of Advertising*, **23**(4), 29-47.

Barwise, P. and Meehan, S. (2010) 'The one thing you must get right when building a brand', *Harvard Business Review*, **88**(12), 80-84.

Dalrymple, T. (2002). Gulf de Luxe – Luxury Hotel in Dubai, *National Review*, May 6.

Fannin, R. (2005). Desert Luxury; a burgeoning oasis, Dubai is the new 'in' place for the vacationing CEO, *The Chief Executive*, May.

France, T. (2011) 'Holidays for health some medical options for two weeks or less', Amazing Thailand.

Hudson, S. and Hudson, D. (2006) 'Branded entertainment: A new advertising technique, or product placement in disguise?' *Journal of Marketing Management*, **22**(5-6), 489-504.

Hudson, S. and Ritchie, J.R.B. (2009) 'Branding a memorable destination experience. The case of Brand Canada', *International Journal of Tourism Research*, **11**(2), 217-228.

Johansmeyer, T. (2010, November 2) 'Delta says customer service isn't dependent upon costs', Huffington Post Blog. Accessed 05/07/2012 from http://www.gadling.com/2010/11/02/delta-says-customer-service-isnt-dependent-upon-costs/

Knight, J. (2009) 'Service that rocks. Hard Rock's strategy for success,' *Alberta Hospitality*, 10-12.

Lovelock, C. and Wirtz, J. (2007) *Services Marketing: People, Technology, Strategy*, 6th edition, New Jersey, USA; Prentice Hall International.

Lunt, N. and Carrera, P. (2010) 'Medical tourism: Assessing the evidence on treatment abroad', *Maturitas*, **66**(1), 27-32.

Matthews, L (2011) 'UlkoTours set to help Russia become a major travel and tourism market', PRWeb. Accessed 04/02/2012 from http://www.prweb.com/printer/8609955.htm

Matilla, A. S. (1999) 'Do emotional appeals work for services?' *International Journal of Service Industry Management*, **10**(3), 292-306.

Ong, J. (2011) 'Interview with 'Can You Service' winner Jacquelyn Yvonne Chan, *Time Out Singapore*. Accessed 04/07/2012 from http://www.timeoutsingapore.com/general/feature/interview-with-jacquelyn-yvonne-chan

Parasuraman, A., Zeithaml, V. A. and Berry, L. L. (1985) 'A conceptual model of service quality and its implications for future research', *Journal of Marketing*, **49**(4), 41–50.

Stoller, G. (2011, May 5) 'Some hotels don't live up to online hype, disappointed guests say', *USA Today*. Accessed 05/25/2012 from http://www.travel.usatoday.com

Talbott, B. (2006) 'The Power of Personal Service', *CHR Industry Perspectives*, No. 1, September, Cornell University.

Tiwsakul, R., Hackley, C. and Szmigin, I. (2005) 'Explicit, non-integrated product placement in british television programmes', *International Journal of Advertising*, **24**(1), 95-111.

Verrastro, N. (2011) 'Medical travel: Through the client's eyes', travelmarket, the voice of the travel seller report.

Woodman, J. (2009) *Patients Beyond Borders: Thailand Edition*, published by Healthy Travel Media.

Zeithaml, V. A., Bitner, M. J., Gremler, D., Mahaffey, T. and Hiltz, B. (2007) *Services Marketing: Integrating Customer Focus Across the Firm*, Canadian Edition, New York: McGraw-Hill.

Scan here to get the hyperlinks in this chapter

11

12 Customer Service Training Handbook

The Exercises

Exercise 1: What is good customer service?

Facilitator's Guide

There is no better way to learn about good customer service practices than to recognize good practices and learn from them. This is the best way to start the dialogue about what good customer service really means.

First of all, ask your participants to identify a company that they feel renders superior service. It doesn't have to be a big brand name like Starbucks or Ritz Carlton (although it can be). It might be their local hairdresser or grocery store.

Then ask them to give three reasons why they chose that company. They will list words/ phrases like friendly, remember my name, personal, customized service, always on time, happy, consistent etc.

Answers can be posted on a white board as you may want to reference them throughout the day.

You may want to point out that customer service means different things for different people. For some it will mean consistency, for others it will be all about friendliness and the willingness to adapt.

You could then focus on a few companies highlighted in the book (they may have already been mentioned by your group) such as Starbucks, Virgin or Walt Disney, (or get the latest list of Customer Service Champions from BusinessWeek) and then explain how they have become 'Customer Service Champs'.

Exercise 1: What is good customer service?

Identify a company that you feel renders superior service. Then give three reasons why you chose that company.

Company: _____

1.

2.

3.

12

Exercise 2: Why do some companies deliver good customer service – and others don't?

Facilitator's Guide

This is a good follow-on from Exercise 1. After discussing the customer service champions you can ask participants why these companies provide superior customer service. What is in it for them?

You should get answers like:

- To keep customer coming back
- To build a relationship with customers
- To increase profits
- To encourage positive word of mouth
- To get good tips

You could then ask why good customer service is not the norm. Why is it that levels of customer service are falling? Reasons offered may be because:

- Companies don't invest in training
- They don't understand the benefits of good customer service
- They don't know how to deliver good customer service
- They just don't care (perhaps they have a monopoly)

Exercise 2: Why do some companies deliver good customer service – and others don't?

List three reasons that some companies deliver excellent customer service.

What is in it for them?

1.

2.

3.

Then list three reasons that other companies don't deliver excellent customer service.

1.

2.

3.

12

Exercise 3: What is your potential for delivering great service?

Facilitator's Guide

This is fun little quiz for you to give your staff before they have undergone any customer service training. It will open up dialogue about their customer service skills and how they can improve different behaviors when dealing with customers.

When they have finished the quiz, ask them to add up the number of the points. When they have finished, you can put up the following results:

- 46-50: You are a saint

- 41-45: You are excellent at service

- 26-40: You are very good, but could improve

- 11-25: You need to work at service

- 10: You should be an accountant (don't use this if you are training accountants!)

At the end of the day, participants could refer back to their scores to see if they have the tools now to improve their customer service skills.

Exercise 3: What is your potential for delivering great service?

Take the test below and find out. Circle the number that's closest to the way you honestly feel, then add up your total number of points at the bottom.

Most of the time I control my moods.	5 4 3 2 1	I have difficulty controlling my moods.
I'm good at remembering names and faces	5 4 3 2 1	I have trouble remembering names or faces.
I like most people and enjoy meeting them.	5 4 3 2 1	It's hard for me to get along with other people.
I don't mind apologizing for mistakes, even if someone else made them.	5 4 3 2 1	I have trouble apologizing for someone else's mistakes.
I can be nice to people who are indifferent to me.	5 4 3 2 1	I can't be pleasant to people who aren't pleasant to me.
I enjoy being of service to others	5 4 3 2 1	I think people should do things for themselves.
Smiling comes naturally to me.	5 4 3 2 1	I tend to be serious.
Seeing others enjoy themselves makes me happy.	5 4 3 2 1	I see no reason to please others, especially if I don't know them.
How I dress and appear to others is important to me.	5 4 3 2 1	I feel that how I dress and appear to others shouldn't be important.
I prefer communicating with others verbally.	5 4 3 2 1	I prefer communicating with others in writing.

Total number of points_____

12

Exercise 4: The WIIFM's of service

Facilitator's Guide

This exercise is best for rejuvenating your staff and its morale; how to get staff to realize that customer service benefits them as well as their employers and customers/clients. This exercise would be perfect for having a one on one discussion with staff members whose morale seems especially low.

When they have finished, you can ask them to compare their list with the following:

- It makes you feel better

- It helps build personal pride

- It generates positive feedback from customers

- It reinforces job security and makes advancement more likely

- It often diminishes on-the-job stress

- It can make the job more fun!

This should lead to further discussion.

Exercise 4: The WIIFMs of service

Service excellence has a clear value to both consumers and businesses. But how about *those who deliver that service*? What's in it for them? (Or as some abbreviate it, what's their WIIFM—What's In It For Me?)

Try to list three ways in which knowing how to provide great service is good for *the employee – OR YOU!*

   1

   2

   3

12

Exercise 5: The Five dimensions of service quality

Put up a list of the five dimensions of service quality (see below). As you go through them, you might refer back to the first exercise as some of them, like empathy and responsiveness, will have been mentioned before.

Reliability - Ability to perform the promised service dependably and accurately.

Assurance - Knowledge and courtesy of employees and their ability to inspire trust and confidence.

Tangibles - Physical facilities, equipment, and appearance of personnel.

 Empathy – Caring, individualized attention the firm provides its customers.

Responsiveness - Willingness to help customers and provide prompt service.

Then give them the following story and ask them to indicate where they see evidence of the five dimensions in practice.

Exercise 5: The five dimensions of service quality

Read the following story and <u>underline</u> where you see the any of the five dimensions of service quality come into play.

Consider this: Exceptional service in an airport?

When people think of exceptional customer service, international airports don't generally come to mind. But just this weekend, Bill and Dora Grant from Florida were downright shocked at just how friendly those airport workers can be. They arrived at Calgary airport on a cold, snowy Friday afternoon, after quite a stressful journey from Banff. They had been involved in the tail-end of a road accident on Highway 1. Although they were not injured, paper-work had taken a lot of time and the road had been closed. After being diverted, they found themselves behind a snowplough for much of the journey, and then arriving at the airport, had trouble finding the car hire drop-off location. So by the time they checked their baggage in, patience was wearing thin. They were both anxious that they would miss their flight, and fond memories of a wonderful holiday in the Canadian Rockies had disappeared. But travel exhaustion soon turned to laughter as the desk clerk greeted them warmly by name and joked about waiting for them just so she could go with them to Florida and warmer climates. Morever, she accompanied the couple through customs in order to ensure they would make their flight, and explained the situation to John, the custom office on duty at the time. John was happy to expedite their route through customs, explaining politely to other waiting passengers that the couple had been delayed due to a road accident. Directing them to security, he wished them a pleasant trip and assured them they had plenty of time to make their flight.

But for Bill, the nightmare wasn't over. Just as he approached security, he realized he had left his lap top on the back seat of the car. The security officer who first greeted them, a smiling giant of a fellow called Brian, could see there was trouble by looking at Bill's face and immediately asked what was wrong. Within seconds, he was on his cell phone to Hertz, and five minutes later, a car rental employee had rushed into the airport and Bill's lap top was soon returned to him. While they were waiting, Brian joked with Dora about some people not being able to leave their work behind when going on holiday. Once again, as their carry-on bags were checked, the couple were reassured by Brian that they had enough time to get to the boarding gate and he directed them on their way, wishing them a pleasant journey as he patted Bill on the back. "Wow", said Bill as they finally boarded the plane, "If only every visit to an airport was like that".

12

Exercise 6: Importance of teamwork

Facilitator's Guide

People in the customer service industry often speak in simple phrases about their job. Things like "The customer is always right" or "Show the customer you care." These phrases may seem very elementary on the surface, but in fact, they are complex. Providing excellent customer service requires the efforts of many people working together.

This activity will demonstrate the importance of teamwork in taking care of the customer, and it will show that serving the customer is complex and requires thinking and creativity.

Divide the participants into four equal groups (teams or pairs). Give each group a card with a customer service statement or slogan (examples are below). Also give each group several sheets of flip chart paper and markers. Suggest they may want to make rough drawings first before re-drawing a large version of their final illustration. Explain that the only rule governing the picture is that no words may be used.

Tell the group that they will be asked at the end of the session to describe how they used the team approach to decide what to draw and who would draw it. While the groups are working, post your flip chart paper showing the four customer service statements.

When time is up, have each group post its picture. Allow two or three minutes for each group to work as a team matching the statements to each picture. Then get them to identify what statement its picture illustrated. This should move quickly and be fun.

Here are some questions to generate discussion:

1.   How did a leader emerge?
2.   Were a lot of different ideas generated at first?
3.   How were ideas presented? How were they accepted?
4.   How did you decide which idea would be your final drawing?
5.   How did you decide who would do the drawing?
6.   How did it feel when the picture was finished?
7.   What would you have done differently if you were to do this activity again?

Possible statements you could use:

- The customer is always right
- Show the customer you care
- We are here to make your day
- We will solve any problem – however small

Exercise 6: Importance of teamwork

"We're going to divide into teams. Each team will select a statement from the cards we have prepared. Your task is to draw a picture that best conveys the statement you have selected. You have 10 minutes to come up with the most creative illustration.

After the time is up, each group will post its illustration. Then all of us will try to match the statement with the pictures.

Then we'll take a look at the team process used to get the picture finished."

Exercise 7: Implications of face-to-face customer service

Facilitator's Guide

Staff members who have worked previously in over the phone or Internet customer service scenarios may be unfamiliar with what is appropriate for face-to-face scenarios; it may be a completely new realm to them. This exercise allows some brainstorming and open dialogue for what is appropriate and why and is a good exercise to use before focusing on specific face-to-face customer service skills.

Exercise 7: Implications of face-to-face customer service

In the face-to-face customer service environment…..	So what should (and shouldn't) you do to give good service?
customers can see what you're wearing	
customers can see your face	
customers can read your body language	

12

Exercise 8: First impressions

Facilitator Guide

First of all, the facilitator will need to gather up some pictures of different people in various physical positions. Try to get a good variety – people in defensive positions (with arms crossed), open positions with hands open, different expressions on their faces, a variety of clothing and hairstyles etc. You can usually get a good cross-section from a magazine.

The idea is that participants will review the pictures to determine the importance of body language. It is a good exercise for both understanding how first impressions can be so important (and misleading), and for learning basic techniques for using body language, appearance and posture to send the intended message.

Pictures can be given out to pairs, who can then discuss what they think that person does for a living, what they are feeling, and what type of personality they might be. They should discuss how they came to these conclusions.

The exercise can lead to a discussion about how body language and attire affects communication: how can you tell a customer you are friendly, confident and interested; what kind of posture can you exhibit to help diffuse a challenging situation?

The exercise may also be used as a way to stress the importance of not jumping to conclusions about someone just because of the way they look – and also for understanding (and having tolerance for) diversity.

Exercise 8: First impressions

In pairs, take a look at the picture given to you, and answer the questions.

What do you think this person does for a living?

_____

_____

_____

_____

What is this person feeling?

_____

_____

_____

_____

What type of personality they might be?

_____

_____

_____

_____

Discuss how you came to these conclusions.

_____

_____

_____

_____

12

Exercise 9: Building rapport with customers

Facilitator's Guide

Especially when dealing with an uncomfortable situation, it is important to build rapport with a customer to make them comfortable and realize that you genuinely care about helping the customer to the best of your ability. This exercise will help your staff members practice building rapport with their customers/clients.

The answers are:

2. Please, Thank you, Information

3. Reasons, No

4. Interest

5. Empathy, Feelings

6. Options

7. Smile

Exercise 9: Building rapport with customers

There are countless ways to build rapport with customers. The puzzle below contains words that complete the following rapport-building techniques. We've done the first one for you.

1. Use the customer's _N A M E_ if possible.

2. Say _____and _____when asking customers for _____.

3. Explain your _____when you have to say _____ to a customer's request.

4. Show your _____in the customer's needs.

5. Show_____for the customer's _____.

6. Let the customer know what his or her _____ are.

7. _____! Even if you're on the phone!

Words can appear horizontally, vertically, or diagonally, and may go in any direction.

Rapport Puzzle

R	M	I	I	K	S	L	E	R	S	T
O	P	M	K	Y	R	E	J	S	W	E
O	T	R	E	E	L	C	N	H	E	E
T	H	A	N	K	Y	O	U	A	S	M
S	E	R	R	A	S	P	B	G	A	P
E	M	A	N	A	A	T	N	M	E	A
R	D	I	E	L	D	I	A	P	L	T
E	Q	R	L	O	L	O	W	I	P	H
T	I	R	E	E	O	N	N	U	Y	Y
N	O	W	E	R	H	S	A	E	L	P
I	N	F	O	R	M	A	T	I	O	N

Source: Carlan, P & Deming, K.V. (1999) *The Big Book of Customer Service Training Games*.

12

Exercise 10: Re-wording in customer service

Facilitator's Guide

This exercise is best for helping staff that deals directly with customers learn how to re-word their dialogue with customers/clients in a more professional manner. Your staff should talk to customers with a positive and optimistic tone, and therefore it is helpful for your staff to do dialogue exercises to improve their reactions and responses with customers.

Exercise 10: Try Rewording for a better tone

Re-phrase the following statements to make the wording positive and tactful. Also strive to solve the caller's concern as efficiently as possible.

1. Bill is out playing golf again. I doubt that he'll be back in the office today.

2. Sarah went to the restroom and then is going to lunch for about an hour or so.

3. Who did you say you were?

4. You say you've been trying to get through? When did you try?

5. Who are you holding for?

6. This is Bobby. What do you need?

7. Hey, sorry about that. I got backed up and couldn't call you back.

8. We don't do that kind of work here.

9. Try again after five, okay?

10. Sally used to work here but we let her go. Maybe I can help.

12

Exercise 11: Customer perceptions

Facilitator's Guide

This is another exercise in re-wording responses to customers. Your staff may think saying something conversational or rather blunt in passing such as "I don't know" or "that's a different department" is helping the customer and is "just being honest". However, for your business, this type of blunt honesty can give your company a poor reputation with respect to customer service. Have your staff complete this exercise and then have an open dialogue about why it is counterproductive to say these types of phrases to customers.

Exercise 11: Customer perceptions

How might a customer negatively interpret the following phrases and how can you re-phrase them?

Phrase	How a customer might interpret it?	How could you rephrase this?
'I don't know'		
'We're really busy'		
'That's not my department'		
'There's nothing I can do'		
'It's company policy'		

12

Exercise 12: How are your phone usage skills and attitudes?

Facilitator Guide

This chart should help your staff isolate any issues they have in over-the-phone customer service, and subsequently, lead them to correct these issues. It may be worth having a group discussion after the fact, as well, discussing why and when these problems occur the most and how to remedy the problem as a group.

Exercise 12: How are your phone usage skills and attitudes?

Circle the appropriate letter for each item: **N = never, SL = seldom, SM = sometimes, O = often, A = always**. Then read the instructions at the end of the form.

How often do you...	Improvement goal					
1. Delay calling someone or fail to return a call?	N	SL	SM	O	A	
2. Answer the phone with a curt or mechanical greeting?	N	SL	SM	O	A	
3. Let the phone ring, hoping the caller will give up?	N	SL	SM	O	A	
4. End the conversation by summarizing what was agreed upon?	A	O	SM	SL	N	
5. Solicit feedback about your customer service phone call?	A	O	SM	SL	N	
6. Put people on hold for more than a few seconds?	N	SL	SM	O	A	
7. Have someone else place your calls for you?	N	SL	SM	O	A	
8. Smile as you speak?	A	O	SM	SL	N	
9. Speak clearly and in pleasant, conversational tones (no 'stage voice')?	A	O	SM	SL	N	

If you circled a letter in the two right columns for any of the items, your telephone techniques can use improvement. In the space provided to the right of these items, set specific goals for improvement in each area needed.

12

Exercise 13: Being alert when serving customers – listening skills

Facilitator's Guide

Even if your employees are present at work, serving customers, they may not be fully 'there' or aware of the information they are giving customers. This can have many reasons, such as external personal problems or other tasks at work they are thinking about. However, it is important to remind your staff that when dealing with external customers, *they* are your #1 priority, and often the reason why your company is in business at all!

What their scores mean:

- 40-50: You are an extremely alert listener
- 35-39: You are a good listener
- 25-34: You pay attention but perhaps should work on your listening skills
- Under 25: Take the cotton wool out!

Exercise 13: Being alert when serving customers – listening skills

Did you ever read a book and suddenly realize that you've read several pages *without being aware of anything you've just read?* Strange, isn't it? Alertness levels vary from minute to minute, even second to second. But as front line staff, it's vital that you remain vigilant for your customer's responses and even to their nonverbal cues. Let's see how good a listener you are. Answer each question by circling the number that applies. At the end, count up your point total.

Question	Never	Occasionally	Often	Usually	Always
When I am listening to someone, do I pay attention, rather than fake it?	1	2	3	4	5
While listening, do I pick up on the feelings and attitudes of the speaker, as well as the mere words?	1	2	3	4	5
Do I block out distractions when listening to somebody?	1	2	3	4	5
Do I manage to avoid letting my own attitudes block out what is being said, if I disagree with the person?	1	2	3	4	5
Do I pick up on nonverbal cues that may communicate what the person is saying over and above his/her words?	1	2	3	4	5
Do I manage to avoid interrupting the person talking?	1	2	3	4	5
Do I succeed in paying attention to slow, rambling, or boring individuals?	1	2	3	4	5
Do I refrain from thinking up what I'm going to say to someone before they're finished talking?	1	2	3	4	5
Do I keep eye contact with the person who's talking to me?	1	2	3	4	5
When the person is done talking, do I verbally indicate that I have understood (or not understood) what they have said?	1	2	3	4	5

Your total score:_____

12

Exercise 14: Pet peeves in customer service

Facilitator's Guide

The best way for your staff to understand what to avoid when dealing with customers is to get them to express what they themselves dislike as customers. Then, it is helpful to talk with your staff members about the best ways to avoid committing these pet peeves when they are handling customers.

Extensive research would predict that some of these *customer turnoffs* **may be on their lists:**

- Being ignored or receiving rude or indifferent service
- Having to wait too long
- Enduring poor quality work (especially on repair jobs) or shoddy products
- Trying to buy sale items that are not in stock
- Finding merchandise prices not marked, forcing a price check at the cashier
- Enduring dirty restaurants or restrooms
- Putting phone calls on hold or forcing you to select from a long menu of choices
- Having employees who lack product knowledge (and try to bluff the customer)
- Putting up with high-pressure sales tactics
- Being talked down to by employees or having them use confusing jargon
- Facing inflexibility when you make a request

Exercise 14: My pet peeves in customer service

Quickly list five specific turnoffs you experience as a customer. What kinds of things irritate you when doing business? Think about several customer contexts: retail, repair services, restaurants, government agencies, and so on. Be as specific as possible about exactly what irritates you. Perhaps cite an example if that helps you express your ideas.

1. _____

2. _____

3. _____

4. _____

5. _____

12

Exercise 15: Dealing with customers from hell

Facilitator's Guide

Anybody working in the service industry, has dealt with difficult customers. Sometimes the best thing to do is to recognize that these types of customers exist, categorize them so that your staff knows how to deal with each type, and discuss the best ways to avoid conflict with these customers and keep them happy. Allow participants to discuss in groups how they would deal with each type (or assign one type to individual groups). Then you can share the material below.

How to deal with them:

- Edgar
    - Appeal to his ego
    - Demonstrate action
    - Don't talk policy
    - Don't let his ego destroy yours
- Betty
    - Ignore her language
    - Force the issue
    - Use selective agreement
- Harold
    - Let him vent
    - Take it backstage
    - Take responsibility for solving the problem

Exercise 15: Dealing with customers from hell

	List ways to work with these characters
Egocentric Edgar Me first, me last, me only—that's his creed. You? You're just a bit player, an extra, an extraneous piece of scenery in that grandest of all productions. "Edgar: The Greatest Story Ever Told." **Sample Behaviors** Won't wait his turn, will only speak to whoever is in charge, intimidates through judicious name dropping, and makes loud demands.	
Bad Mouth Betty Her mother would be proud. Such an extensive vocabulary! It takes timing, talent, and a total lack of shame to swear like a trooper, but Betty makes it look easy. **Sample Behaviors** Uses language and has a demeanor that is caustic, crude, cruel, and foul.	
Hysterical Harold He's a screamer. If it's true that there is a child in all of us yearning to break free, Harold demonstrates the dark side of that happy thought. He is the classic tantrum-thrower, the adult embodiment of the terrible twos. Only louder. Much louder. **Sample Behaviors** Screams, is rabid and extremely animated, jumps around, and invades the personal space of others.	

12

Exercise 16: Handling customers & strategies

Facilitator's Guide

This exercise would be best for helping your staff prepare to deal with difficult customer service situations and to help prevent service breakdown or aid in service recovery. Based on your staff's responses to the following statements, you as the manager should assist staff in finding resources to broaden their knowledge base as a customer service representative. This may be an opportunity to present some of the material from the book on the importance of service recovery, such as the customer complain iceberg.

Exercise 16: Handling customers & strategies

Respond to the following responses. Discuss these questions – and your answers – with your co-workers or classmates. This can ultimately help improve your own skills, employee morale, and service to customers.

I can approach what I believe to be a difficult customer with a positive attitude and believe that I can turn the situation around.	YES/NO
In dealing with customers, I seek to determine their true needs before offering a service solution.	YES/NO
I consciously monitor my language, and elicit feedback from peers on it to ensure that I typically use positive words and phrases when communicating.	YES/NO
When dealing with the types of difficult customers described earlier, I maintain my professionalism and actively listen in order to better serve their needs.	YES/NO
What actions or circumstances have you noticed lead to service breakdowns in organizations where you were either a customer or service provider?	
When you were a customer and service broke down, what recovery strategies were effectively used to help "make you whole"?	

12

Exercise 17: What are your feelings about dealing with difficult customers?

Facilitator Guide

Difficult customers exist and we've all had to deal with them at least once. This exercise should create some dialogue with your staff about experiences they've had with difficult customers, and rather than a 'venting' session or complaining, you can turn these experiences into learning opportunities for your staff.

The exercise should challenge your staff to think critically about how to deal with a difficult customer effectively next time they are faced with this situation.

Exercise 17: What are your feelings about dealing with difficult customers?

Below is a list of words that may describe the ways you feel about dealing with upset customers. Select the five that best describe your general feelings. Discuss your results in a small group, asking for their feedback on how to deal with the feelings you have.

Afraid	Confident	Foolish	Relieved
Angry	Confused	Frustrated	Sad
Anxious	Contented	Glad	Silly
Apathetic	Distraught	Hesitant	Uncomfortable
Bored	Eager	Humiliated	Uneasy
Calm	Ecstatic	Joyful	Wishful
Cautious	Elated	Nervous	
Comfortable	Excited	Proud	

My top five:

_____

_____

_____

_____

_____

Probes:

How can you re-frame these feelings – change the negative into potential positive – when adopting an attitude of opportunity?

To what extent are these feelings irrational or unreasonable? Is it possible that some may reflect fears or discomfort that you could learn to manage? Give an example of what you might do.

12

Exercise 18: The law of the garbage truck

Facilitator's Guide

This simple reading is 'food for thought' for your staff members to take with them in the back of their mind when serving difficult customers.

Exercise 18: The law of the garbage truck

One day I hopped in a taxi and we took off for the airport. We were driving in the right lane when suddenly a black car jumped out of a parking space right in front of us. My taxi driver slammed on his breaks, skidded, and missed the other car by just inches! The driver of the other car whipped his head around and started yelling at us. My taxi driver just smiled and waved at the guy. And, I mean, he was really friendly.

So I asked, 'Why did you just do that? This guy almost caused an accident and sent us to the hospital!' This is when my taxi driver taught me what I now call, 'The Law of the Garbage Truck.'

He explained that many people are like garbage trucks. They run around full of garbage, full of frustration, full of anger, full of disappointment and rage. As their garbage piles up, they need a place to dump it and sometimes they'll dump it on you. Don't take it personally. Just smile, wave, wish them well, and move on. Don't pick up their garbage and spread it to other people in your life, whether at work, at home, or to people that you don't even know on the streets.

Always remember that good people do not let garbage trucks take over their day. Life's too short to wake up in the morning with regrets, so.....

'Love the people who treat you right and forgive and pray for the ones who don't.'

12

Exercise 19: How motivating a manager would you be?

Facilitator's Guide

This exercise would best be used with staff members that you feel fill a leadership role in your organization or staff members you feel would have potential in a leadership role. Have them answer these questions and then have a one-on-one discussion with these staff members about how they see themselves in leadership roles and where you see them in these roles in the future.

Scoring:

- 41-50 points: You're a strong team manager and motivator.
- 31-40 points: You're able to build a strong team.
- 21-30 points: You need to work on your managerial and motivating skills.
- 10-20 points: You're like the boss in 'The Office'.

(courtesy of Cruise Lines International Association)

Exercise 19: How motivating a manager would you be?

For each of the following statements, rate yourself from 1 to 5 (with 5 being the best) and total your score. If you're not a manager, answer according to what you would do if you actually were. At the bottom of the page, you'll see how to interpret your score.

I extend a pleasant greeting to each employee each day.	1	2	3	4	5
I praise and reward employees for good work.	1	2	3	4	5
I offer constructive criticism in private.	1	2	3	4	5
I encourage training and skill development.	1	2	3	4	5
I succeed in resolving employee conflicts.	1	2	3	4	5
I encourage employees to make suggestions.	1	2	3	4	5
I respond quickly to employee requests.	1	2	3	4	5
I keep staff informed.	1	2	3	4	5
I encourage my staff to accept new challenges.	1	2	3	4	5
I see myself as a team leader.	1	2	3	4	5

Your total score: _____

12

Exercise 20: Observing customer service behavior

Facilitator's Guide

Sometimes the best way to learn how to do something is to watch how it's done well and even observe how not to do something. Customer service behavior is no exception. As a part of a consumer culture, we are constantly encountering opportunities to learn the best ways to practice exceptional customer service. So this exercise is best for your staff to observe behaviors that they would like to adopt in the future and behaviors that they will learn not to repeat.

Exercise 20: Observing customer service behavior

Go to a restaurant—either full-service or fast food—and sit at a strategic table (one where you can observe the employees). Watch the behavior of these people. How good is each, based on things you consider to be good customer service practices? (Some concepts that apply to travel may not be relevant to the dining industry). Then fill out the following:

Important note: You should be as subtle and unobtrusive about this exercise as possible. If anyone asks what you're doing, explain that it's part of a class you're taking.

1. How are customers greeted? (For a full-service restaurant: at the entrance; at a fast food place: at the food service counter). Describe what you observe.

2. Have you noticed one person who is doing his or her job especially well? What is it about that person that makes him or her so effective?

3. Have you noticed one person who is not doing his or her job very well? What made you conclude this?

4. Does the restaurant have any positive "atmospheres" that helps customers feel good about their experience? Any negative ones?

12

Exercise 21: Role of the Internet in your organization's customer service

Facilitator's Guide

This exercise is best for getting your employees to be aware of what Internet options your organization offers to customers. This exercise could be especially useful for companies with new staff members that want to get their new staff comfortable with the organization's customer service options on the Web.

Exercise 21: Role of the Internet in your organization's customer service

E-service guru, Greg Gianforte has developed a short "SQ" (service quotient) test for assessing the health of an organization's web-mediated customer service. If you are currently working in an organization with a website, take a minute and complete the following survey. If you do not work in such an organization, select the website of a company you have visited, put yourself in the role of one of the company's leaders and answer as many of the questions as you can.

SQ Test	Yes	No	Don't know
Can your customers quickly find answers to their most frequently asked questions on your website?			
Can they easily check on the status of the response they previously requested?			
Do you respond to all customer emails or social media comments within one business day?			
Does the e-service content on your site change automatically based on customer input?			
Are the most useful and/or commonly requested knowledge items presented first?			
Do customers have an easy way to get to a human support staffer?			
Do your customers consistently return to your site to get information? Do you have any way of determining whether or not they do?			
Are you tracking activity that has taken place on your site on a week-by-week basis? Do these reports help you determine the return of investment (ROI) of the site?			
Do you give visitors an option to have updates sent to them automatically by email or via a social media platform?			
Are you consistently using the Internet to capture and publish useful information that's currently only in the heads of your best staff?			
Does your call center only handle queries that couldn't be handled automatically by your website?			
Do customers ever praise your company because they found your site especially helpful?			
Can you view both the email and call history of any given incident from a single interface?			
Are the answers you give your customers on the phone the same as the ones you give them on your website?			

(Scoring: According to Gianforte, a "yes" answer on 10 or more items indicates that your organization's e-service health is excellent. Anything less should prompt you to re-examine some of your online customer service strategies.)

12

Index